D1617567

Family
Sexual
Abuse

Family
Sexual
Abuse

Frontline Research and Evaluation

HQ
78
,U53
F36
1991
WEST

Edited by
Michael Quinn Patton

This book is published during the 50th anniversary celebration of The Saint Paul Foundation, Incorporated, with the assistance of The Saint Paul Foundation, the F. R. Bigelow Foundation, Mardag Foundation, Cowles Media Foundation, Edwards Memorial Trust, First Bank Systems, and The Saint Paul Companies.

SAGE PUBLICATIONS
The International Professional Publishers
Newbury Park   London   New Delhi

For information address:

SAGE Publications, Inc.
2455 Teller Road
Newbury Park, California 91320

SAGE Pubications Ltd.
6 Bonhill Street
London EC2A 4PU
United Kingdom

SAGE Publications India Pvt. ltd.
M-32 Market
Greater Kailish I
New Delhi 110 048 India

Printed in the United States of America

Library of Congress Cataloging-in-Publication Data

Main entry under title:
Family sexual abuse : frontline research and evaluation / edited by
Michael Quinn Patton.
        p.   cm.
    Includes bibliographic references.
    ISBN 0-8039-3960-4. -- ISBN 0-8039-3961-2 (pbk.)
    1. Child molesting--United States. 2. Sexually abused children-
-Services for--United States. 3. Problem families--Services for-
-United States.   I. Patton, Michael Quinn.
HQ72.U53F36   1991
362.7'6--dc20   90-19706
                                                         CIP

FIRST PRINTING, 1991

Sage Production Editor: Judith L. Hunter

Contents

Preface

The Family Sexual Abuse Project was created to support the process of inquiry that would strengthen the field of family sexual abuse intervention. In funding the research and evaluation projects described in this book, the project strove to make connections between information and action.

The first connection was through selection of projects to fund; they typically were conducted in action environments. Then we talked about what we were learning. We wrote about the projects in our periodic newsletter. We spoke to policymakers. We convened the researchers to discuss themes and issues, both substantive and methodological. We invited practitioners and researchers to annual conferences at which the project findings were presented and participants enabled to carry on further discussion about the implications for practice.

This book is a logical extension of our desire to share what we are learning—and, we hope, to continue the process of inquiry. Here we present the projects and invite each reader to ask what the next questions are for policy, practice, and future research.

A unique aspect of the Family Sexual Abuse Project is that it was undertaken by a small collaboration of funders, with leadership from The Saint Paul Foundation. These funders believed that a great deal could be accomplished, even with relatively modest funding. They believed that, by conducting all the activities referred to above, we could extend the impact of the work beyond the individual programs and researchers. We are enormously grateful to the funders who shared the vision of The Saint Paul Foundation and made this work possible: the F. R. Bigelow Foundation, First Bank Saint Paul, the Mardag Foundation, the Minneapolis Star and Tribune/Cowles Media Company, and the St. Paul Companies.

We owe a special thanks to members of a peer review panel who agreed to critique the component chapters of this book in preparation for publication. They are Ann C. Jaede, manager, Criminal Justice Program of the Minnesota State Planning Agency; Terry M. Lindeke, Ramsey County, director, intergovernmental relations; and Paul W. Mattessich, director, Wilder Research Center. Gretchen Shafer coordinated the communications among authors and assisted in finalizing chapters.

Finally, an enormous debt of thanks is owed to our many dedicated advisers, who served unwaveringly over the years. Their creativity, knowledge, humor, and occasional prodding have helped this project come to full flower. Thank you to Gay Bakken, Cheryl Champion, Donna Fehrenbach, Arthur Fleischer, Pat Genereux, Paul Gerber, Ann Jaede, Terry Lindeke, Alan Listiak, Maribeth Lundeen, Anne McBean, James H. Michel, Dick Merwin, Frank Pasnecker, Michael Patton, Gretchen Shafer, Carol Seefeldt, Fran Sepler, Larry Simon, Joan Sykora and Joan Velasquez.

—Margaret J. Bringewatt
Saint Paul, Minnesota

PART I
CONTEXT:
DEVELOPMENT OF
FAMILY SEXUAL
ABUSE RESEARCH
AND PRACTICE

1

Child Sexual Abuse:
Looking Backward and Forward

JON R. CONTE

The majority of child sexual abuse professionals working today, fate willing, are likely to be around to see the profession's and the public's responses to this social problem in the year 2001. Widespread current awareness of the problem in modern times is only a bit over a decade old as this is written in early 1990. The last decade has witnessed considerable work and effort, with some significant accomplishments and a few activities that may not turn out to be worth the effort.

This chapter looks briefly at the development of child sexual abuse as a multidisciplinary subspecialty and the social context in which professionals carry out their various tasks and responsibilities in responding to sexually abused children and the adults who share and influence their lives. Space prohibits a full analysis of the field's history, including a few professional misadventures along the way. Nor will it be possible to critique fully the social policies that directly support and limit the capacity of professionals to respond to the problem of child sexual abuse. I do hope that this chapter will further a discussion among professionals about the directions necessary to reach our goals by the year 2001. By both reviewing the field's historical development and looking ahead to new directions, I would hope this chapter provides a current national context for the kind of frontline research and evaluation presented in the other chapters of this book.

EARLY BEGINNINGS

It is generally recognized that there has been adult sexual use of children from earliest recorded history. It was a practice in ancient

Rome to castrate boys to make them more pleasing sexual partners for rich Romans. The field has come to mark Freud's discussion of the link between "hysterical illness" in eighteen of his patients and their reports of childhood sexual experiences with adults as the beginning of professional awareness of the problem (see Lerman, 1988). It is also generally recognized that from Freud's time until the mid-1970s, most professionals simply did not consider adult sexual use of children to be much of a problem. The first phase of professional development in responding to child sexual abuse was characterized by efforts to recognize that the problem was in fact a common problem of childhood.

Recognizing sexual abuse for what it is has been an ongoing struggle for the public and professionals alike. At a psychological level, we understand that adult sexual abuse of children is anxiety producing and emotionally difficult. It requires adults to face material that is difficult for most, including issues of sexuality, deviant behavior, abuse and terror of children, and the violation of social norms. It requires recognition that members of our families, communities, and social institutions, such as schools and churches, regularly sexually abuse children.

Psychological defenses inherent to the human species operate within individuals to protect them from the anxiety-producing and painful knowledge that older persons regularly abuse younger persons. At their most extreme (albeit for different reasons), these defenses are seen in the minimization, rationalization, distortion, and denial of the sexual offender (Conte, 1985). Defense mechanisms also operate in the loved ones of victims, who struggle to understand what young victims tell them, often in disguised ways, about sexual abuse. These defenses also help us understand why victims may not recall their own abuse for a number of years, only much later to begin regaining memory and enter treatment.

Helping victims and their families understand sexual abuse is an inherent component of mental health treatment. Treatment aims to help them understand that sexual abuse is real, what it really consists of, and how victim reactions (commonly referred to as the effects of abuse or mental health symptoms) are a natural response to abuse. It is difficult for me to imagine that it will ever become easier for victims or their families to overcome psychological defenses without intervention. The intervention of professionals in this regard is likely to continue to be part of our work well into the next century.

What is more problematic is the extent to which professionals and professional knowledge appear to be defensive in nature. I believe that many of our cherished ideas serve in practice to make it easier for us as professionals to deal with this problem rather than to provide accurate reflections of the problem. Related to this problem of professional defenses has been a tendency over the last few years to believe things that only a few years later we have recognized as naive or impressionistic, or things we should not have believed because they were simply not true. We have to recognize that these erroneous ideas have been used in the past to make decisions that influenced the lives of real people. To illustrate I will provide a few examples of erroneous ideas.

Behavior Proves Sexual Abuse: An Erroneous Idea

It was common until just a few years ago to read in professional reports and in the literature that a child was or was not abused because she or he did or did not present with the "core symptoms" (e.g., behavioral regression, somatic complaints, fearfulness). Anecdotal experience suggests that cases were "substantiated" or not, based on little more than professional judgment about these behaviors. More recently we have come to recognize that these behaviors are indicators of stress in childhood, and stressors may be any of a number of events common to childhood (e.g., divorce or school difficulties). In a study of the impact of sexual abuse on children that Lucy Berliner (Harborview Medical Center in Seattle) and I conducted in the early 1980s, 21% of the children were without any of these core symptoms (Conte & Schuerman, 1987). There has been recent discussion that the one sure sign of sexual abuse is one of the set of "sexual behaviors" (sexual knowledge, sex play, or sexual talk that is not developmentally appropriate or sexual behavior). Although there has been some important recent research on sexual behaviors (see, e.g., Deblinger, McLeer, Atkins, Ralphie, & Foa, 1989; Kolko, Moser, & Weldy, 1988), it appears that not all abused children will exhibit these behaviors and that some nonabused children will exhibit them. Chapter 4 in this book falls within this tradition of research.

There is a real need for studies that help us understand variation across developmental stages and ethnic and class groups in normal "sexual" behaviors. Little is known about what effects the increasing availability of "adults-only" videos and cable TV have had on children's knowledge or experimentation. Little is known about the range of behaviors (e.g., nudity or touching) regarded as acceptable in families or at what ages specific types of sexual behavior emerge naturally. Nevertheless, even without these normative studies, behavior in children indicative of stress or problem functioning is regarded as a potential symptom of a number of problems (including sexual abuse) deserving further assessment.

Erroneous Ideas About the Nature of Sexual Abuse

Perhaps no other area within the study of sexual abuse has been the subject of so many erroneous concepts as that of sexual offenders. Elsewhere I have devoted some attention to these ideas, so I will only highlight the issues here (see Conte, 1985, 1986).

One erroneous idea about the nature of sexual abuse is that incest is a unique clinical problem. Incest offenders have long been believed to represent a clinical problem distinct and different from nonincestuous offenders (i.e., pedophiles). This belief is at the foundation of current social policy, which tends to support community-based treatment for the incest offender who is not regarded as dangerous to society as a whole. Although there is as much variation among family-oriented views of adult sexual use of children as there is between family and nonfamily views, I have suggested that all *family* views of the problem rest on two key assumptions: Incestuous fathers and stepfathers do not act out sexually outside of the home, and incest is the sexual expression of nonsexual needs (Conte, 1986).

The first assumption, the belief that incest offenders do not act out sexually outside of the family, is regarded as both an empirical statement about reality and a statement about the nature of incest. Incest is a family problem in which every member of the family contributes to the development and maintenance of the sexual relationship between father/stepfather and daughter. This belief is the basis for the assumption that incest offenders are not dangerous to children who live outside of their homes and, in most cases, can be left safely in the community (although perhaps not in the same house) during treatment.

Preliminary data have seriously challenged this core belief about incest. Abel, Becker, Cunningham-Rathner, Mittleman, and Rouleau (1988) indicate that 49% of the incestuous fathers and stepfathers referred for outpatient treatment at their clinics abused children outside of the family at the same time they were abusing their own children. Moreover, 18% of these men were raping adult women at the same time they were sexually abusing their own children. While replication of these data is critical to understanding how generalizable they are, they do raise questions about the validity of the assumption that the initial referral diagnosis (e.g., father or stepfather incest) has any significance in understanding the nature of the incestuous father or stepfather's problem.

The second assumption, the belief that incest is the sexual expression of nonsexual needs, has led generations of professionals to direct attention toward nonsexual problems typically found in incest offenders (e.g., depression, poor self-esteem, difficulties in relationships with adult women). Virtually all sexual behavior may include sexual (i.e., tactile, physiological) and nonsexual (e.g., affectional or recreational) aspects. It is not clear why sexual use of children by a father or stepfather should be regarded as a special kind of *sexual* behavior. There has been some research in which the sexual arousal of incest offenders was actually assessed in the laboratory. For example, Quinsey, Chaplin, and Carrigan (1979) evaluated nine incestuous and seven non-incestuous child molesters and found that incestuous (father or stepfather) offenders exhibited more appropriate (i.e., adult) sexual arousal than nonincestuous child molesters. Abel, Becker, Murphy, and Flanagan (1981) found that incest offenders were sexually aroused to children. Marshall, Barbaree, and Christophe (1986) evaluated 40 child molesters, 21 incest offenders, and 22 normal controls. The normals demonstrated minimal arousal to children younger than age 12, slight arousal to children ages 12–14, and a dramatic increase in and substantial arousal to children 14 years and older. Child molesters showed considerable arousal to children, with the largest amount of arousal to 9-year-olds, decreasing arousal to children ages 11–13, and a gradually increasing arousal to 14–24-year-olds. The finding that child molesters are aroused to children and adults is surprising and not consistent with other research. Incest offenders more closely paralleled normals, although they showed no dramatic arousal increase to children over 14 (as did normals). There were significant differences between normals and incest offenders in the magnitude of their arousal to 14–24-year-olds, with the incest offenders showing less arousal to older persons.

The data regarding the extent and nature of incest fathers' and stepfathers' sexual arousal to children are contradictory and limited. There have been problems with some of the research on sexual arousal and incest. For example, as Marshall et al. (1986) point out, many studies have mixed natural fathers, stepfathers, and adoptive fathers in a single incest sample. It may well be that the level of arousal to children will vary across these subsamples. Other problems in the studies of sexual arousal in incestuous and nonincestuous offenders include small sample sizes, selection of nonrepresentative samples or samples of unknown representativeness, lack of raters blind to the hypotheses, and lack of control groups (Avery-Clark, O'Neil, & Laws, 1981). Notwithstanding these problems and the somewhat limited and preliminary data on incest fathers' arousal, it is simply not possible to know how many incest offenders have abused children outside the home or what the nature of their arousal pattern is. Knowing the reason for referral (e.g., for incest) is not sufficient to answer these other questions. These can be determined only through specialized assessment (see Earls & Marshall, 1983; Laws & Osborn, 1983).

Most sexual abuse of children is not even sexual. There has been recent discussion making much of the fact that most sexual abuse is of a "less sexual" nature. For example, in a thought-provoking chapter, Plummer (1981) suggests that it is a "stereotype that the sex act itself is damaging and dangerous and may even lead to such things as child murder" (p. 225). He then cites as evidence for this statement the high rate of occurrence of the "less sexual (e.g., fondling) behaviors" and the low incidence of child sexual murders.

It is true that in many cases, fondling occurs most often. For example, Kendall-Tackett and Simon (1987), in their description of 365 adults sexually abused in childhood, report the following abuse experiences: 64% fondled from the waist up, 92% fondled from the waist down, 48% oral sex, 19% attempted intercourse, 10% simulated intercourse, 44% intercourse, and 9% anal intercourse. Kercher and McShane (1984) describe the sexual behaviors to which a sample of 619 children were exposed: 19% exhibitionism by perpetrator, 42% fondling by perpetrator, 39% heterosexual intercourse, 6% homosexual intercourse, 14% oral sex on victim, 14% oral sex on perpetrator, 8% perpetrator masturbates self, 2% photographing child nude or in sexual act, 2% prostitution of victim, 2% sale/distribution of erotic material to victim, and 3% sexual performance by child.

The problem is what to make of the relatively more frequent occurrence of "less sexual behaviors." To suggest that such behaviors are "not serious" ignores the feelings of victims who may find even "less sexual behaviors" such as fondling or kissing painful, intrusive, and frightening. It may be that fondling behavior serves to desensitize children to touch, thereby conditioning or "grooming" them for more sexual behavior. Some offenders may be identified early in the grooming process, thus accounting for the larger proportion of "less serious" sexual abuse.

Whatever the case, the point is that professionals in the field do not know what to make of current findings on the prevalence of various sexual behaviors. The common error made in practice is to accept the offender's view of the behavior, given that the self-reports of sexual offenders are known to be unreliable (Abel et al., 1981; Marshall & Christie, 1981; Quinsey, 1984; Quinsey, Steinman, Bergersen, & Holmes, 1975). In accepting the offender's view that his motivation is not really sexual or his behavior does not really hurt children, professionals accept a view of the problem that may well make it easier for them to interact with sexual offenders. However, such interactions may minimize or distort the nature of the behavior experienced by the victim, thereby doing little to help either the victim or the offender.

Prevention Harms Children: Another Erroneous Idea

That prevention harms children is another prevalent but erroneous belief. For some time it has been suggested that sexual abuse prevention programs may cause more harm than good to the extent that they are associated with unanticipated negative consequences. Recently, Reppucci and Haugaard (1989) have suggested that prevention programs may be associated with negative consequences such as the following:

> A first grade child interpreted the message that she had the right to say "no" as generalizing to all realms of behavior. For several weeks following the prevention program she frequently told her parents that she had the right to say "no" to any requests that she did not like or made her feel uncomfortable. The parents reported much anguish and frustration on their part about this behavior and about the fact that they had to punish her in order to convince her that she did not have the right to disobey them whenever she wanted. (p. 1273)

I don't know where or in what kind of family the parents described in the article live, but I have never met a parent whose child does not frequently say no. It is not clear why this is such a negative finding. Indeed, one might wonder why a first-grade child could not be reasoned with and helped by her parents to understand when saying no is appropriate and when it is inappropriate. Perhaps something else is going on in this family that we are not told about.

More to the point, there is a growing body of research that has failed to identify any unanticipated consequences of prevention training. Generally, research on prevention training has found positive results (Binder & McNiel, 1987; Kenning, Gallmeier, Jackson, & Plemons, 1987; Miltenberger & Thiesse-Duffy, 1988; Swan, Press, & Briggs, 1987; Wolfe, MacPherson, Blount, & Wolfe, 1986; Wurtele, Kast, Miller-Perrin, & Kondrick, 1988; Wurtele, Marrs, & Miller-Perrin,

1987). For example, Binder and McNiel (1987) found no significant increases in behavior problems recorded by parents' ratings after prevention programs in a sample of 5- through 12-year-olds, but did find a decrease in 3 of 18 problem behaviors. Similarly, no significant increases in children's State-Trait Anxiety Inventory scores or in scores on the adapted version of Quay and Peterson's Problem Behaviors Checklist (using four subscales only: conduct disorders, anxiety withdrawal, attention problem, and motor excess) completed by parents were found following implementation of the Talking About Touching curriculum (Kenning et al., 1987). In another study designed to assess the negative consequences of prevention programs, no increases in the child's fear, as reported by the child and parent, were found (Wurtele et al., 1987). Three significant changes in pre- to posttest behavior problems were found according to parents' ratings, but these were all decreases.

Miltenberger and Thiesse-Duffy (1988) found no new behavioral problems, nightmares, or other lasting emotional reactions, according to parent reports, but nearly a third of the children were "a little more scared" and more than two-thirds were more cautious. Similarly, Garbarino (1987) found that a sizable minority of children of both sexes and in each of three grades reported that reading a Spiderman comic on sexual abuse prevention worried or scared them (from 17% to 50%). The reason given most often was that they realized "it" might happen to them.

A number of evaluations have assessed children's more general reactions to prevention programs. Most children reported feeling "much safer" (64%) or "somewhat safer" and better able to take care of themselves (94%) after a school-based training, while only 3% felt "somewhat more scared" (Binder & McNiel, 1987). When children were asked how they liked the prevention programs, most reported enjoying them (Swan et al., 1987; Wolfe et al., 1986). For example, in one study 65% of the second through fifth graders who viewed the *Bubbylonian Encounter* video either "liked the play" or "liked the play a lot" (Swan et al., 1987).

The possibility that prevention programs could create an exaggerated suspiciousness about all touch has also been explored by researchers. By learning the lessons of such programs "too well," children may be inclined to see abuse where there is none, or to avoid even nurturing touch. Evidence from evaluation studies is mixed. One study found that first through third graders were significantly better at discriminating good touches—that is, labeling nurturing, nonsexual touch correctly—after a one-hour role-play-based prevention training session (Blumberg, Chadwick, Fogarty, Speth, & Chadwick, 1988). In another study, fifth graders did not report feeling more negative about touch between people at posttest, but "overall, they were less willing to trust in, believe, obey and rely on any and all adults" (Plummer, 1984). One study reported that preschoolers had "an increase in the degree to which they associated ambiguous touches (tickling and bathing) with feeling sad" and "a decrease in their association of these touches with happy feelings" following training (Gilbert, Daro, Duerr, LeProhn, & Nyman, 1988).

While no research is currently available indicating that children actually use prevention content to prevent, avoid, or escape their own abuse, there is also no research indicating that prevention efforts are not worth the small amount of funds they require. Indeed, it is not clear how many children would have to employ what they learn in a prevention program successfully to escape abuse before society would say that such programs are worth the cost. I suppose if the child saved from abuse were your own, you would think it well worth it.

An End to the Beginning?

Some pages ago I suggested that the first phase of professional development in child sexual abuse was characterized by efforts to recognize that the problem was in fact a problem. While we as professionals have made significant gains in recognizing that many children are sexually abused (for review of incidence studies, see Peters, Wyatt, & Finkelhor, 1986) and new research findings continuously challenge cherished beliefs, we have a long way to go. Patton takes up the theme of dispelling common myths in the final chapter of this book. Still, there is much we have not yet learned about childhood sexual abuse. To name only a few current "hot" topics, note how little is known about ritualistic abuse, the connection between child pornography and sexual interest in adults, whether sexual and physical child abuse are different phenomena, whether repressed or dissociated experiences can always be brought into active consciousness, or what the most effective treatments are for childhood sexual abuse.

While it appears that there will always be a battle with the psychological defenses inherent in humans against recognizing childhood sexual abuse for what it is, it is clear that ever-increasing numbers of professionals are interested in, aware of, and willing to work in this problem area. The last few years have witnessed the births of three new journals devoted to interpersonal violence that publish (among other things) research on childhood sexual abuse. It is a rare social science journal that does not publish something in each volume on childhood sexual abuse. A new multidisciplinary professional society, the American Professional Society on the Abuse of Children, has a focus, in part, on childhood sexual abuse. Most professional meetings and many regional and state conferences devote attention to this problem. While there may be a long way to go, it appears that development of the field has reached the point where (to borrow from Winston Churchill) it is safe to say we have reached the end of the beginning.

THE MIDDLE PHASE

The middle phase of the field's professional development (approximately from the mid-1970s to early 1980s) was a period in which professionals were concerned with preventing "system-induced trauma." This notion arose early in professional efforts to identify abuse, support disclosures from children, and mobilize "the system" in response. The field viewed childhood sexual abuse as a multidisciplinary problem with legal, medical, social service, public policy, and mental health components. Professionals from each of these fields had a legitimate and unique role to play in responding to the problem. But there was concern that all these professionals, each carrying out some assigned task, would traumatize child victims.

As a result of this concern a great deal of effort was expended in training police officers and medical personnel, adopting innovations in the justice system (e.g., by having the same prosecutor carry the case throughout the process, so the victim would not have to relate to more than prosecutor), creating multidisciplinary teams where one or two professionals would interview the child victim about "what happened" with other professionals observing and taking notes, and a host of other "innovations" (see MacFarlane & Bulkley, 1982). While these may all be fine things to do, it is interesting to note that prior to these solutions, there were no data documenting that "system-induced trauma" was a common problem resulting from interactions with the professional intervention system.

While it is a laudable goal to prevent harm as a consequence of helping, it is not clear that we have strived to attain it in everything we do. Indeed, it is not at all clear that the intervention system is really concerned about children, a point to which I shall return. Although there are many social goals to which lip service is paid (e.g., keeping families together, prosecuting sexual offenders, and reducing public spending), I believe that an evaluation would show that time and time again children do not benefit from these efforts. While there are few data currently available on this matter, ample anecdotal cases exist that point to the damage done to children in the pursuit of such social goals.

Decline in Support for Rehabilitation

During this same period, two major social changes were under way. First, the period witnessed a general decline in public support for rehabilitation and a corresponding increase in support for incarceration. Second, these values were coupled with strong leanings among child sexual abuse professionals toward the prosecution of offenders. These changes resulted in the view that the prosecution of sexual offenders was synonymous with appropriate social response.

It is very difficult to get a true picture of how the intervention system actually operates. No national data are currently available, but a glimpse can be generated by piecing information together. In a recent survey, 276 mental health professionals from around the country reported how sexual offense cases are handled in their communities. They estimated that in 41% of cases the offenders are charged with sexual abuse. Of these, in 30% of cases the offender receives probation; in 26%, there is a civil finding of abuse; in 26%, there is a criminal finding of abuse; and in 18%, the offender goes to jail (Conte, Fogarty, & Collins, 1990).

In a follow-up study of 150 children seen at the Sexual Assault Center in Seattle, Washington, Conte and Berliner (1990) report that 15% received no treatment and 23% were treated for one month or less. Of those who received treatment in the community, the average number of months in treatment was 3.6 (fewer than 16 sessions). National data indicate that about 40% of reports to child protective services of sexual abuse are determined by investigation to be unfounded.

Gradually over the last decade, child protection approaches have shifted from identifying conditions that place children at risk in families and providing services to alter those conditions to an approach that emphasizes *finding fault*. Increasingly child protection is viewed within a legal formulation where finding fault is the major goal. Considerable attention has been paid in the press to state mandates that child sexual abuse cases be investigated within 24 hours of the report. Reports about individuals arrested for sexual abuse of children appear in the nation's newspapers frequently.

Public sentiment, elected officials' rhetoric, and periodic press stories leave the public with the impression that sexually abused children are being taken care of and that sexual offenders are adjudicated and imprisoned. Although available estimates are based on very inadequate data, it appears that most victims do not receive adequate intervention and most sexual offenders do not go to prison. These factors have resulted in several unfortunate consequences.

Emphasis on Professional Procedures

Over the last half decade or so, there has been increasing effort by adults accused of child sexual abuse to retain defense council and vigorously fight the charges. While few Americans would argue against the cherished rights of the accused to defend themselves under our laws, on occasion this defense has involved distortions of child development knowledge (e.g., children can never be accurate reporters of events) and attacks on the procedures and processes used by professionals to support children's disclosures.

The defense strategy of attacking the professional has resulted in defense claims in court that are without empirical support. For example, it is frequently suggested that professionals who have histories of childhood sexual abuse are more likely to see abuse where none has taken place. Although there are no data currently available one way or the other on this matter, it is just as reasonable to expect that since minimization and memory loss are frequent components of the adult's reaction to childhood abuse, abuse survivors are *less* likely to find abuse because they are psychologically defensive. Whatever the reality, the point is that no data exist to inform this issue.

Attacks on professionals have also focused on the procedures used to support children's disclosures. For example, the use of anatomically detailed dolls has been criticized because it is argued that the sexual parts of the dolls overstimulate children and increase the likelihood that they will make false reports of abuse. No data exist supporting this argument. Indeed, recent research by Goodman and Rosenberg (1987) found that 3- and 5-year-old children were no more suggestive when interviewed using anatomically detailed dolls than when interviewed with other dolls or without dolls.

Goodman's research illustrates the nature of the attack on professionals currently under way by the defense and its allies (see, e.g., Goodman & Aman, in press; Goodman, Aman, & Hirschma, 1987; Goodman & Reed, 1986; Goodman, Rudy, Bottoms, & Aman, in press). In a recent *Newsweek* story, Goodman's research over the last few years was criticized for methodological weaknesses (Gelman, 1989). The only evidence cited for these weaknesses was an unpublished research project. Goodman's work does in fact stand out for its methodological rigor involving random assignment to conditions, careful attention to procedures, detailed measurement and analysis, and cautious interpretation of results. Much of it has either been published in or is under review at peer-reviewed scientific journals.

Attacks on Goodman's research and on professionals in general are likely to continue because they make it possible for those who do not really want to believe that children are abused to be more comfortable in not believing and because such attacks may be useful in getting adults accused of sexual abuse out of legal trouble. For the moment these attacks are likely to continue. Over time, however, it is increasingly clear that the attacks will not be successful because the data will not support them. The cautious, rigorous, and planned sequence of studies carried out by Goodman and her colleagues illustrates that research findings support much of what professionals do and believe.

The difficult task for professionals until more research becomes available is to *know what we know and know what we don't know*. Professionals working in child sexual abuse cannot have it both ways. They cannot demand proof for ideas they do not agree with and not demand the same proof for their own ideas. There is little question that on occasion we, as professionals, have become sloppy and not expected the same rigor of ourselves that we demand of others. I recently read a transcript of a court case in which a professional told the judge that there was a high level of confidence that a child had been abused because the child used red ink in her drawings. I have been unable to locate any research suggesting that red ink is a sure sign of anything. Although there is promising research on abused children's art (e.g., Burgess & Grant, 1988; Kelly, 1984), it has not yet progressed to a point that would support the statement made by this professional.

Consensus alone is not sufficient to lay the foundation for forensic practice. In a recent survey of professionals engaged in such work, Conte et al. (1990) report generally high levels of consensus among 212 professionals on 41 criteria or indicators for substantiating reports of sexual abuse. However, notwithstanding the high levels of consensus, it is not clear how much research support exists for many of the criteria. For example, a number of the criteria with higher support are those that involve comparing the child's description of abuse either with itself over time (e.g., "child's statement relates progression of sexual activity") or with a "known" abuse scenario (e.g., "child's statement relates progression of sexual activity" or "child's description of abuse relates elements of pressure or coercion"). There are a number of concerns with such criteria. For example, little is known about what consistency one can expect in children's reports of events. Lack of consistency over time may involve a child's providing progressively more information or different information over time. In the case of more detail over time, the child may be recalling more detail, describing several different incidents of sexual abuse, or supplying fabricated information. Current knowledge simply does not make it possible to determine which of these alternatives is correct in a given case.

Comparing children's descriptions of abuse to known or typical abuse cases is quite problematic, because it is increasingly clear that sexual abuse is a complex behavior in which the offender, the victim, and the situation can experience variation in what happens. Some abuse involves force; some does not. Some abuse involves a slow seduction or grooming process; other abuse does not. The known or common pattern is limited by the professional's training, currency with the literature, professional experience in sexual abuse, and, most important, the state of current knowledge. A child's statements may vary, even quite dramatically, from the "known" or common pattern, and this variation may reflect true variation in the phenomenon or an extreme form of abuse. Although some have argued that it is unlikely that such high levels of consensus are wrong (e.g., Myers et al., 1989), I believe the history of our new field indicates that we have often been wrong, even when we believed things passionately, and many of us have tended to believe the same things without supporting evidence.

Emphasis on Identification and Intake

As a result of increasing emphasis in rhetoric (if not in actual practice) on legal handling of child sexual abuse cases and the resulting efforts to challenge professional practice, there has been undue emphasis placed on the front end of service—identification, validation, and adjudication. These have taken up more energy than what is likely to be more important: treatment of victims and offenders. Clearly, identification of victims and offenders, determining "true" cases from "false" cases, and initiating the processes of intervention are all important undertakings. They may well be thought of as "necessary but not sufficient conditions" for an effective social response.

If society actually punished the majority of adults who have sex with children, it could be argued that something was being done about the problem. I personally doubt that placement of sexual offenders in correctional facilities, where they may spend a proportion of their time masturbating to images of sex with children, is in society's long-term interest. More critically, no information currently available suggests that most offenders are in fact incarcerated. As noted above, the data are quite impressionistic but suggest that most cases simply do not complete the justice system.

When professionals argued (e.g., Conte, 1984) that there was a role for the justice system in child sexual abuse cases, it was to encourage adult offenders to accept responsibility for their behavior and enter treatment. Some have even suggested that sexual abuse should be decriminalized. Such an action would serve to give the wrong message to offenders about the nature of their behavior and society's feelings about it. National data are not available, but it appears that fewer communities now have community-based alternatives to incarceration and that more adults are willing to run the risk of trial because the new defense tactics are successful in some cases.

THE FUTURE AGENDA

It is time for a reanalysis of current social policy regarding sexual abuse. Clearly there are multiple goals. Although it appears that adult sexual use of children is a more common experience of childhood than heretofore believed, no reasonable person argues that sexual abuse of children is desirable or should be tolerated. Society through its laws establishes guidelines for behavior, criteria for full participation in a free society, and sanctions to protect society from those who violate those guidelines and thereby forfeit their freedom. Few would disagree that society has a special obligation to its weakest and youngest members, its children. Nevertheless, there is considerable disagreement between conservative and liberal political philosophies about the appropriate and desirable roles of government and nongovernment institutions in meeting society's obligations to children. These issues are beyond the scope of this chapter but they are an important part of the future agenda for the field. This chapter closes by highlighting a number of social policy principles that can help frame the future agenda as the field of child sexual abuse moves into a maturing phase.

The Need for a Long-Range View

There needs to be serious discussion about the long-term goals of society. Sexual abuse in childhood has been clearly linked to significant mental health and social problems in childhood and adulthood (e.g., Browne & Finkelhor, 1986; Courtois & Sprei, 1988). Early identification of victims is important, as is the provision of a range of social and mental health services likely to facilitate recovery and prevent long-term negative consequences of abuse. These interventions are likely to have significant implications for society.

No one has yet calculated the financial costs of childhood sexual abuse in terms of social problems, lost individual potential, and human suffering, but they are likely to be substantial. Effective and early treatment should help reduce these costs, but providing that treatment will require a major sustained and organized effort to educate the public. The public needs to know about the current lack of treatment, the long-term costs and negative consequences of childhood sexual abuse, and our failure to treat the victims of family sexual abuse effectively. It is increasingly clear that eliciting public support for effective treatment will require leadership willing to point out the current failures of society's organized response to childhood sexual abuse and to suggest practical programs and policies for a new way of responding. Healing the invisible wounds of childhood sexual abuse and other forms of child maltreatment must be as much a national priority as rebuilding the infrastructure, maintaining the national defense, or protecting the natural environment.

Protection of Children as Core Policy

In a climate where there are competing social goals, principles should be articulated for selecting among alternative goals or courses of action. One such principle, it seems to me, is protection of children as a core policy. Research is needed to operationalize such a policy. Whether or not prosecution of offenders prevents future child abuse, the effects of longer or shorter prison sentences, the results of community treatment for offenders on probation, and what types of treatment are more effective—these are questions that research can answer if society is willing to support such research. It is also clear that research is needed that will help us understand the consequences for children of various intervention decisions. For example, what happens when a case is determined to be "unfounded" at the child protection level? What happens to a child who may have been abused when a prosecutor declines prosecution? What happens when an adult accused of sexual abuse of his own child is removed from the home? These are only a few of the kinds of questions that need to be addressed if the public and professionals are to understand how the child protection system operates and its effects on children. Several chapters in this book address these kinds of issues.

As suggested above, it is not clear the extent to which effective interventions are made available to children. There appears to be a lack of mental health services in most communities to meet the needs of sexually abused children, and it is not clear the extent to which supportive social services (e.g., supervised day care, job training programs) are available to the families of abused children to make it possible for those families to provide protective and supportive environments.

Obviously there are many avenues through which society may protect children and assure their development. If successfully pursued, incarceration of adults who abuse children is likely to stop some abuse. Effective community-based or prison-based treatment programs, if available in sufficient numbers to meet current needs, may help prevent some abuse, at least abuse by those offenders who are treated. Continued efforts to identify victims and offenders as early as possible may decrease the duration of some children's sexual abuse. While data are lacking on overall societal patterns, it does not appear that we are all that successful in incarcerating sexual offenders or in providing effective treatment to those offenders who may benefit from it. More clearly, to the extent that we have information on child victims, it currently appears that most are not being treated at all.

I suggest that there can be no more central guiding mission for society than the protection of children. There will certainly be considerable debate over society's responsibility to children versus other groups (e.g., the elderly and the chronically ill). Some of us may argue that there is enough money to support all the truly deserving, but others will argue that there is not, so priorities must be established. As professionals working in child abuse, it seems important to refocus on our central mission: *protecting children*. It may prove to be a fruitful exercise to ask ourselves the extent to which our efforts, and each specific case decision we make, serve to protect children.

Initially, we may find more debate than expected within our own ranks about the extent to which our actions really do protect children or what social and individual interventions are more likely to result in the greatest benefits for children. In the long run, such an exercise may help us to see that by the year 2001 children really are protected and really do come first.

NOTE

1. The American Professional Society on the Abuse of Children can be contacted at 332 N. Michigan Ave. N., Chicago, IL.

REFERENCES

Abel, G., Becker, J., Cunningham-Rathner, J., Mittleman, M., & Rouleau, J. L. (1988). Multiple paraphiliac diagnoses among sex offenders. *Bulletin of the American Academy of Psychiatry and the Law, 16*(2), 153–168.

Abel, G., Becker, J., Murphy, W., & Flanagan, B. (1981). Identifying dangerous child molesters. In R. Stuart (Ed.), *Violent behavior: Social learning approaches to prediction, management, and treatment.* New York: Brunner/Mazel.

Avery-Clark, C., O'Neil, J. A., & Laws, D. R. (1981). A comparison of intrafamilial sexual and physical child abuse. In M. Cook & K. Howell (Eds.), *Adult sexual interest in children* (pp. 3–39). Toronto: Academic Press.

Binder, R. L., & McNiel, D. E. (1987). Evaluation of a school-based sexual abuse prevention program: Cognitive and emotional effects. *Child Abuse and Neglect, 11,* 497–506.

Blumberg, E., Chadwick, M. W., Fogarty, L. A., Speth, T., & Chadwick, D. (1988). *The good touch/bad touch component of a sexual abuse prevention program: Unanticipated positive consequences.* Unpublished manuscript.

Browne, A., & Finkelhor, D. (1986). Initial and long-term effects: A review of the research. In D. Finkelhor & Associates, *A sourcebook on child sexual abuse* (pp. 143–179). Beverly Hills, CA: Sage.

Burgess, A. W., & Grant, C. A. (1988). *Children traumatized in sex rings.* Washington, DC: National Center for Missing and Exploited Children.

Conte, J. R. (1984). The justice system and sexual abuse of children. *Social Service Review, 58*(10), 556–568.

Conte, J. R. (1985). The effects of sexual abuse on children: A critique and suggestions for future research. *Victimology, 10,* 110–130.

Conte, J. R. (1986). Child sexual abuse and the family: A critical analysis. *Journal of Psychotherapy and the Family, 2*(2), 113–126.

Conte, J. R., & Berliner, L. (1990). *What happens to sexually abused children after disclosure.* (Available from J. R. Conte, School of Social Work, University of Washington JH-30, Seattle, WA 98195)

Conte, J. R., Fogarty, L., & Collins, M. E. (1990). *National survey of professional practice in child sexual abuse.* (Available from J. R. Conte, School of Social Work, University of Washington JH-30, Seattle, WA 98195)

Conte, J. R., & Schuerman, J. R. (1987). Factors associated with an increased impact of child sexual abuse. *Child Abuse and Neglect, 11,* 201–211.

Conte, J. R., Sorenson, E., Fogarty, L., & Rosa, J. D. (in press). Validating allegations of sexual abuse: The state of knowledge. *American Journal of Occupational Therapy.*

Courtois, C. A., & Sprei, J. E. (1988). Retrospective incest therapy for women. In L. Walker (Ed.), *Handbook on sexual abuse of children* (pp. 270–308). New York: Springer.

Deblinger, E., McLeer, S. V., Atkins, M. S., Ralphe, D., & Foa, E. (1989). Post-traumatic stress in sexually abused, physically abused, and nonabused children. *Child Abuse and Neglect, 13,* 403–408.

Earls, C., & Marshall, W. L. (1983). The current state of technology in the laboratory assessment of sexual arousal patterns. In J. G. Greer & I. R. Stuart (Eds.), *The sexual aggressor: Current perspectives on treatment.* New York: Van Nostrand Reinhold.

Garbarino, J. (1987). Children's response to a sexual abuse prevention program: A study of the *Spiderman* comic. *Child Abuse and Neglect, 11,* 143–148.

Gelman, D. (1989, November 13). The sex-abuse puzzle. *Newsweek,* pp. 99–100.

Gilbert, N., Daro, D., Duerr, J., LeProhn, N., & Nyman, N. (1988). *Child sexual abuse prevention: Evaluation of educational materials for pre-school programs* (Department of Health and Human Services, National Center on Child Abuse and Neglect, Grant 90-CA-1163). Berkeley: University of California, School of Social Welfare, Family Welfare Research Group.

Goodman, G. S., & Aman, C. (in press). Children's use of anatomically detailed dolls to recount an event. *Child Development.*

Goodman, G. S., Aman, C., & Hirschma, J. (1987). Child sexual and physical abuse: Children's testimony. In S. J. Ceci, M. P. Togila, & D. F. Ross (Eds.), *Children's eyewitness memory.* New York: Springer-Verlag.

Goodman, G. S., & Reed, R. S. (1986). Age differences in eyewitness testimony. *Law and Human Behavior, 10,* 317–332.

Goodman, G. S., & Rosenberg, M. S. (1987). The child witness to family violence: Clinical and legal considerations. In D. Sonkin (Ed.), *Domestic violence on trial.* New York: Springer.

Goodman, G. S., Rudy, L., Bottoms, B. L., & Aman, C. (in press). Children's concerns and memory: Issues of ecological validity in children's testimony. In R. Fivush & J. Hudson (Eds.), *What young children remember and know.* New York: Cambridge University Press.

Kelly, S. J. (1984). The use of art therapy for sexually abused children. *Journal of Psychosocial Nursing, 22*(12), 13–18.

Kendall-Tackett, K. A., & Simon, A. F. (1987). Perpetrators and their acts: Data from 365 adults molested as children. *Child Abuse and Neglect, 11,* 237–246.

Kenning, M., Gallmeier, T., Jackson, T. L., & Plemons, S. (1987). *Evaluation of child sexual abuse prevention programs: A summary of two studies.* Paper presented at the National Conference on Family Violence, Durham, NH.

Kercher, G., & McShane, M. (1984). Characterizing child sexual abuse on the basis of a multi-agency sample. *Victimology, 9,* 364–382.

Kolko, D. J., Moser, J. T., & Weldy, S. R. (1988). Behavioral/emotional indicators of sexual abuse in child psychiatric inpatients: A controlled comparison with physical abuse. *Child Abuse and Neglect, 12,* 529–541.

Laws, D. R., & Osborn, C. A. (1983). How to build and operate a behavioral laboratory to evaluate and treat sexual defiance. In J. G. Greer & I. R. Stuart (Eds.), *The sexual aggressor: Current perspectives on treatment.* New York: Van Nostrand Reinhold.

Lerman, H. (1988). The psychoanalytic legacy: From whence we came. In L. Walker (Ed.), *Handbook on Sexual Abuse of Children.* New York: Springer.

MacFarlane, K., & Bulkley, J. (1982). Treating child sexual abuse: An overview of current program models. *Journal of Social Work and Human Sexuality, 1,* 69–91.

Marshall, W. L., Barbaree, H. E., & Christophe, D. (1986). Sexual offenders against female children: Sexual preferences for age of victims and type of behaviour. *Canadian Journal of Behavioral Science, 18,* 424–439.

Marshall, W. L., & Christie, M. M. (1981). Pedophilia and aggression. *Criminal Justice and Behavior, 8,* 145–158.

Miltenberger, R. G., & Thiesse-Duffy, E. (1988). Evaluation of home-based programs for teaching personal safety skills to children. *Journal of Applied Behavior Analysis, 21,* 81–87.

Myers, J., Bays, J., Becker, J., Berliner, L., Corwin, D. L., & Saywitz, K. J. (1989). Expert testimony in child sexual abuse litigation. *Nebraska Law Review, 68*(1/2).

Peters, S. D., Wyatt, G. E., & Finkelhor, D. (1986). Prevalence. In D. Finkelhor & Associates, *A sourcebook on child sexual abuse* (pp. 15–59). Beverly Hills, CA: Sage.

Plummer, K. (1981). Pedophilia: Constructing a sociological baseline. In M. Cook & K. Howell (Eds.), *Adult sexual interest in children* (pp. 221–250). New York: Academic Press.

Plummer, C. (1984, April 26–28). *Research on prevention: What school programs teach children.* Paper presented at the Third National Conference on Sexual Victimization of Children. Washington, DC. (Available from C. Plummer, P.O. Box 421, Kalamazoo, MI 49005–0421)

Quinsey, V. L. (1984). Sexual aggression: Studies of offenders against women. In D. Weisstub (Ed.), *Law and mental health: International perspectives.* New York: Pergamon.

Quinsey, V. L., Chaplin, T. C., & Carrigan, W. F. (1979). Sexual preferences among incestuous and nonincestuous child molesters. *Behavior Therapy, 10,* 562–565.

Quinsey, V. L., Steinman, C. M., Bergersen, S. G., & Holmes, T. F. (1975). Penile circumference, skin conductance, and ranking responses of child molesters and normals to sexual and nonsexual visual stimuli. *Behavior Therapy, 6,* 213–219.

Reppucci, N. D., & Haugaard, J. J. (1989). Prevention of child sexual abuse: Myth or reality. *American Psychologist, 44,* 1266–1275.

Swan, H. L., Press, A. N., & Briggs, S. C. (1987). Child sexual abuse prevention: Does it work? *Child Welfare, 64,* 395–405.

Wolfe, D. A., MacPherson, T., Blount, R., & Wolfe, V. V. (1986). Evaluation of a brief intervention for educating school children in awareness of physical and sexual abuse. *Child Abuse and Neglect, 10,* 85–92.

Wurtele, S. K., Kast, L. C., Miller-Perrin, C. L., & Kondrick, P. A. (1989). A comparison of programs for teaching personal safety skills to pre-schoolers. *Journal of Consulting and Clinical Psychology.*

Wurtele, S. K., Marrs, S. R., & Miller-Perrin, C. L. (1987). An evaluation of side effects associated with participation in a child sexual abuse prevention program. *Journal of School Health, 57*(6), 228–231.

2

The Minnesota Family
Sexual Abuse Project

MARGARET J. BRINGEWATT

This chapter provides a context for this book by recounting the story of the Family Sexual Abuse Project (FSAP) in Minnesota. A five-year effort (1985–1990) sponsored by The Saint Paul Foundation, FSAP promoted and funded research and evaluation projects aimed at studying the effectiveness of different intervention and treatment approaches to problems of family sexual abuse. Most of these projects focused specifically on the relationships between selected interventions and the status and functioning of the family. The chapters in this book present the major findings of 11 studies funded through FSAP.

The Family Sexual Abuse Project has demonstrated the importance of studying interventions and family systems at the local level. Large, national studies provide data on major trends, but the real impacts of family sexual abuse interventions take place at the local program level, in the context of specific community systems. The FSAP studies are relatively small in scale and narrow in focus, but they concentrate their inquiries where the action is—with local practitioners dealing with local problems. These studies, and the Family Sexual Abuse Project in general, demonstrate the kinds of contributions small studies and specific program evaluations can make to the field of family sexual abuse research and practice.

To understand the nature, workings, and contributions of the Family Sexual Abuse Project, it helps to place it in the joint contexts of national trends and of Minnesota's particular configuration of politics, philosophy, and practice. Jon Conte established a national context in Chapter 1. This chapter further establishes the context for FSAP by summarizing the evolution of Minnesota's responses to child abuse and then to child sexual abuse, including family sexual abuse. With that distinctive backdrop in place, FSAP's origins and outcomes can be described and assessed.

MINNESOTA POLITICS, PRACTICE, AND PHILOSOPHY

Beginnings: 1960s and 1970s

Responses to Child Abuse

The Minnesota legislature first passed a law specifically addressing maltreatment of minors in 1975. The focus of that law was physical abuse of children rather than sexual abuse. However, coordination of services for physically abused children in Minnesota preceded that law by at least a decade. Responding to the exposure of the child abuse phenomenon in the early 1960s, a few public and private sector professionals in the Twin Cities of Minneapolis and Saint Paul saw a need to coordinate the efforts of the many different people who were (or thought they should be) involved with abused children and their families.

The Kempe National Center for Protection and Treatment of Child Abuse and Neglect, founded in 1972 in Denver, Colorado, provided a hospital-based model of multidisciplinary coordination. In the early 1970s, Ramsey County (which includes the city of Saint Paul) adapted the Kempe Center approach and created what was, as far as we know, the first community-based, multidisciplinary child protection team in the nation. This team included representatives from child protection, law enforcement, the county attorney's office, county corrections, the courts (criminal, juvenile, and family), and mental health services (both public and private).

The innovative aspect of the community-based model was its independence from any institutional base (i.e., the welfare, medical, or legal systems). The strength of this model rests in the collaboration of team members with diverse backgrounds and professional bases (although its necessary reliance on shared philosophy can make it difficult to get going). With encouragement from the Minnesota Department of Human Services, this community-based team approach to child abuse has been adopted by nearly half of the 87 counties in Minnesota.

Recognition of Child Sexual Abuse

In 1963 Minnesota enacted the Incest Law, which, for the first time, defined sexual relations between two people related by blood as criminal. At that time incest was thought to be extremely rare. No services for sexually abused children existed. Cases that arose were regarded as the province of either the medical profession or the legal system.

The extent and complexity of intrafamilial sexual abuse began to come to light in Minnesota in the late 1970s through two parallel routes. Juvenile females, typically runaways, recounted stories of long-standing sexual abuse within their families. Concurrently, adult women in shelters and other settings began to describe their abusive family histories. These stories provided the first glimpse of how widespread child sexual abuse is, and of the complex and long-term effects of that trauma. At about the same time, amendments to the Minnesota Child Abuse Reporting Law greatly expanded the types of professionals who were required to report suspected abuse, including sexual abuse. This law, and the training its enactment prompted, heightened awareness of physicians, teachers, school nurses, and others who worked with children to the possibility of child sexual abuse.

When child sexual abuse, including intrafamilial abuse, began to emerge as an issue in the mid-1970s, the multidisciplinary team model was fairly well established in Minnesota as an approach that many believed served the best interests of the child. The late 1970s saw the initiation of various programs to treat victims of sexual abuse, including the first family treatment program in Minnesota.

In addition to treatment programs, new initiatives focused on the prevention of child abuse, including sexual abuse. Minnesota chapters of the Committee for the Prevention of Child Abuse and of Parents Anonymous were established. The innovative Illusion Theater developed prevention plays titled *Touch* and *No Easy Answers*. These productions have toured extensively to spread prevention messages. The formation of Responses to End Child Abuse, a collaborative effort of concerned corporations, insurers, courts, public agencies, and health care entities, represented another innovative response to the need for prevention efforts.

In part because of their early recognition of the issue and their participation in community-based teams, professionals in Minnesota tended to regard themselves to some extent as pioneers in the development of child sexual abuse treatment and prevention approaches. This perspective, and the exposure to multidisciplinary viewpoints, seemed to foster not only innovation but also a corresponding willingness to accept diversity and to experiment with different models. There was a sense that everyone was still learning, and thus a keen interest in sharing information.

The 1980s: Watershed Years

Sexual Abuse in the Forefront

In 1981 the Minnesota legislature passed a new law dealing directly with intrafamilial sexual abuse. This law broadened the definition of *familial*, expanded coverage to all sexual acts, and established guidelines concerning some aspects of defense and testimony. Since that time, reporting and prosecuting of child sexual abuse, including intrafamilial abuse, have increased greatly. The first half of the 1980s saw dramatic increases in both reported cases of sexual abuse and substantiation rates. Minnesota's situation mirrored national data from the National Center on Child Abuse and Neglect (1988) in that reported cases of child sexual abuse increased threefold between 1980 and 1986.

Difficulties in obtaining valid and reliable data on the extent of child sexual abuse perpetuate a broad continuum of beliefs in Minnesota about prevalence. Some maintain that most reported cases do not warrant government intrusion. Research indicates, however, that child sexual abuse continues to be dramatically underreported (Peters, Wyatt, & Finkelhor, 1986).

This diversity of beliefs contributes to a diversity of responses in terms of available services, treatment modalities, court prosecutions, and legislation. Against this uncertain backdrop, child abuse legislation has continued to be enacted, and has continued to generate controversy. The Minnesota Child Abuse Reporting Law alone has been amended more than 100 times since its enactment in 1975.

The art and practice of working with family sexual abuse cases blossomed during the 1980s. Numerous private sector programs were established as professionals realized that family sexual abuse presented a distinct set of issues with treatment implications requiring tailored programs. Programs and models of intervention evolved that were suited to various types of clients. In addition, as offenders came to be regarded as persons who needed treatment, assessment and intervention programs for adult and adolescent offenders also began to emerge. This period of service development left important legacies, among them realization that the treatment process is complex, expensive, and of uncertain effectiveness.

A final significant event of the mid-1980s was Project Abuse, a production of CBS affiliate WCCO-TV, which offered a solid week of programming for all ages, classroom discussion guides, and special news reports. A hot line set up to respond to viewers' questions and concerns received 700 calls in two weeks. Project Abuse drew attention to child sexual abuse as no previous local event had, and prompted discussion at all levels throughout the community.

The Scott County Case

Beginning in 1981, several widely publicized cases of child sexual abuse heightened public awareness of the extent of such abuse across all social, economic, and ethnic groups. The most famous case brought family sexual abuse to the public's attention in a prolonged and spectacular way, and brought this sensitive topic into the open in Minnesota.

In 1984, the county attorney in Scott County (a suburban/rural county adjacent to the Twin Cities metropolitan area) filed charges against 24 adults following an extensive investigation of reported child sexual abuse. Allegations of child pornography, a child sex abuse ring, and homicides surfaced. Statements from alleged child victims reported sex parties, pornographic photos, murders of young children, and repeated incidents of sexual abuse involving multiple adults. By October of that year, enormous controversy had been generated over the handling of the case. After only one conviction, charges against the other citizens accused of child sexual abuse were dropped.

Both the Minnesota Bureau of Criminal Apprehension and the Federal Bureau of Investigation subsequently conducted investigations and found insufficient evidence to justify the filing of any new charges. The official report on the case from the Minnesota Attorney General's Office emphasized that at least some of the children were in fact sexually abused, but that the seriously flawed investigation prohibited successful prosecution (Humphrey, 1985).

The investigations found that many of the children had been questioned about sex abuse repeatedly, even dozens of times, often by several individuals. Most of this repeated questioning went undocumented. Many families were separated while the investigation continued. In many cases, even when children denied having been sexually abused, they were removed from their homes and isolated from all family contact for prolonged periods. The investigation further uncovered instances in which children were told that reunification with their families would be facilitated by admissions of sex abuse by their parents and other adults. In some instances, under questioning over an extended period of time, children's allegations of sexual abuse turned to stories of mutilations and eventually homicide. There were numerous instances of "cross-germination" of allegations, when witnesses were interviewed together or informed of what other witnesses had stated. A thorough search for corroboration of a child's allegations was generally not completed prior to arrests. The suspects themselves were seldom, if ever, interviewed prior to being charged.

Aftermath of Scott County

While the Scott County case was clearly an anomaly in both its scope and Minnesota's practice of handling child sexual abuse, it brought to light a number of serious issues and had multiple repercussions through the late 1980s. A 1986 report from the Attorney General's Office contained more than 100 recommendations for changes in laws, practices, and procedures (Attorney General's Task Force on Child Abuse Within the Family, 1986). A flurry of legislative activity resulted. A massive set of legislative hearings dramatically framed the issues for policymakers. Multiple changes in courtroom practices and investigative procedures ensued as policymakers tried to assure fair trial of an accused adult, protection of the child from harm, and viability of child testimony.

In addition to prompting legal and procedural changes, the Scott County case generated widespread, vociferous debate about protection of children versus family privacy and integrity. As a result, the notion of balance between the child's interests and the family's interests gained credence. Parental rights groups emerged in an organized and visible way to question the believability of children's testimony and to advocate for interventions less disruptive to the family.

The Scott County case also had profound effects on professionals who work with sexually abused children. The roles of treatment professionals and of investigators began to be delineated more clearly. Medical providers established protocols for evidentiary exams. Professionals realized the need for more standardized approaches and for documentation that would withstand intense review. Prosecutorial practices received close scrutiny. Reactions from professionals could be characterized on a continuum from extreme caution and reluctance to take on cases aggressively to willingness to take the hard lessons from Scott County as impetus to sharpen professional skills.

Two more significant effects of the Scott County case deserve mention. First, the case and its prolonged and intensive media coverage dramatically raised the general public's awareness of intrafamilial sexual abuse. Second, the scramble for answers in the wake of the case underscored just how little was known about intrafamilial sexual abuse and its effects, thus pointing out the need for research and evaluation.

EVOLVING MINNESOTA CLIMATE

Policy Directions

A great many people have put a great deal of effort into dealing with child sexual abuse in Minnesota. The result, over time, has been a genuine responsiveness from professionals, public officials, and the general public, and a corresponding willingness to tackle the problem in all its complexity. Beginning in the 1970s, both administrative and legislative efforts reflected state-level leadership and a commitment to multidisciplinary approaches. Interagency task forces have included, for example, the Governor's Task Force on Criminal Justice Policy, the Interagency Child Abuse and Neglect Team, and the Task Force on Child Safety. In 1990 the Omnibus Child Protection Revitalization Bill was passed by the Minnesota Legislature; among other provisions it mandates that all counties create multidisciplinary child abuse teams.

Most recently, Project IMPACT (a 1986–1989 project funded through the U.S. Department of Justice) provided statewide, multidisciplinary training and team building for professionals who work with child sexual abuse victims. Project IMPACT explicitly emphasized building community partnerships. The project's final publication, *Child Sexual Abuse: Impact and Aftershocks* (Freese, 1989), offers a useful overview of the current state of knowledge about child sexual abuse from a variety of perspectives.

Fran Sepler (1989), executive director of the Minnesota Crime Victim and Witness Advisory Council, has identified the emergence of three general trends in public policy over the last decade. The first of these is the aforementioned movement toward *balancing the often competing rights of children and rights of families.* Active prevention and early intervention efforts may offer hope of maintaining an appropriate balance, since such efforts, if appropriately directed and effective, support family integrity and avoid intrusive public action. The recent findings of a Minnesota legislative commission continue to fuel the debate about balance with a series of recommendations that strongly articulate "the child's best interest" as the paramount consideration for the courts (Child Protection System Study Commission, 1990).

The second trend, toward *increasing sanctions for criminal sexual conduct*, including intrafamilial sexual abuse, reflects a more general policy trend of getting tougher on crime. As recently as 1980 very few intrafamilial sexual abuse cases were prosecuted in Minnesota. Debate has evolved over the last decade away from "treatment versus incarceration" and toward finding an appropriate balance of treatment and court involvement.

The third public policy advance has been in the area of *making the processes of investigation and prosecution as "child friendly" as possible*. Multiple procedural changes have addressed the special needs of child witnesses, including admissibility of evidence and adequacy of protection. Child testimony has been greatly facilitated through a variety of technical accommodations as well as legislative actions.

Importance of Evaluation

Minnesota's strong expertise in evaluation research constitutes yet another factor in the development of child sexual abuse services and policy—and a factor in the establishment of the Family Sexual Abuse Project as well. Broadly defined, evaluation involves using research to improve and/or judge a program's effectiveness. Beginning in the 1970s, Minnesota provided leadership in defining and exploring the emergent field of evaluation research, especially through an interdisciplinary, NIMH-supported fellowship program at the University of Minnesota.

Evaluation research has been used extensively in Minnesota to improve programs, guide policy, and inform practice. Michael Quinn Patton (1978, 1986), a Minnesota-based leader in this field, created an approach called "utilization-focused evaluation," which emphasizes increasing the usefulness of evaluation results by identifying primary intended users; determining what information will best inform their forthcoming decisions on planning, funding, and practice; designing the evaluation so as to obtain needed and desired information; and then working with the primary intended users to apply findings for program improvement and decision making.

In 1980, Ramsey County developed a formative model of evaluation focused on client outcomes; it was implemented among all of the county's contracted mental health and social service providers (U.S. Department of Human Services, 1984). According to Joan Velasquez, director of research and evaluation for Ramsey County Human Services, Ramsey was the first county in the nation to develop such an approach, and it has been widely adopted across the country. Another nationally recognized evaluation system (Kamerman & Kahn, 1989) has been instituted in the Community Services Department of Hennepin County (Minneapolis), which includes child protection. Its strong formative emphasis gives program staff the opportunity to help develop criteria, interpret results, and implement program changes based upon evaluation findings.

This local leadership and expertise in evaluation research is an important part of the context for understanding developments in child sexual abuse research and evaluation in Minnesota. The emergence of evaluation research in Minnesota intersected with the acknowledgment of gaps in knowledge about child sexual abuse in general and concerns about the effectiveness of various interventions in particular. Encouraging evaluation research directed at family sexual abuse programs was a logical next step. Thus service, policy, and evaluation trends combined to create a climate ripe for genesis of the Family Sexual Abuse Project.

THE FAMILY SEXUAL ABUSE PROJECT

Beginnings: The Bigelow Study

In 1984, before the Scott County case burst on the scene, the F. R. Bigelow Foundation of Saint Paul commissioned a study on intrafamilial sexual abuse in the three eastern counties of the Twin Cities metropolitan area (McBean, 1984). The study report brought into focus the range of problems and needs concerning intrafamilial sexual abuse. The report also delineated options for philanthropic organizations that wanted to have an impact on this issue.

Using the F. R. Bigelow study as background and rationale, The Saint Paul Foundation, a community foundation serving the east metro region, decided to create a project that would focus on one significant aspect of intrafamilial sexual abuse. Accordingly, it assembled an advisory group that considered the numerous recommendations of the F. R. Bigelow Foundation report.

That advisory group settled on the strategy of creating a grant-making program to fund research and evaluation projects that would study the effectiveness of various interventions. In the second and third grant-making rounds, the focus was more specifically on the relationship of family structure or functioning to various interventions, rather than on the study of victims or offenders alone. The Saint Paul Foundation contributed funds and spearheaded fund-raising efforts from other sources—and the Family Sexual Abuse Project was born.

Rationale for Research and Evaluation

Treatment effectiveness was, and continues to be, one of the major unknown variables in this field. Everyone involved wants to know what works, for whom, and for how long, but there were virtually no local studies of any aspect of family sexual abuse policies or treatment programs, much less systematic evaluations. Were any families in treatment healing? If so, which ones, and what made the difference? A huge knowledge deficit provided one major rationale for focusing on treatment effectiveness.

The potential "ripple effect" of new knowledge offered another compelling reason to focus on intervention approaches. In the short term, the children and families being served by the agencies participating in the research would benefit. More broadly, FSAP's explicit commitment to sharing information could assist professionals in a number of related fields (child protection agencies; treatment programs; legislative, judicial, and law enforcement systems; and health care organizations and the health insurance industry). Furthermore, Minnesota's diverse systems and treatment approaches offered a natural laboratory for studies of effectiveness.

Project Structure

The Family Sexual Abuse Project was designed as a five-year program that would make grants from a pool of funds contributed by several corporate and foundation sources (see the preface to this volume for a list of contributors). FSAP was formally created by The Saint Paul Foundation in 1985. After a start-up period, FSAP conducted three grant-making rounds, soliciting proposals through annual Requests for Proposals (RFPs) issued in 1986, 1987, and 1988. In these three rounds, 12 grants were awarded, for a total disbursement of $253,475 in grant funds.

The RFPs outlined two program options: (a) evaluation of existing treatment and intervention efforts and (b) original research conducted either by career researchers or by practitioners in the field. These relatively broad options for research and evaluation reflected the fact that no single research priority could be identified as most urgent.

Because no consensus on treatment models existed, numerous approaches were being tried. Thus it seemed important to learn to what extent those approaches could be evaluated and, if successful, regarded as models. FSAP deliberately chose to support research by and for practitioners in the hope that resultant advancements in knowledge would prove useful in the daily decisions professionals in the field need to make.

FSAP Goals

Given all of these considerations, the Family Sexual Abuse Project articulated four goals:

1. Advance knowledge about the effectiveness of treatment and intervention for family sexual abuse through research and evaluation.
2. Improve the effectiveness of treatment and intervention programs providing services to families experiencing sexual abuse.
3. Stimulate interest in conducting and using high-quality research on family sexual abuse interventions and treatments.
4. Inform professionals and policymakers about new knowledge regarding family sexual abuse, program improvements in intervention and treatment, and effective evaluation and / or research approaches.

The Studies

Diversity continues to flourish in family sexual abuse prevention and treatment in Minnesota. This diversity marks not only comprehensiveness of services and models of treatments, but also record keeping, data gathering, and readiness to undertake related research. Such diversity befits an evolving field in a changing political climate. However, Minnesota's climate of diversity does not lend itself to large, standardized research studies, or to controlled comparisons of treatment options.

The state of practice dictates the nature of research that can appropriately be undertaken. Thus our research studies on family sexual abuse consist of situationally specific studies, the value of which lies in their individual and collective ability to illuminate some of the fundamental questions that have arisen out of a dozen years of Minnesota's experience with family sexual abuse. Chapters 3 through 13 of this book contribute to a better understanding of six very central questions.

What are we learning about offenders? What variables are associated with sibling incest (Chapter 5)? What characteristics distinguish women who sexually abuse children (Chapter 13)? What processes support or interrupt the transition from victim to perpetrator (Chapter 6)?

What are the effects of offender removal and treatment? How do offenders respond to treatment during incarceration, and what impact does such treatment have on family formation or reformation following release (Chapter 12)? How are families affected by removing offenders from the home (Chapter 9)? What factors contribute to positive or negative reunification experiences (Chapter 10)?

What is the experience of abuse for young children? What behavioral effects are seen in sexually abused preschoolers (Chapter 4)? What lasting problems result for child victims of sexual abuse (Chapter 3)?

What are we learning about the design and effects of various treatments? What are the lasting impacts of treatment for victims and families (Chapter 8)? What treatment goals and strategies can be identified for working with adolescent offenders (Chapter 5)? To what extent do female sex offenders benefit from psychological treatment in an outpatient setting (Chapter 13)?

What are we learning about families in which sexual abuse occurs? What parental and family characteristics affect children's adjustment after abuse (Chapter 4)? What are the patterns of sexual interaction in incest families, and what variables contribute to sexual health (Chapter 11)? What is an appropriate working definition of *family* when dealing with sexual abuse in American Indian cultures (Chapter 7)?

What are we learning about the service and legal systems and their effects on families? How adequate are system interventions (Chapter 3)? What are the patterns of service utilization for American Indian families (Chapter 7)? What are the adjustment patterns of family members other than the victim or the offender (Chapters 3 and 8)? How do families experience the decision-making authority of the system (Chapters 3, 5, and 9)?

CONCLUSION

The Family Sexual Abuse Project set out to provide insight into the diversity and complexity of the field rather than to find definitive answers to any one question. Yet there are important reinforcing patterns among the separate studies. The final chapter, written by editor Michael Quinn Patton, provides an overview and synthesis of the findings of these 11 projects.

When the FSAP advisory committee began working in 1985, we could not have known that we were embarking on this project during what has been described by Fran Sepler, executive director of the Minnesota Crime Victim and Witness Advisory Council, as "the last ten minutes of calm" in the Minnesota experience with child sexual abuse. Since our beginnings in 1985, the field has grown more diverse and complex, and the political environment has become more highly contentious.

This chapter has reviewed the distinctive philosophical and political environment in Minnesota that shaped the focus and findings of the FSAP projects. The state of the art in family sexual abuse research will continue to evolve as practitioners find ways to ask questions of importance to the field, and search for answers that can inform their actions. The FSAP practitioner-researchers have contributed information and insights—and posed new questions—that challenge us to examine both programs and policies in the field of family sexual abuse.

REFERENCES

Attorney General's Task Force on Child Abuse Within the Family. (1986). *A report to Hubert H. Humphrey III, attorney general.* Saint Paul: State of Minnesota.

Child Protection System Study Commission. (1990). *Final report.* Saint Paul: State of Minnesota.

Freese, S. (1989). *Child sexual abuse: Impact and aftershocks.* Saint Paul: Government Training Service.

Humphrey, H. H., III. (1985). *Report on Scott County investigations.* Saint Paul: State of Minnesota.

Kamerman, S. B., & Kahn, A. J. (1989). *Social services for children, youth and families in the United States.* Greenwich, CT: Annie E. Casey Foundation.

McBean, A. J. (1984). *Intrafamilial sexual abuse: Considering the next steps.* Saint Paul: F. R. Bigelow Foundation.

National Center on Child Abuse and Neglect. (1988). *Study of national incidence and prevalence of child abuse and neglect.* Washington, DC: U.S. Department of Health and Human Services.

Patton, M. Q. (1978). *Utilization-focused evaluation.* Beverly Hills, CA: Sage.

Patton, M. Q. (1986). *Utilization-focused evaluation* (2nd ed.). Newbury Park, CA: Sage.

Peters, S. D., Wyatt, G. E., & Finkelhor, D. (1986). Prevalence. In D. Finkelhor & Associates, *A sourcebook on child sexual abuse.* Beverly Hills, CA: Sage.

Sepler, F. (1989). *Proceedings from Special Project IMPACT Forum.* Saint Paul: Government Training Service.

U.S. Department of Human Services. (1984). *Formative program evaluation: Research report and training manual.* Washington, DC: Government Printing Office.

PART II
UNDERSTANDING FAMILY SEXUAL ABUSE AND ITS EFFECTS

3

Families After Sexual Abuse: What Helps? What Is Needed?

CAROLYN J. LEVITT
GREG OWEN
JEANETTE TRUCHSESS

Public awareness and reporting of child sexual abuse has increased significantly in the last 10–15 years (Finkelhor, 1984). In Minnesota, for example, the number of reported cases of sexual maltreatment of children increased 133% from 1982 to 1984. Reported cases rose another 18.6% from 1984 to 1987, with a total of 8,392 cases reported in 1987, the last year for which data are available (Berry, 1990). The large and increasing number of reports has overloaded county child protection and social service systems, and has had a significant impact on the criminal justice system and mental health treatment services as well (League of Women Voters of Minnesota, 1986). Information is generally lacking regarding what happens to these families and children beyond the initial reporting and intervention efforts (Finkelhor, 1988).

PRIMARY RESEARCH QUESTIONS

Children's Hospital of Saint Paul, Minnesota, has been a primary evaluation center in the Upper Midwest for children who are suspected of being sexually abused. Between 1982 and 1986 more than 900 children were referred to this hospital for medical evaluation of suspected sexual abuse, and a medical protocol was developed for the evaluation of these children (Levitt, 1986). In 1987 a study was instituted to follow up families of children who had been examined for suspected sexual abuse during 1985 and 1986. The study sought answers to the following questions:

1. What were the parents' or primary caretakers' perceptions of the impact of sexual abuse on the victims?
2. What were the respondents' perceptions of the impact of sexual abuse on the family?
3. What services did children and families receive after disclosure of sexual abuse?
4. What were the respondents' evaluations of the services received?
5. What additional needs for services and barriers to service use were identified by the respondents?

SIGNIFICANCE OF RESEARCH QUESTIONS

The disclosure of sexual abuse in a family usually precipitates a crisis, often in an already dysfunctional family system. It brings with it numerous potential losses, such as the loss of spouse or parent, income, and/or housing, and the possible removal of the child from the home. The family's structure and functioning are disrupted as members react to the disclosure and ensuing events (Meddin & Hansen, 1985).

Incest families are often described as closed systems, where contact with people outside the family is very restricted and family members rely solely upon each other for meeting personal needs (MacFarlane & Waterman, 1986). These families may find themselves "intruded upon" by a number of agencies following the disclosure of sexual abuse. Minimally, they are required to have contact with child protection service personnel and/or the police. They may also find themselves interacting with social services, the court system, and the media, as well as clergy, neighbors, and extended family members.

The various service providers often have different agendas for treating incest victims and their families. This can lead to confusion. In addition, often communication and coordination of services are inadequate. As a result, victims and their families may be retraumatized by those who are mandated to help them (Berliner & Stevens, 1982; Finkelhor, 1983; Fontana, 1986; Herman, 1981; MacFarlane & Bulkley, 1982; Marron, 1988). There is growing concern about the potential for "secondary victimization," particularly by legal procedures in the criminal prosecution of child sexual abuse cases (Shafer, 1988). Conversely, in other cases parents and their children have felt the need to become part of an "underground railroad" to flee the system they believe is failing to protect their children from abusive ex-partners (Podesta & Van Biema, 1989).

The purpose of this study was to determine what services child sexual abuse victims and their families received related to the abuse and whether these services were meeting their needs. The findings help delineate the range of child abuse intervention and treatment efforts as experienced and appraised by the family. By obtaining information from families up to two years after the disclosure of abuse, the follow-up study provides important information about how victims and their families cope with the aftermath of abuse and its disclosure. The study yields data about the needs of the child and the family postdisclosure, and identifies the difficulties they experience in obtaining adequate and appropriate services. Methodologically, this follow-up study is a simple, relatively straightforward means of conducting a needs assessment. It suggests that community programs might use such an approach to identify more clearly the needs of this population.

METHODS

The target study population consisted of all children (482) evaluated for sexual abuse by the first author during 1985 and 1986. The Sexual Abuse Consultation records of these children were reviewed for inclusion in the study. Criteria included a determination by the physician that sexual abuse had most likely occurred (confirmed by the child's history and/or physical examination or by admission of guilt by the perpetrator), that the alleged perpetrator was a relative or person entrusted with the child's care, and that the victim was under 18 years of age. Of those evaluated, 258 children from 220 families fit these criteria. Of the 220 families, 119 primary caretakers provided complete interviews. (The single most important factor affecting the response rate was the inability of researchers to locate families more than one year after the disclosure of abuse. It is possible that such a sampling bias underrepresents the seriousness of the postdisclosure problems in families.) The sample selection process is illustrated in Figure 3.1.

Data collection involved the review of individual medical records and a follow-up telephone interview. Information regarding family composition, the disclosure of abuse, the severity of abuse, and the offender(s) involved was extracted from the medical records.

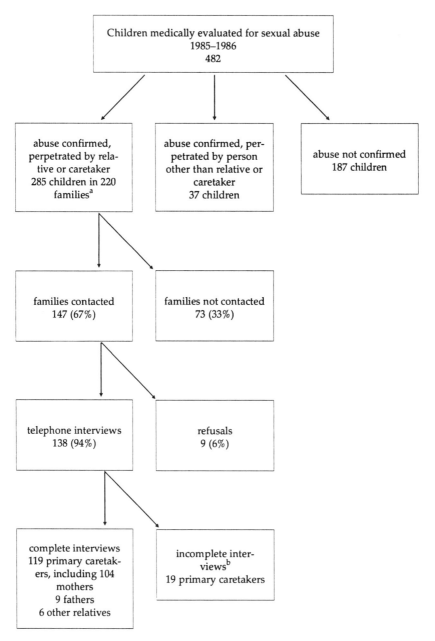

a. When more than one child in a family had been abused, a focus child was randomly selected for purposes of this study
b. interviews were incomplete because respondents were foster mothers or other caregivers who had not been responsible for the care of the victim for the entire period since disclosure.

Figure 3.1 Selection of the Sample

The telephone interview schedule was developed over several months with input from an advisory committee of researchers and child sexual abuse experts. The interview schedule was pretested in face-to-face interviews and revised. The final form included questions about family composition, identification and evaluation of service providers, experience and satisfaction with the criminal justice system, impact of the sexual abuse on the child and family, child and family functioning, demographics, and child sexual abuse prevention and reoccurrence.

In order to secure consent for follow-up contact, Dr. Levitt contacted the primary caretaker in each case by telephone, rather than sending a letter requesting participation in the study. This was done to ensure confidentiality of the victims and primary caretakers. We believe this personal call was a major factor in the low refusal rate of 6%.

FINDINGS

Background Characteristics of the Abuse

Tables 3.1 and 3.2 show characteristics of the victims and of the perpetrators, respectively. The victims in the sample were primarily white females under the age of 10 years. Among the victims, 45% experienced vaginal, anal, or oral intercourse or attempted intercourse; 47% experienced vaginal or anal penetration digitally or with objects, genital fondling (of the child or of the offender), or simulated intercourse; 8% experienced nongenital sexual touching, voyeurism, and/or exhibitionism. One case with physical findings could not be classified according to the most serious act.

A total of 54% ($N = 61$) of the perpetrators in the sample were males between 20 and 39 years of age, while 36% ($N = 40$) of the perpetrators were 19 or younger. The perpetrators were predominantly white, and nearly half had never been married. The majority of perpetrators were fathers, uncles, stepfathers, or male babysitters.

The respondents (primary caretakers of victims) were female in 97% of the cases, and the majority were between 26 and 35 years of age; 87% were mothers of victims, and 97% were white. The majority were married (45%) or separated (10%); 31% were divorced, 13% were single, and one was widowed. One-third had incomes below the poverty level, but the average family income was $28,500. A total of 88% had at least a high school diploma, with the majority of respondents having had some education beyond high school.

Table 3.1
Characteristics of Victims in Sample (N = 119)

	N	%[a]
Gender		
female	102	86
male	17	14
Age Abuse Ended[b]		
1–4 years	46	38
5–9 years	51	43
10–17 years	22	18
Race		
white	115	97
Hispanic	3	3
black	1	1
Most Serious Sexual Offense Experienced		
vaginal intercourse	11	9.3
anal intercourse	15	12.7
oral—on child	12	10.2
oral—to perpetrator	5	4.2
attempted intercourse	10	8.5
digital penetration—vaginal	28	23.7
digital penetration—anal	4	3.4
fondling—child	22	18.6
fondling—offender	0	0
simulated intercourse	1	.8
exhibitionism	2	1.7
voyeurism	3	2.5
nongenital sexual touching	5	4.2
unknown[c]	1	
Total	119	

a. Percentages may not total 100% because of rounding.
b. $\bar{X} = 6.2$; $SD = 3.2$.
c. One case with physical findings could not be classified according to most serious act.

Impacts on the Child

Each respondent was asked several questions about the victim's functioning and about problems the child had experienced associated with the sexual abuse. Responses to these questions are summarized in Table 3.3. When asked about problems their children had related to the abuse, 45% of the respondents said the abuse caused "more than a few," "many," or "a great many" problems. When asked to assess their children's overall current functioning (one to two years after the disclosure of abuse), most respondents said that the victims were

Table 3.2
Characteristics of Perpetrators in Sample (N = 119)

	N	$\%^a$
Gender		
female	11	9
male	108	91
Age^b		
7–12	10	9
13–19	30	27
20–29	24	21
30–39	37	33
40–49	7	6
> 50	5	4
missing	6	5
Race		
white	108	91
black	1	1
Hispanic	3	3
American Indian	2	2
other	5	4
Marital Status at Time of Abuse		
never married	54	45
married	36	30
separated	6	5
divorced	22	19
missing	1	1
Relationship to Victim		
father	34	29
uncle	14	12
grandfather	4	3
stepfather	8	7
adoptive or foster father	2	2
natural brother	7	6
step- or foster brother	7	6
male cousin	2	2
boyfriend of parent	7	6
male sitter	11	9
all other males in caretaking role (e.g., husband of daycare provider)	12	10
mother	1	1
grandmother	1	1
female sitter	5	4
all other females in caretaking role (e.g., parent's girlfriend, female cousin)	4	4

a. Percentages may not total 100% due to rounding.
b. 30% of the perpetrators were juveniles (17 years or younger); 16% of the juvenile perpetrators were female.

doing relatively well. Table 3.3 also shows that when the child's current functioning is examined more specifically, the greatest numbers of problems cited by respondents were in the area of emotional health. The type of emotional problems reported included both internalized and externalized behaviors and feelings. Internalized behaviors mentioned most often were withdrawal, sadness, depression, suicidal feelings or behavior, fearfulness, and low self-esteem. Externalized behaviors included anger, physical or verbal aggressiveness, and lying or stealing. Other difficulties noted were toileting problems, compulsive behaviors, eating problems, and psychosomatic symptoms.

When asked about inappropriate sexual behavior, 32% of respondents indicated that the victims exhibited such behaviors as inappropriate touching of self or others, as well as verbal and nonverbal behavior indicative of being "too sexy," flirtatious, provocative, and so on. Other comments referred to promiscuous sex, lack of trust in males, confusion regarding appropriate sexuality, and overreacting to sexual connotations and things to which most children of the same age would not respond.

Impacts on Families

Respondents were asked to rate the number of problems their families had experienced resulting from the abuse and to rate their overall current family functioning. Table 3.3 shows that most respondents indicated the abuse had a significant impact on the family as well as on the child. These responses highlight the need for service providers and the criminal justice system to recognize and respond to child sexual abuse as a crisis affecting the whole family system, not only the victim.

One respondent spoke of her own "sleeplessness, feeling of trauma, guilt-ridden, feeling [like a] victim of rape who's had no help." Another respondent talked about the brother of the victim, who "was very damaged by the incident. [He] was in the same room during the abuse and was threatened not to tell. [He] was close to the perpetrator. It was a big loss to him when the perpetrator left." Another respondent said:

> I think it is real difficult—financially and emotionally. It's difficult being a single-parent family. To regain that trust for me is real difficult with the father. We still have stuff to work through and [I] turned out to be the bad guy to her [victim]. Her father is real clear to her [in denying any wrongdoing] . . . that she doesn't understand. She's too young. She thinks I did something bad.

Table 3.3 Impacts of Abuse

Respondents' perceptions of the number of problems for the child and family resulting from the abuse[a]

	Few Problems		Many problems	
	N	%	N	%
Child	65	54	53	45
Family	36	30	83	70

Respondents' perceptions of overall current functioning of the child and of the family[b]

	Poor		Good	
	N	%	N	%
Child	16	14	102	86
Family	16	13	103	87

Respondents' perception of current functioning of the child within specified areas

	No Problems at all		Very Few Problems		A Few Problems		More than a Few Problems		Many Problems		A Great Many Problems		X[d]
	N	%	N	%	N	%	N	%	N	%	N	%	
Physical health	85	71	14	12	10	8	3	3	4	3	2	2	1.59
Emotional health	36	30	24	20	26	22	20	17	6	5	6	5	2.71
Relationships with family/friends	73	61	18	15	17	14	6	5	3	3	1	1	1.95
Inappropriate sexual behavior	78	66	20	17	11	9	4	3	1	1	2	2	1.65
School adjustment[c]	47	67	6	9	9	13	2	3	3	4	3	4	1.81

NOTE: Numbers of cases vary slightly because of missing values
a. Derived from a 6-point scale where 1 = no problems at all, 2 = very few problems, 3 = a few problems, 4 = more than a few problems, 5 = many problems, and 6 = a great many problems. The scale was dichotomized: few problems = values 1–3; many problems = values 4–6.
b. Derived from a 6-point scale where 1 = very poor, 2 = poor, 3 = fair, 4 = good, 5 = very good, and 6 = excellent.
c. N = 70 because of omission of preschool children.
d. Mean scores based on the following range of values: 1 = no problem at all, 6 = a great many problems.

Table 3.4
Comparison of Stressful Life Events in Two Samples (in percentages)

Stressful Event	Sexual Abuse Study Sample[a] N = 119	General Population Sample[b] N = 1,000, weighted
Serious marital conflict between parents	60%	23%
Parent arrested or jailed	29%	5%
Violence in the family	38%	8%
Drug or alcohol problems of a parent	38%	12%
Physical abuse apart from the sexual abuse	25%	3%
Severe financial hardship	42%	19%
Parent treated for mental illness	7%	3%
Brother or sister in trouble with the law	17%	5%

a. Includes events for previous three years only.
b. Includes events during child's lifetime. Figures weighted to include ages 0–17 years.

An additional perspective on these families was gained by asking respondents to identify what major life changes had occurred in their families in the last three years. These answers were compared to the results of a recent survey in which a randomly selected group of parents in Ramsey County, Minnesota, were asked what stressful family events had occurred during their children's lifetimes (Mueller & Cooper, 1987). Table 3.4 shows markedly higher percentages of families in the sexual abuse study sample reporting numerous stressful life events, compared with the random sample of families from the same community.

Whether the numerous stressful life events the families in the study experienced occurred prior to or subsequent to the abuse is unknown, but in cases where the perpetrator was the father, many respondents reported marital dissolution and resulting loss of financial support after the disclosure of abuse. Even when child support payments had been court ordered, they were not necessarily forthcoming. Several respondents reported losing their homes, spending considerable money on lawyers' fees, and experiencing financial crises subsequent to the abuse.

One respondent noted that she "lost all of her savings, her home and her job as a result of the time and expense of defending the offender's court action against the victim and herself." Another respondent, who had just lost her job, said, "Even when I was working, it was impossible to make ends meet. I made $800 monthly and off the top of that came the $340 per month for the loan I took out to pay attorney's fees, plus day-care expenses for the kids." She also said she does not get the $500 monthly support payments that her ex-husband is supposed to send, "except occasionally," and has spent $30,000 in attorney's fees.

In this context the impact of the abuse on the families was striking. When respondents were asked to name the most stressful event that had occurred in their families in the last three years, 82% identified the sexual abuse and/or its aftermath.

Evaluation of Services Received

Respondents were asked to identify the services or agencies with which they had contact regarding the sexual abuse, and to evaluate each one. Table 3.5 provides information on these services, the helpfulness ratings, and the percentage of ratings indicating lack of helpfulness. In general, respondents were satisfied with the services received. However, it is important to note that each service type rated, with three exceptions (medical evaluation, guardian *ad litem*, and victim witness assistant), received over 25% of ratings in the "less than helpful" range of 1–3. In addition, when asked to rate their overall satisfaction with all agencies/services, 32% of respondents gave ratings from "less than satisfied" to "somewhat satisfied," while 67% said they were "satisfied" to "extremely satisfied." Thus it appears that while services were generally found to be helpful, one-fourth to one-third of respondents found them to be less than satisfactory.

Respondents were also asked which service was most helpful, which was least helpful, and why. The reasons given indicated similar concerns regardless of which service was identified. Reasons given most frequently for finding a particular service most helpful include the following:

- The professional was supportive, understanding, reassuring.
- The service provider worked hard for the benefit of the victim and family, did a good job, got results.
- The agency provided needed information and workers explained things adequately.

Table 3.5
Utilization and Evaluation of Services

Agency	Respondents Who Received Services from This Type of Agency		$\overline{X}$ Help-fulness[a] Rating	SD	Reporting Service as Less Helpful (Score Range 1–3)	
	N	%			N	%
Physician	119	100	5.47	.96	7	6
Child protection[b]	116	98	4.05	1.98	54	38
Police	104	87	4.26	1.83	35	29
Counseling	96	81	4.50	1.77	56	28
Legal[c]	73	61	4.26	1.90	30	29
School	53	45	4.40	1.81	17	26
Church	25	21	4.11	2.14	10	37
Guardian ad litem	13	11	5.00	1.36	1	7
Victim-witness assistant	11	9	5.09	1.04	1	9

a. Derived from a 6-point scale where 1 = Not at all helpful, 2 = Slightly helpful, 3 = Somewhat helpful, 4 = Helpful, 5 = Very helpful, and 6 = Extremely helpful.
b. Includes social services.
c. Includes public and private lawyers.

- The service provider was respectful, established trust and rapport with the victim and family, and handled the child well, often helping the victim talk about the abuse.
- Workers stayed very involved with the victim and family throughout the process.
- Program staff displayed expertise and professionalism, and were readily available to talk things out and work through feelings.

The reasons some agencies were rated least helpful also showed similarities across services. The reasons given most often were the following:

- Workers showed insensitivity to victim and family needs, lack of support and caring.
- There was not enough follow-up or action.
- Personnel were incompetent or inadequately trained.
- Workers showed lack of rapport or trust; behavior described as harsh, traumatizing, or unethical.

- Workers did not provide enough information, referrals, or advice.
- Workers displayed negative attitudes or disbelief of victim.
- Lack of coordination or poor communication among agencies was evident.

Additional Services Needed

When asked if there were additional services for the victim that would have been or could now be helpful, 40% answered affirmatively, with recommendations including counseling—such as additional individual, family, and group counseling—and support services, and availability of professional child abuse experts to evaluate and provide counseling for the child (N = 40), and long-term follow-up to evaluate and address needs (N = 8). Other responses included recommendations for more prosecution of perpetrators, additional protection for victims from perpetrators, requests for more help with and improvement of the court system, better coordination of services, and more information and referral services.

One respondent said she would "like to believe that a more professional approach will be taken in the future regarding sexual abuse—that a person who is specially trained would come in and manage the case right away (especially when seeking answers from the child) and to provide for adequate follow-up for the family and the victim." Another respondent recommended "a follow-up service to coordinate among the professionals, so the information gets to everyone." Many spoke of further counseling needs, such as "to help [the victim] in dealing with the aftermath, someone to talk to, to give support, show her she's okay, allay her fears," or "to learn to deal with the guilt the victim's parents laid on her for disclosing," or "where she can learn about her own sexuality and what a normal family is," and again "to relieve her shame and guilt."

Several respondents talked about long-term follow-up needs such as "more follow-up after treatment to see if perhaps the child's problems need any further attention," or "someone staying aware of and sensitive to arising problems, maybe counseling in the future." Other respondents recommended "a legal advocate to speed up the court process" and efforts to "make the court system easier for kids. . . . Court is harder than the abuse. . . . Something to help them through."

When respondents were asked whether additional services for themselves or their family would have been or could now be helpful, 51% answered yes, with recommendations including the following:

- additional counseling, including suggestions for counseling for parents, siblings, relatives, and/or perpetrator (*N* = 59)
- education for parents about sexual abuse, including how to prevent abuse and how to cope with behaviors subsequent to sexual abuse (*N* = 8)
- protection from the perpetrator, supervised visitation (*N* = 8)
- advice and help regarding how to proceed with the social service and legal systems (*N* = 6)
- improved court services, additional legal help (*N* = 6)
- financial help for counseling, child care, and health insurance (*N* = 4)

Toward the end of the interview, each respondent was again asked if there were problems that the family was currently having for which they were not receiving the help they would like. Some 32% answered affirmatively. The two major themes were the need for counseling and support groups for all family members, and financial help, whether it be for counseling, medical bills, legal help, or housing.

Barriers to Services

When asked if there had been anything that kept them from getting the help they needed, 46% of the respondents identified barriers to obtaining needed services. Lack of financial resources and/or inadequate health care coverage most often prevented respondents from obtaining needed services. This obstructed many things, from access to counseling and legal services to having the means of transportation needed to get to the services.

As one respondent put it, money was a major obstacle:

> For me, I needed to leave the marriage. He wouldn't get therapy. There should be financial assistance for women who have to leave the marriage. It was rough enough emotionally, but the survival was tougher.

Another respondent, recently divorced, talked of needing counseling but "[I] can't afford it. Haven't been able to get free services because my income is too high, but all the money goes to rent and living expenses for myself and the boys." The second barrier discussed was lack of available or appropriate services, primarily counseling, and lack of information about available services. One respondent spoke about going to the local county mental health program: "Their services were so poor we didn't get the kind of counseling we needed. We didn't have a choice in clinics. The cost of going to another place was prohibitive." Another had major insurance hassles.

Lack of information about how to get help from the social services and criminal justice systems was also cited. Other responses included negative experiences with counselors and human service providers, resistance on the part of the victim and/or family members, mistrust of human service workers, and logistical problems, such as difficulties with transportation, child care, and the scheduling of appointments.

Limitations of the Study

This follow-up study was descriptive and, as such, did not attempt to test any hypotheses or break new ground in assessing the emotional impact of abuse on the victim. However, it does offer a perspective on the problems and needs of these children and their families after a significant period of time has passed since the disclosure of abuse.

Only one person's perspective on the problems was solicited, that of the child's primary caretaker. It is possible this method may have resulted in some minimization of the problems experienced by the child, due to the parent's or caretaker's desire to believe that the child is all right. When seeking definitive information on the child's psychological status, such a follow-up interview with parent/caretaker is no substitute for a direct clinical assessment of the child. It should also be noted that the design of this study, relying upon the information of the protective parent or caretaker, does not lead itself to an understanding of those cases in which both parents were involved in the abusive treatment of the child.

IMPLICATIONS FOR PRACTICE

Results of the follow-up survey of parents caring for sexually abused children show that the emotional effects of abusive events can be both significant and long lasting. Of great significance for the families is the fact that income and resources are often depleted as a result of both marital dissolution and the expense of services and treatment. In addition, services are fragmented and often lack consistency. The time-limited nature of county intervention efforts means that once initial intervention and legal action are completed, the child and family are often confronted with a lack of services and resources to help with continuing problems of a practical and/or emotional nature.

The study shows that a comprehensive medical evaluation is helpful to families, and that this represents a good point at which to supply other types of services, including referral to counseling, social, and legal services. The emotional health of victims and families appears to be strengthened and supported when there is continued involvement by at least one outside party available to talk with and advise the child's primary caregiver. This represents a significant opportunity to assist these families toward a lasting recovery. It also offers longer-term help for the emotional or behavioral problems that are so often associated with untreated victimization. It is not clear from the data that any one type of service is best equipped to provide such long-term support. In this study, the services that received highest ratings from families include the evaluating physician, victim and witness assistance services, guardians *ad litem*, and professional counseling services.

It should be noted, however, that counseling was often perceived as less than helpful by respondents. This was usually attributed to a lack of needed expertise and specialized training and skills on the part of the counselor. Such evaluations were associated primarily with situations in which the family did not have choices about counseling, but had to rely on a "closed panel" of mental health services as part of a prepaid health insurance program.

The current study suggests a need for centralized service delivery from a nonprosecutorial or investigative source. County social service efforts as well as police and child protection investigators are not necessarily in the best position to provide long-term, ongoing support to a child victim and his or her primary caregiver. The importance of adequate long-term services is underscored by the finding that 32% of the abuse victims in this study continued to have contact with the perpetrator up to two years after disclosure and county intervention.

Nonprofit private medical and counseling services appear to be better suited than county services to meeting the long-term needs of these families. However, the lack of financial resources often obstructs provision of these services. One needed change would occur if more prepaid health insurance plans allowed payment for specialized services in child abuse cases, provided by appropriately trained staff, rather than restricting these families to generic mental health services.

IMPLICATIONS FOR RESEARCH

We found the telephone interview using a structured questionnaire to be a satisfactory method of collecting follow-up information. As discussed above, this does not serve as a substitute for an in-person assessment of the child. However, it does yield rough indicators of the problems confronting these families and the extent to which they are receiving services. Thus the telephone interview would appear to be a useful tool for treatment centers and other community programs interested in conducting similar follow-up studies.

In conducting such a follow-up study, it is important to identify an appropriate respondent, which is not always easy. We sought respondents who functioned in a protective capacity on behalf of the child victim, and who were able to identify the needs and concerns of the child. Obviously this is not always the mother. Sadly, in some cases it is not possible to find such a caregiver.

We would recommend including a follow-up school assessment to augment information collected from the parent or caretaker. Without such an assessment, it is impossible to know about the child's school functioning. Emotional issues that the parent does not see may well be displayed in school.

Finally, the issue of reabuse and the legal requirement that professionals report any knowledge of abuse to the authorities must be considered. In this study, the interviewer told respondents of the reporting obligation prior to asking whether any reabuse had occurred. A total of 8% of the respondents indicated that some further abuse had occurred. In considering this issue, we felt morally bound as social service professionals to act on behalf of the child. We, of course, do not know to what extent alerting the respondents to our requirement to report affected their answers to questions about further abuse. Clearly, any service agency following up child abuse cases is going to have to address this issue.

REFERENCES

Berliner, L., & Stevens, D. (1982). Clinical issues in child sexual abuse. In J. Conte & D. Shore (Eds.), *Social work and child sexual abuse* (pp. 93–108). New York: Haworth.

Berry, D. (1990). [Preliminary data]. Minnesota Department of Human Services, Community Social Services Division, Research and Planning Section, Saint Paul.

Finkelhor, D. (1983). Removing the child—prosecuting the offender in cases of sexual abuse: Evidence from the national reporting system for child abuse and neglect. *Child Abuse and Neglect, 7,* 195–205.

Finkelhor, D. (1984). *Child sexual abuse: New theory and research.* New York: Free Press.

Finkelhor, D., with Hotaling, G. T., & Yllo, K. (1988). *Stopping family violence: Research priorities for the next decade.* Newbury Park, CA: Sage.

Fontana, V. J. (1986). When systems fail: Protecting the victim of child sexual abuse. In D. C. Haden (Ed.), *Out of harm's way: Readings on child sexual abuse, its prevention and treatments* (pp. 129–136). Phoenix, AZ: Oryx.

Herman, J. L. (1981). *Father-daughter incest.* Cambridge, MA: Harvard University Press.

League of Women Voters of Minnesota. (1986). *Protecting Minnesota's children: Public issues.* Minneapolis: Author.

Levitt, C. J. (1986). Sexual abuse in children: A compassionate yet thorough approach to evaluation. *Postgraduate Medicine, 80,* 201–215.

MacFarlane, K., & Bulkley, J. (1982). Treating child sexual abuse: An overview of current program models. In J. Conte & D. Shore (Eds.), *Social work and child sexual abuse* (pp. 69–91). New York: Haworth.

MacFarlane, K., & Waterman, J. (Eds.). (1986). *Sexual abuse of young children: Evaluation and treatment.* New York: Guilford.

Marron, K. (1988). *Ritual abuse.* Toronto: McClelland-Bantam.

Meddin, B. J., & Hansen, I. (1985). The services provided during a child abuse and/or neglect case investigation and the barriers that exist to service provision. *Child Abuse and Neglect, 9,* 175–182.

Mueller, D., & Cooper, P. (1987). *Caring for children: Family change, parent-child relations and child care.* Saint Paul: Wilder Research Center.

Podesta, J. S. & Van Biema, D. (1989, January 23). Running for their lives. *People,* pp. 70–80.

Shafer, G. (1988). The child victim in criminal court. *Looking Ahead: Innovation and Inquiry in Family Sexual Abuse Intervention, 2*(3), 1.

4

Effects of Probable Sexual Abuse on Preschool Children

S. K. HEWITT

W. N. FRIEDRICH

Despite the fact that the sexual abuse of children is recognized as a significant problem, our understanding of the preschool sexually abused child is minimal. Yet at Midwest Children's Resource Center, a specialty child abuse service of Children's Hospital Inc. of Saint Paul, Minnesota, 65% of the referrals for suspected sexual abuse are children ages 5 and under. Approximately 50% of referrals seen for suspected abuse at the Mayo Clinic Section of Psychology are also 5 and under.

This study examines several questions derived from our clinical practice. First, what are the typical characteristics of sexually abused preschool children regarding their developmental level, quality of behavioral adjustment, and degree of sexualized behavior? Second, can sexually abused preschoolers be distinguished on standardized measures from children who have been determined not to have been sexually abused, and also from children for whom a determination of sexual abuse could not be made because of either developmental compromise or deleterious life circumstances? A third question was derived from our understanding that the younger the child, the more likely he or she is to be affected by family circumstances: How do family variables help us understand the impact of child sexual abuse on the preschool child? A final question, also derived from developmental theory and sensitive to the fact that preschool children are rapidly changing, concerns the persisting negative effects of sexual abuse over time: How do sexually abused children appear on psychological dimensions one year following the initial investigation, and what types of naturally occurring variables positively or negatively affect the child's short-term adjustment?

Given our training in developmental psychology and child psychopathology, we developed an assessment battery that evaluated a wide range of behavioral, developmental, and cognitive functions in children; examined for the quality of parental functioning and consistent family environment; and examined for critical legal and therapeutic interventions that might have affected the child's current status in the year following abuse.

SIGNIFICANCE OF THE RESEARCH

To date, there has been no systematic survey of behavior problems and developmental status in even a moderate-sized sample of preschoolers who allegedly have been sexually abused. In some studies with reasonably large sample sizes (e.g., Friedrich, Bielke, & Urquiza, 1987) preschoolers comprised a significant minority of the larger sample, but for purposes of analysis, children ranging in age from 3 to 12 were combined. This reflects the fact that very young children are frequently not interviewed or evaluated despite allegations of sexual abuse. This is due in part to the belief that preschoolers cannot provide reliable reports. In addition, the lability of their behavior is often thought to interfere with the reliable assessment of behavior problems in very young children—that is, children 1 to 3 years old. Only recently, for example, has a widely used and well-developed measure of a broad range of child behavior problems in 2- to 3-year-olds become available (Achenbach, 1986).

The need for data to help us gain a greater understanding of sexually abused preschoolers is very clear from statistics regarding the incidence of sexual abuse in both local (G. Lyle, statistician, Ramsey County, personal communication, spring 1989) and national (Finkelhor & Associates, 1986) settings. The incidence levels depict a bimodal distribution in alleged sexual abuse cases. Although the largest number of reported cases involves children ages 10–12, the second largest grouping involves children ages 3–5. Frequently there are very few resources for evaluation or treatment of these young children. The behavior of sexually abused preschoolers is not well understood, and there is certainly a lower level of reporting and substantiation for preverbal or minimally verbal children.

The need to understand simultaneously the sexually abused child's family and the child comes from ecological child development (Kegan, 1982). Kegan emphasizes that the young child is embedded in his or her social environment and in many respects is a barometer of family functioning. Given Friedrich's (1988) contention that the impact of sexual abuse in children is compounded by poor family functioning (findings derived with older sexually abused children), it is imperative to study family functioning in sexually abused pre-schoolers.

METHODS

The methodology used in this study was based on our belief that a valid assessment of these children required obtaining information directly from children, parent figures, and trained clinicians regarding child and family functioning. In addition, we designed a follow-up evaluation to be conducted over the telephone one year after the initial appointment.

The child's primary caretaker completed the Child Behavior Checklist (CBCL; Achenbach & Edelbrock, 1983), the Minnesota Child Development Inventory (MCDI; Ireton & Thwing, 1974), and the Child Sexual Behavior Inventory (CSBI; Friedrich, 1990). Often, the Peabody Picture Vocabulary Test—Revised (PPVT-R) was administered to the child as another measure of language development. These measures provided information on the children's overall behavior, level of development (including expressive language development), and degree of sexualization (i.e., sexual behavior). In addition, information from the caretaker was obtained on stressful family events, maternal depression, and maternal social support. The therapist rated a number of additional dimensions of family functioning, including the degree to which the child was supported by the family, whether or not the child's autonomy was encouraged, verbal and physical conflict in the family, and whether or not the mother had a history of sexual abuse herself. (The questionnaires used are available from the authors.)

The therapists made a judgment regarding the validity of the sexual abuse allegations after an extensive psychological evaluation of the child. The psychological evaluation involved the completion of a thorough developmental history; a review of file records (some of which include an extensive social service involvement besides the history of allegations); assessment of cognitive, behavioral, social, and emotional status; and a developmentally appropriate interview via direct verbal interaction, with pencil-and-paper drawings, with small dolls in a doll house, or with the supplemental use of sexually anatomically correct dolls. Cases were discussed with other staff members in order to arrive at a consensus regarding abuse. These multiple criteria for abuse integrate aspects of work encompassed in the writings of Faller (1986) and MacFarlane and Waterman (1986).

At the end of the evaluation period, 64 children had been identified as having a probable history of sexual abuse (*probably abused* group), 19 were judged not to have been abused (*nonabused* group), and for an additional 28, abuse status was indeterminate one way or the other (*abuse-uncertain* group).

SAMPLE CHARACTERISTICS

For purposes of analysis, our overall sample of 111 children was divided into children ages 1 to 3 and children ages 4 to 5. We compared the three groups (probably abused, nonabused, and abuse uncertain) on a variety of demographic variables, such as age of the child, parents' education level, and family income. No significant differences were noted among our three groups for children ages 1 to 3 on any of the demographic variables. The average child in this age group was approximately 2½ years old, was one of two to three children in the family, had parents with slightly more than high school education, and lived in a family with an annual income below $15,000. Approximately three-fourths of these 1- to 3-year-olds were female. The nonabused children tended to have somewhat better-educated fathers, and lived in families where the income was relatively greater than for the probably abused and abuse-uncertain children, but the differences were not statistically significant.

Because at this age level even a few months' development can make a difference in the child's communication abilities, we assessed this younger group more carefully with regard to age in months. Contributing to our difficulties in assessing the children in the abuse-uncertain group is the fact that only slightly more than 16% of these children were above 36 months in age. This is in direct contrast to the fact that 62% of children in the probably abused group were above 36 months in age, and 54% of the children in the nonabused group were above 36 months of age. Although these differences were not statistically significant, they do explain why assessment of children in the abuse-uncertain group was more problematic overall.

In the 4- to 5-year-old sample the only significant difference among groups was that mothers of children in the nonabused group were significantly better educated than mothers of children for whom we could not determine abuse status (X = 14.4 years of education versus 12.0 years of education).

FINDINGS

Initial Impact

We measured the initial impact for all three groups and for two age groups (children ages 1 to 3 and children ages 4 to 5). This was done for developmental reasons, given our belief that children ages 1 to 3 constitute a developmentally different group than children 4 to 5, and also because the main behavioral problems rating scale, the Child Behavior Checklist, is considerably different for these two age groups. Differences between groups were calculated with the Mann-Whitney U Test unless otherwise indicated.

Tables 4.1–4.3 graphically represent the findings for the three groups regarding children ages 1 to 3. As illustrated in Table 4.1, which represents the differences among the three groups on sexual behavior as assessed with the Child Sexual Behavior Inventory and general behavior problems as assessed with the Child Behavior Checklist, the probably abused children differ from the nonabused children with regard to greater levels of sexual behavior and significantly more problems with sleep. The abuse-uncertain group appeared to be even more compromised than the probably abused children in that it differs from the nonabused children on sexual behavior, sleep problems, and greater levels of overall difficulties with internalizing behavior and externalizing behavior as assessed by the CBCL. (Internalizing behavior includes difficulties with social withdrawal, depression, sleep problems, and somatic problems, whereas externalizing behavior is related to aggression and destructive behavior.)

Table 4.2 illustrates the differences among the three groups on developmental variables, as derived from the Peabody Picture Vocabulary Test and the Minnesota Child Development Inventory. The probably abused children are significantly better off than the abuse-uncertain children on a measure of receptive language (PPVT-R) and

Table 4.1

Behavior Checklist Results: Ages 1–3

Variable	Probably Abused (N = 31)		Nonabused (N = 12)		Abuse Uncertain (N = 7)	
	Mean	SD	Mean	SD	Mean	SD
CSBI	*24.6	12.4	10.6	7.4	**24.0	12.6
CBCL1 (social withdrawal)	62.1	8.8	59.4	6.3	65.8	7.4
CBCL2 (depressed)	61.3	6.4	62.1	6.2	66.8	3.7
CBCL3 (sleep problems)	*75.1	12.0	63.3	7.2	**71.6	14.4
CBCL4 (somatic problems)	64.7	8.7	61.0	6.1	68.8	13.1
CBCL5 (aggression)	62.0	8.4	56.8	5.2	64.4	10.8
CBCL6 (destructive behavior)	62.3	8.8	58.7	7.9	65.8	9.2
CBCL, Internalizing	63.6	9.1	58.8	9.9	**67.2	8.6
CBCL, Externalizing	59.8	12.3	53.3	9.0	**64.2	7.2

* 1 versus 2 ($p < .05$); ** 2 versus 3 ($p < .05$)

on gross motor skills on the MCDI. The abuse-uncertain children are more immature than the nonabused children on the same two variables and, in addition, are lower on overall general development, expressive language, situation comprehension, and self-help skills, all of which are assessed with the MCDI.

There were no differences among the three groups with regard to maternal levels of depression and social support, nor were there differences in the therapist ratings of family functioning (e.g., family cohesion, verbal and physical conflict, support of the child) across 11 variables. However, using a chi-square test, children in the probably abused and abuse-uncertain groups had experienced significantly more parental separation and parental battering than had the nonabused children (see Table 4.3). This latter finding provides further evidence that children with a history of sexual abuse, and children for whom a history could not be determined, come from more compromised families.

Table 4.2
Developmental Variables: Ages 1–3

Variable	Probably Abused (N = 31)		Nonabused (N = 13)		Abuse Uncertain (N = 10)	
	Mean	SD	Mean	SD	Mean	SD
PPVT-R	*97.9	13.1	99.4	10.5	**85.5	9.4
MCDI general development	0.0	8.9	3.3	6.8	**–5.0	8.0
MCDI gross motor skills	*3.2	11.9	1.1	10.4	**–4.6	8.0
MCDI fine motor skills	1.1	9.6	1.0	8.7	–4.2	10.2
MCDI expressive language	–1.0	8.8	2.3	8.2	**–6.0	7.2
MCDI concept comprehension	–1.1	9.6	1.6	6.2	–5.2	7.8
MCDI situation comprehension	3.2	10.3	9.2	18.8	**–2.2	18.5
MCDI self-help	1.8	7.0	3.4	12.2	**–6.8	8.7
MCDI personal/ social skills	–8.1	7.2	–1.83	3.6	–6.0	8.8

* 1 versus 3 ($p < .05$); ** 2 versus 3 ($p < .05$)

The initial impact of alleged abuse for children ages 4 to 5 is graphically illustrated in Tables 4.4–4.6. As shown in Table 4.4, children with a probable history of sexual abuse exhibit significantly more sexual behavior (i.e., are more sexualized) than do nonabused children, and children in the abuse-uncertain group exhibit significantly more internalizing behavior problems than do nonabused children. Because separate norms exist for males and females in this age group, differences for males and females were calculated on individual subscales from the CBCL. Due in part to small sample sizes (from three to nine, depending on group), no significant differences were noted among the three groups of boys on the eight subscales of the CBCL. However, abuse-uncertain females at this age level were significantly more anxious than nonabused females.

More differences were noted on the developmental variables (see Table 4.5), with probably abused children exhibiting significantly better situation comprehension as assessed by the MCDI than nonabused

Table 4.3
Life Events Experienced by Child: Ages 1–3

	Probably Abused (N = 31)	Nonabused (N = 12)	Abuse Uncertain (N = 7)
Event			
Parental illness	48.4	33.3	33.3
Parental death	0	0	0
Divorce	35.5	33.3	50
Separation*	67.7	8.3	100
Other family death	19.4	8.3	0
Physical abuse	45.2	33.3	50
Foster care	35.5	33.3	50
Adoption	3.2	0	0
Child illness	25.8	25	25
Parental battering*	67.7	33.3	75

* $p < .05$

children, and probably abused children exhibiting higher levels of expressive language development and situation comprehension than abuse-uncertain children. Finally, nonabused children also had better receptive language skills as measured by the PPVT-R than did children in the abuse-uncertain group.

As was the case with children ages 1 to 3, no differences were noted among groups on levels of maternal depression and social support or on levels of family functioning as rated by the therapist. Similar levels of compromised functioning were observed across the majority of the families. Abuse-uncertain children were significantly more likely than nonabused children to have experienced physical abuse and foster care in their short lives, as assessed with the chi-square statistic. (See Table 4.6 for more details.)

Contributors to Behavior

Given the nonparametric nature of our test data, Spearman correlations were calculated between the demographic, maternal, and family ratings and three variables: sexual behavior as determined by the

Table 4.4
Behavior Checklist Results: Ages 4–5

Variable	Probably Abused (N = 33)		Nonabused (N = 7)		Abuse Uncertain (N = 18)	
	Mean	SD	Mean	SD	Mean	SD
CSBI	*26.2	12.9	13.7	12.8	19.8	10.1
CBCL, Internalizing	65.1	7.5	58.6	14.5	**70.2	11.6
CBCL, Externalizing	66.7	9.3	61.5	13.5	70.9	11.5

* $p < .05$ (1 versus 2); ** $p < .05$ (2 versus 3)

Table 4.5
Developmental Variables: Ages 4–5

Variable	Probably Abused (N = 33)		Nonabused (N = 7)		Abuse Uncertain (N = 18)	
	Mean	SD	Mean	SD	Mean	SD
PPVT-R	97.6	6.8	***98.4	5.8	**84.3	9.9
MCDI general development	1.6	12.0	−5.6	.7	−3.8	8.2
MCDI gross motor skills	7.0	16.3	−6.2	18.4	−7.9	20.5
MCDI fine motor skills	1.4	14.7	−3.0	5.7	−2.0	17.9
MCDI expressive language	2.9	17.7	−4.0	11.3	**−14.5	12.8
MCDI concept comprehension	2.0	13.4	−10.6	10.6	−3.0	10.6
MCDI situation comprehension	*10.0	16.4	−11.2	7.8	**−6.6	16.4
MCDI self-help	8.9	11.0	−14.4	11.3	0.9	11.0
MCDI person/ social skills	−5.3	15.6	−5.5	5.0	−14.7	9.6

* 1 versus 2 ($p < .05$); ** 1 versus 3 ($p < .05$); *** 2 versus 3 ($p < .05$).

Table 4.6
Life Events Experienced by Child: Ages 4–5 (in percentages)

	Probably Abused (N = 33)	Nonabused (N = 7)	Abuse Uncertain (N = 18)
Life Event			
Parental illness	33.3	28.6	33.3
Parental death	3.0	0	0
Divorce	48.5	57.1	77.7
Separation	48.5	42.9	72.2
Other family death	30.3	14.3	16.6
Physical abuse*	30.3	14.3	66.6
Foster care*	33.3	14.3	56.6
Adoption	0	0	0
Child illness	18.2	0	33.3
Parental battering	51.5	42.9	77.7

* $p < .05$.

CSBI, and internalizing behavior and externalizing behavior, both of which were measured by the CBCL. The entire sample, ages 1 to 5, was used in these analyses. Sexual behavior in children is correlated significantly with 8 of the 32 variables entered into the correlation matrix. Sexual behavior is *inversely* related to (a) family income, (b) a measure of the child's social development (i.e., how well the child gets along with friends), (c) family cohesion, (d) family expressiveness, and (e) the degree to which the child's autonomy is fostered by the family. It is correlated *directly* with (a) total life events, (b) maternal history of sexual abuse, and (c) whether or not the perpetrator was in the home (i.e., reflective of both longer abuse and probable incest). The implications of this finding are that less socialized children from poorer and more problematic families, whose early years have been quite stressful, who have mothers with histories of sexual abuse and who have been molested (most likely in an incestuous situation) are the most sexualized.

Internalizing behavior was correlated with the same dependent variables, with 12 significant correlations. Internalizing behavior is correlated *inversely* with the degree to which the mother feels (a) supported and (b) satisfied with her social support, (c) whether or not the child is valued, and the degree to which the family is (d) cohesive and (e) expressive, and (f) fosters the child's autonomy. It is *directly* correlated with (a) stressful life events, (b) maternal depression, (c) presence of physical abuse, (d) presence of verbal conflict, and (e) presence of physical conflict in the home, and (f) a maternal history of sexual abuse. Children who have more internalizing problems have mothers who are not only more depressed, but feel less satisfied with their social support. These children live in stressful families in which verbal and physical abuse are likely. They tend not to be valued, and the family environment does not foster their development. In addition, the mother is more likely to have a history of sexual abuse.

Finally, 17 variables correlated significantly with externalizing behavior at a significant level. Externalizing behavior is related *inversely* to such indices of social development in the child as (a) number of friends and (b) whether the child gets along with friends, (c) whether or not the child is believed, and (d) whether the parent is supportive of the child; and several dimensions of family functioning, including (e) whether or not the child is valued, (f) the degree of family expressiveness, (g) cohesion in the family, and (h) the degree to which the child's autonomy is fostered. It is correlated *directly* with (a) stressful life events, (b) maternal depression, and the child having experienced either (c) physical abuse or (d) neglect. Verbal and physical conflict are also *directly* correlated with externalizing behavior, as is a history of chemical dependency in one or more parent figures. The more severe the abuse, the more externalizing behavior exhibited, with severity of abuse determined for purposes of our analyses by whether or not penetration was attempted or completed. Finally, a maternal history of sexual abuse was also significantly correlated in a direct fashion with the level of externalizing behavior exhibited in the child.

The results of these correlations, although certainly not indicative of a cause-and-effect relationship, do indicate that the level of behavioral disturbance in a child in which sexual abuse is suspected is directly related to deleterious family variables. For example, the degree to which a child's autonomy is supported in a family that is cohesive and expressive constituted important "buffering" variables for all three variables used for outcome (i.e., CSBI, CBCL Internalizing and Externalizing). In addition, the level of the child's social development and the degree to which the mother is depressed and lacks social support were also quite important. Cutting across all three variables is the impact of a maternal history of sexual abuse. This history may operate in a number of ways, including interfering with the mother's effectiveness as a parent, and possibly causing her to view her child and her parenting ability more negatively. Unresolved sexual abuse may also have contributed to the mother's choice of mate, another risk factor.

It is interesting that abuse variables were only minimally related to child behavior. This is due in large part, we believe, to the fact that it is difficult to determine the severity and extent of the abuse young children experience. For example, complete information on sexual abuse was available for only 16 children, with partial information present on another 12. The two relationships that were noted—that is, perpetrator present in the home (related to sexual behavior) and abuse severity (related to externalizing behavior)—certainly make sense given the circumstances.

One-Year Follow-Up

After a one-year period we were able to follow up with 26 children from the probably abused group and 7 nonabused children. We were unable to follow up with any children from the abuse-uncertain group, which suggests that this group of children experienced greater levels of family chaos and disruption than did the others. The child's caretaker was interviewed over the telephone and completed the Child Sexual Behavior Inventory, the Child Behavior Checklist, the Minnesota Child Development Inventory, and the measure of maternal depression used earlier. The analyses have not yet been completed, but preliminary findings regarding follow-up are summarized in Tables 4.7–4.9.

Significant comparisons between Time 1 and Time 2 on our most robust and empirically rigorous outcome variables were noted only in the area of sexual behavior, which had dropped off significantly after a one-year period. Although differences were certainly in the right direction for probably abused children on internalizing and externalizing behaviors, they did not reach significance. We were unable to measure differences between Time 1 and Time 2 on the more specific CBCL scales, since the majority of children were assessed on a different version of the scale because they were then older.

Given the small sample sizes of children for whom the same test could be used both times, we decided to assess for the degree to which the children clinically improved. We defined clinical improve-

Table 4.7
Follow-Up Assessment

Variable	Time 1	Time 2
	Mean (SD)	Mean (SD)
Probably abused (N = 26)		
CSBI	17.4 (7.8)	*8.4 (5.0)
CBCL Internalizing	64.1 (9.2)	54.9 (8.1)
CBCL Externalizing	62.4 (8.9)	57.1 (7.9)
MCDI general development	+1.0 month	+.56 month
Nonabused (N = 7)		
CSBI	15.1 (14.1)	8.7 (8.1)
CBCL Internalizing	56.3 (7.3)	59.6 (7.2)
CBCL Externalizing	57.3 (8.2)	58.6 (9.1)
MCDI general development	+0.0 month	−1.1 month

* $p < .01$.

Table 4.8
Clinical Improvement, Time 1 to Time 2

Variable	N	%
Probably Abused (N = 26)		
improved	17	65.4
deteriorated	5[a]	19.2
no change	4	15.4
Nonabused (N = 7)		
improved	2	28.6
deteriorated	2	28.6
no change	3	42.8

NOTE: Clinical improvement is change by at least .5 SD in both CBCL Internalizing and Externalizing scores. Deterioration is the inverse.

a. Of these 5, 4 were male.

Table 4.9
Correlations with Change Scores

Improvement Correlated with	r	p
Sexual Behavior		
sex of child (female)	.43	<.01
time in therapy	.38	<.01
Internalizing Behavior		
sex of child (female)	.35	<.01
time in therapy	.42	<.01
age of child (older)	.36	<.01

NOTE: Improvement in externalizing behavior is not significantly correlated with child or family variables

ment as a change of at least .5 standard deviation in both internalizing and externalizing scores from the Child Behavior Checklist. According to parent reports, approximately two-thirds of the probably abused children improved, using our definition of clinical improvement. Approximately one out of five of the children deteriorated, and four of these were male. The remaining children neither improved nor deteriorated over this time period. Table 4.8 shows that nonabused children varied widely regarding outcome, although the majority of them were completely within normal limits at the time of first assessment.

What variables were related to improvement in the child after a one-year period? Improvement was calculated by the degree of change between Time 1 and Time 2 on sexual behavior, internalizing behavior, and externalizing behavior. These change scores have not been transformed, and their nonnormal distribution may be related to the paucity of relationships noted. See Table 4.9 for results.

Improvement with regard to sexual behavior was directly related to female gender for the children ($r = .43, p < .01$) and the length of the time the child spent in therapy ($r = .38, p < .01$). Internalizing behavior was also related to the child being female ($r = .35, p < .01$) and time in therapy ($r = .42, p < .01$). In addition, the age of the child was directly related to the degree of improvement ($r = .36, p < .01$). Change scores for externalizing were not significantly correlated with any of the variables assessed at follow-up. This may be due in part to the fact that less change was noted on the average with our externalizing scores, thus allowing less variance to be examined.

One could make an argument from these data that females improve more than males, but an equally logical argument is that females, who tend to be better socialized than male children at this age, may simply have learned how to inhibit the overt expression of sexual and internalizing behaviors. Thus they may overtly appear to be improved, but in reality may not be. Support for this hypothesis comes from the fact that the majority of children who deteriorated over time were male.

These results also provide some support for the utility of therapy with sexually abused children. When therapy was provided, it appeared that a focus on parental functioning was often a component. However, families who are able to focus on the therapy process and get their children to appointments as needed tend to be families that are more organized, and in which children are supported.

IMPLICATIONS FOR PRACTICE

The results of this study have implications for assessment, treatment, and case management of preschool children with alleged sexual abuse. Regarding assessment, it seems clear from our data that allegations of sexual abuse in this age group should be taken seriously. Not only is sexual abuse associated with significant behavioral impacts, but using careful observation, extensive history taking, and empirically based assessments, we were able to evaluate the veracity of sexual abuse allegations in the majority of children in this group of preschoolers. However, despite our ability to assess the majority of these children, they were almost never given the opportunity to testify, and the perpetrators were usually not confronted with their misdeeds.

The behavioral impact of sexual abuse in very young children seems to be related to the degree to which children are able to regulate themselves (e.g., sleep disorders as assessed on the CBCL). Children ages 1 to 3 are newly mastering sleeping, and traumatic events cause disregulation. In addition, elevated sexual behavior also appears to yield an empirically based difference in children ages 1 to 5 who have been sexually abused when contrasted with those who have not.

Sexual abuse also appears to be related to developmental differences, although in ways we did not necessarily predict. It is the abuse-uncertain children who appear to be the most compromised developmentally. These children, for whom we were unable to make a determination one way or the other as to the veracity of the sexual abuse allegations, are very disquieting to us. We realize that many of these children may have been sexually abused, but because of their delayed development and the confounds of numerous other family problems, clear determinations could not be made. Moreover, given that their families are some of the most problematic in our study, it is likely that they are at great risk for further maltreatment. To discontinue protective services for these children seems clearly inappropriate. Rather, seriously managing these cases in the manner described by Hewitt (1991) may be an option, along with continued casework involvement and possible placement in enrichment programs that address these children's clear developmental needs. Documentation of delays and handicaps can help qualify a child for specialized intervention at a number of levels. By placing an at-risk child in environments where monitoring by caregivers and educators can occur, some protection can be facilitated.

It is also clear that child sexual abuse is not an isolated event for the children in our sample. Their abuse occurs in the context of impaired family functioning. The frequency of such elements as concomitant marital discord, parental battering, financial problems, and physical child abuse is extremely high. We cannot emphasize enough that *these families are highly distressed*, and the sexual abuse, albeit important, is only one of the many negative life circumstances facing these children and their families. Our findings underscore the need for broad-based intervention in these cases. Child, family, and parent therapy appear routinely necessary.

In many of the cases in our study the mother had also been sexually abused, and her child's sexual abuse may have activated previous issues that she had not resolved, resulting in considerable emotional turmoil. At the time that her child needed her most, she may have been struggling with her own issues and hence was less available emotionally. To ignore the fact that over 50% of the mothers of probably abused children had histories of sexual abuse is to do a disservice to these children. Both mother and child have treatment needs; both should receive treatment.

In addition to direct therapy, the child and family may need intervention on social and academic levels as a result of the abuse. Many of these children do need specialized educational assistance, but a clinician needs to be available to provide consultation in the school setting, given our experience that such children present a wide variety of problems, both developmental and behavioral.

Child protection services and the police are responsible for the investigation of child sexual abuse. In some communities the police screen child abuse cases and call child protection workers only if they determine there is a solid case. This process of investigation is of particular concern for preverbal children. For example, it is a policy in some major communities not to investigate allegations of abuse unless the child can talk. This research would clearly argue against that policy. The investigator for abuse among preverbal children needs to have a strong background in early childhood growth and development. Few police officers have such a background. Although many social workers have some training in child development, rarely is this component specialized for the preverbal child. Professionals with extensive background in child development at young ages are most often not trained in the process of investigation. Investigation and evaluation are separate activities, yet the needs of these young children demand both. We need to consider carefully the process of investigation to determine how such services can best be offered to these young children.

IMPLICATIONS FOR RESEARCH

Based upon this initial study, it seems clear that future research on young children who have a history of maltreatment needs to move beyond initial assessment and emphasize follow-up research. In addition, given the primacy of maternal and family variables, the research must be ecological and developmental. Future research must exert the effort to train therapists to be reliable raters of family functioning. This will allow us to understand more fully how family variables contribute not only to abuse onset but also to the nature and course of symptoms that result. In addition to telephone interviewing, face-to-face interviewing and a complete reevaluation of the child at selected follow-up times should be used. Also, this study relied heavily upon parental reports; obtaining collaborative report data is highly recommended. For example, many of these children were in preschool, and teacher evaluations could have added to the validity and ecological soundness of this study.

Researchers must anticipate that these families are often fractured and chaotic. We often lost valuable maternal data because a foster mother brought the child to the interview. Being able to interview even noncustodial biological mothers may have added validity to our findings.

Assessing outcome is also difficult, and simple change scores are not enough. An opportunity must be provided for the family to report on whether anything has changed and how, and family members' perceptions should be compared to standardized measures. This requires that a larger qualitative element be added to future research, to go beyond the largely quantitative focus of this study. In these ways researchers can make substantial contributions to our understanding of the effects of sexual abuse on preschool children and provide solid guidance for investigation, intervention, and treatment.

REFERENCES

Achenbach, T. M. (1986). *Child Behavior Checklist for Ages 2–3*. Burlington: University of Vermont.

Achenbach, T. M., & Edelbrock, C. (1983). *Manual for the Child Behavior Checklist and Revised Child Behavior Profile*. Burlington, VT: Queen City.

Faller, K. C. (1986). *Child sexual abuse*. New York: Columbia University Press.

Finkelhor, D., & Associates. (1986). *A sourcebook on child sexual abuse*. Beverly Hills, CA: Sage.

Friedrich, W. N. (1988). Behavior problems in sexually abused children: An adaptational perspective. In G. E. Wyatt & G. J. Powell (Eds.), *Lasting effects of child sexual abuse* (pp. 171–191). Newbury Park, CA: Sage.

Friedrich, W. N. (1990, April 27). *The Child Sexual Behavior Inventory: Normative and clinical findings*. Paper presented at the National Symposium on Child Victimization, Atlanta, GA.

Friedrich, W. N., Bielke, R. L., & Urquiza, A. J. (1987). Children from sexually abusive families: A behavioral comparison. *Journal of Interpersonal Violence, 2*, 391–402.

Hewitt, S. K. (1991). Therapeutic management of preschool cases of alleged but unsubstantiated sexual abuse. *Child Welfare*.

Ireton, H., & Thwing, E. (1974). *The Minnesota Child Development Inventory*. Minneapolis: Behavior Science Systems.

Kegan, R. (1982). *The evolving self*. Cambridge, MA: Harvard University Press.

MacFarlane, K., & Waterman, J. (Eds.). (1986). *Sexual abuse of young children: Evaluation and treatment*. New York: Guilford.

5

Taking Sibling Incest Seriously

MICHAEL J. O'BRIEN

There has been an explosion of publications over the past two decades on the subject of family sexual abuse, reflecting society's awareness and recognition of a problem previously hidden behind a cultural veil of denial, secrecy, and disbelief. While the literature has focused most attention on father-daughter incest, there is general agreement that the most prevalent type of incestuous behavior occurs between siblings (Finkelhor, 1980; Lindzey, 1967). Despite its prevalence, however, sexual behavior between siblings is often regarded as mere "sex play" that is exploratory, mutually consenting, mutually enjoyable, and benign in its effects on later psychological, social, or sexual development. Consequently, the research literature on family sexual abuse has largely ignored sibling incest, dismissing it as relatively harmless.

Writers and practitioners in social science and criminal justice have generally failed to distinguish between sexual activity engaged in by mutually consenting near-same-age siblings and sexual behavior that is clearly exploitive in nature (i.e., where there is a significant age difference or where force, violence, or intimidation is employed). Finkelhor (1980) found in his college student survey sample that at least a quarter of the students who had sibling sexual experiences during their childhoods reported that there was an abusive quality to them and, in 23% of the cases, there was more than a five-year age difference between siblings. The majority of the respondents who had been threatened or forced and those whose sibling abusers were much older rated their experience as negative.

A recent study comparing the experiences and affective reactions of adult women survivors of brother-sister sexual abuse with adult women survivors of father-daughter incest found no differences between the groups in the frequency of reported self-abusive behaviors, physical problems, sexual problems, or level of guilt and shame about the experiences (Cole, 1990). This supported earlier research that found serious long-term effects resulting from brother-sister incest (e.g., Mieselman, 1978; Russell, 1986).

There is little in the literature about the characteristics of sibling incest perpetrators. Only one study could be found that presented descriptive data on a meaningful sample of sibling incest offenders. Becker, Kaplan, Cunningham-Rathner, and Kavoussi (1986) describe 22 adolescent males who had been charged with sexual crimes against siblings, and suggest that sexual experimentation is not a very useful explanation for the incestuous behavior, nor is prior sexual victimization particularly significant as an explanation. These authors stress that a unified profile of the adolescent incest perpetrator did not emerge from their study. They were limited by a relatively small sample size and the omission of comparison groups.

RESEARCH FOCUS AND METHODS

The purpose of this study was to identify demographic, sexual, individual, and family factors that differentiate male adolescent sibling incest offenders from other types of adolescent sex offenders. Clinicians have suggested several factors that may have etiological significance: prior sexual abuse, prior physical abuse, lack of impulse control, learning and school problems, low self-esteem, conduct disorder, poor social skills, exposure to pornography, drug/alcohol abuse, lack of appropriate male role models, lack of sexual experience and information, and family pathology. Learning what distinguishes sibling incest offenders from other adolescent sex offenders might shed some light on the factors responsible for this behavior.

The subjects were 170 adolescent male sex offenders (mean age 15.2, range 12–19) referred for evaluation and/or treatment to the Program for Healthy Adolescent Sexual Expression (PHASE) of East Communities Family Service, a nonprofit, outpatient mental health clinic in Saint Paul, Minnesota. The sample included all male adolescents referred to the program between January 1986 and June 1987 who had undergone at least the program intake process. (See Table 5.1; because some intake items were not completed for all offenders, the number of subjects referred to in several tables does not equal 170.)

The sample was further subdivided into four groups on the basis of primary sexual offending behavior. Group 1 consisted of adolescents who had victimized siblings. The definition of *sibling* included

Table 5.1
Sample Groups

	N	%
Sibling incest offender	50	29.4
Child molester—nonfamily	57	33.5
Nonchild offender	38	22.4
Mixed offender	25	14.7
Total	170	100.0%

stepsiblings, half siblings, and adoptive siblings. Group 2 was made up of adolescents who had victimized extrafamilial (nonsibling) children. Group 3 was made up of adolescents who had sexually victimized peers and/or adults. Group 4, a residual category, was made up of adolescents who had multiple victims who may have included siblings, nonfamilial children, and/or peers and adults and could not be placed in any of the first three groups. Ages did not vary significantly among the four groups.

There were several sources of data for the study:

1. *Confidential Family Questionnaire (CFQ):* a 14-page questionnaire filled out by the parents of the adolescents prior to intake
2. *Intake Data Form:* a 27-item form completed by intake clinicians based on client responses to a structured clinical interview focusing on the clients' social and family histories
3. *Demographic Description Report:* a 33-item form detailing client background data and offense history completed by the case manager who worked with the adolescent and his family throughout the assessment and/or treatment process

Only clients who signed the research consent form at intake and whose parent(s) signed the consent form were included in this study.

FINDINGS

Background Characteristics

Most of the study subjects were white (95%), and 75% lived in the five counties making up the Minneapolis/Saint Paul metropolitan area. One-fourth, however, were from rural counties. A slightly larger

Table 5.2
Mean Acts per Offender Admitted at Intake

Offender Group	Mean	Standard Deviation
Incest offender	18.0	50.6
Child molester	4.2	7.6
Nonchild offender	7.4	24.5
Mixed	8.5	13.5
Total sample	9.6	30.8

proportion of the sibling incest offender group (31%) was from rural Minnesota and Wisconsin. Most of the adolescents who victimized peers or adults (Group 3) were from the metropolitan area (86%).

Offense Characteristics

The sample of adolescent sex offenders (N = 170) admitted at intake to having committed a total of 1,636 criminal sexual acts against 461 victims, a mean of 9.6 criminal sexual acts per offender and 2.7 victims per offender overall. Table 5.2 presents criminal sexual acts admitted by the offender types. Incest offenders committed on average the largest number of offenses of the four groups, a mean of 18 separate sexual incidents with their sibling victims, compared with a mean of 4.2 acts admitted to by the child molesters and a mean of 7.4 acts by the nonchild offenders.

There was considerable difference as well in the length of the sexual abuse careers among the various offender types. Table 5.3 reveals that the incest offenders had longer careers on average than either child molesters or nonchild offenders. Nearly 45% of the sibling offenders had durations of abuse that extended beyond one year, while only 23% of the extrafamilial child molesters and 24% of the nonchild offenders had careers beyond one year.

The differences in both numbers of acts and duration of the abuse among the offender groups can be explained most easily by considering the comparative availability of the victim to the offender. In the sibling incest situation the victim is obviously much more available to the offender, hence the opportunity for multiple acts over an extended duration.

Table 5.3
Duration of Offending Behavior (in percentages)

Offender Group	One event	6 Months or less	6–12 Months	1–3 Years	Over 3 years
Incest offender	10.2	38.8	6.1	30.6	14.3
Child molester	29.8	43.9	3.5	17.5	5.3
Nonchild offender	44.7	23.7	7.9	15.8	7.9

Note: Chi-square, incest versus nonincest child molester, $p < .05$; chi-square, incest versus all others $p < .05$

The nature of the relationship may be a significant factor militating against disclosure in the sibling incest situation. Since the victim is a sibling, the consequences of disclosure—retribution by the offender, disbelief and/or punishment by the parents, removal from the home of either or both the victim and offender, and family disruption—may be relatively more immediate or salient.

Types of Offenses and Victim Characteristics

The data reveal that the sibling incest offenders were more likely to engage in sexual intercourse with their victims than were the nonincest offenders. Nearly half (46%) of the sibling offenders committed offenses involving penile penetration of the victim's vagina or anus, compared with 28% of the child molesters and only 13% of the nonchild offenders. This finding is perhaps best explained by the victim's availability and the duration of the abuse. Since, in the majority of these study cases, the incestuous involvement extended beyond six months and involved numerous sexual contacts, it is more likely that the incest offenders would have progressed to acts of intercourse with their sibling victims than those sex offenders whose victims were less available and involved with them for shorter durations.

Also, clinical experience reveals that victims of sibling incest are likely to be implicated gradually as coconspirators by the abusive sibling so they will share in the responsibility, blame, and punishment for the behavior if the "secret" is disclosed. Once established, this dynamic makes it difficult for victims to resist offenders' more intrusive sexual demands.

The data also reveal that sibling incest offenders were more likely to have two or more victims (53%) than were extrafamilial child molesters (42%), suggesting that the incest offender does not usually confine his sexual abuse to a single sibling in the family.

In general, the extrafamilial child molesters chose younger victims. Incest offenders' victims were generally older. However, over three-fourths (76%) of the incest offenders victimized children under the age of 9. Since the average age of the incest offenders in this study was 15 years, it is clear that the victims were most often much younger than the offenders. But in just over one-fourth of the cases, the victims might be considered the sibling offenders' peers (within three years of age).

The possibility that the occurrence of sibling incest is a function of the greater availability of siblings to the adolescent abuser, compared with the adolescent who molests children outside his family, was explored by comparing the number of siblings living with the adolescent offenders. Of the families for whom information regarding siblings was provided (CFQ, $N = 127$), the mean number of siblings per offender was 1.76. An examination of the data revealed that incest offenders generally had more siblings than the other groups, but the differences were not great. However, an examination of the gender of the siblings revealed that the sibling offenders were likely to have more female siblings living at home. The availability of more sisters may be important, at least as it relates to victim gender.

It is important to note, however, that while the child molesters were almost equally likely to have siblings in the home, at least one of whom was likely to be a sister, their victims were chosen from outside the family. Clearly, other factors besides siblings in the home are crucial in determining whether sexual behavior between siblings will occur.

ETIOLOGICAL FACTORS

The literature on adolescent sex offenders suggests a number of etiological factors that may have significance. Among these factors are family functioning, social adjustment, school performance, social skills, friendship patterns, and experience as a victim of sexual abuse. This section will explore these factors, presenting comparative findings for the three major groups.

Family Environment

The literature on incest is replete with references to the pathological nature of incest families. They are described as families that have role

Table 5.4
Types of Abuse in Families of Adolescent Sex Offenders

Offender Group	Nuclear Family Incest[a]	Physical Abuse	Chemical Abuse
Incest offender (N = 49)	22.4	61.2	56.3
Child molester (N = 57)	14.0	44.6	56.1
Nonchild offender (N = 38)	2.7	36.8	52.6

a. Not including the sibling incest committed by study subjects.

reversals, blurred generational and interpersonal boundaries, and dysfunctional communication styles, and in which other types of abuse (emotional, physical, and chemical) take place. Magal and Winnec (1968) describe five sibling incest families in treatment in a psychiatric facility in Israel. They report that all five families were dysfunctional. Mieselman (1978), in studying eight sibling incest cases, found the lack of parental supervision of children to be the most consistent factor among the families.

Table 5.4 illustrates the prevalence of physical, sexual, or chemical abuse (alcohol/drugs) within the families of the adolescent offenders in the study sample. The table also shows the prevalence of sexual abuse in the families of the incest sibling perpetrators compared with the other two groups. In 22% of these families there was incestuous behavior in addition to that perpetrated by the subject. Unfortunately, the demographic data form did not specify whether this was intergenerational (parent-child) or sibling incest involving siblings other than the subject.

Earlier studies have suggested that paternal incest in particular may be a causative factor for sibling incest by sexualizing the children prematurely and modeling exploitive sexual behavior for sons (see, e.g., Magal & Winnec, 1968; Weinberg, 1955). Data on the sexual victimization experiences of the sibling incest offenders demonstrate that as a group these study subjects were more likely than the other offender groups to have been sexually victimized by their fathers. Of the sibling incest perpetrators who had been sexually abused, two out of three were abused by family members or relatives, compared with half of the abused child molesters and less than one-fifth of the abused nonchild offenders. However, only a minority of sibling offenders had prior experience of sexual abuse within the family. Thus a previously existing incestuous family culture does not appear to be a sufficient causal factor in sibling incest.

Table 5.5
Offenders' Parents as Victims of Sexual Abuse (in percentages)

Offender Group	Mother Sex Abuse Victim	Father Sex Abuse Victim
Incest offender	36.0	10.0
Child molester	9.1	5.5
Nonchild offender	13.2	—

The families of sibling incest offenders were more likely to be physically abusive (61%) than those of the child molesters (45%) or the nonchild offenders (37%). There was little difference among the groups concerning the presence of chemical abuse within the families. Abuse of alcohol and/or drugs occurred in the majority of the subjects' families.

The literature on family sexual abuse has long held that incest is multigenerational, that is, that it is passed down from the father or mother to the children and grandchildren. Goodwin, McCarthy, and DiVasto (1981) compared 100 mothers of physically or sexually abused children with 500 mothers matched for age and ethnicity whose children were not known to have been physically or sexually abused. They found that 24% of the mothers of abused children had been sexually abused as children, compared with only 3% of the comparison group. Prior sexual victimization was not more common, however, among mothers of incest victims than among mothers of physically abused children.

Table 5.5 shows that 36% of the mothers and 10% of the fathers of the sibling incest perpetrators in this sample were themselves victims of sexual abuse as children, compared with only 9.1% of the mothers and 5.5% of the fathers of the extrafamilial child molesters. The mothers of the incest perpetrators were significantly more likely to have been victims of sexual abuse than were the mothers of adolescents in the two other groups (chi-square; $p < .001$). This finding lends support to the multigenerational transmission hypothesis, though the mechanism of transmission is unclear.

Family Functioning

For the purposes of the study, case managers were asked to rate the families as healthy, midrange, or severely disturbed using Robert Beavers's (1977) levels of family health as a guide. Nearly half (47%)

Table 5.6
Levels of Family Health (in percentages)

Offender Group	Healthy	Midrange	Severely Disturbed
Incest offender (N = 40)	2.5	45.0	52.5
Child molester (N = 44)	13.6	40.9	45.5
Nonchild offender (N = 29)	13.8	51.7	34.5

of all the families were judged to be severely disturbed. Table 5.6 shows ratings of family health levels by the three groups. Perhaps family disturbance plays an important role in the psychological or social development of the male adolescent that predisposes him to molest children. For instance, family dysfunction might lead to arrested emotional or psychological development, low self-worth, and social skills deficits, possibly putting these teens at greater risk to act out sexually with younger children.

Psychological Adjustment

One common assumption about adolescents who commit sex offenses is that the sexual acting out represents one feature of their general psychological and social maladjustment. While studies comparing the offense histories of other adolescents are lacking, the research indicates that other behavioral problems are often present in the histories of adolescent sex offenders (Becker et al., 1986; Fehrenbach, Smith, Monastersky, & Deisher, 1986). In this study sample, 41% of the adolescents had prior involvement with the juvenile justice system. The majority of the offenses for all groups were status or property offenses, and were not significantly different relative to offender type.

Crimes against persons, however, were more likely to have been committed by nonchild offenders. Over one-fourth (26%) of this group had prior involvement with the juvenile justice system because of crimes against persons. The incest offenders (11%) and the child molesters (18%) were much less likely to have been apprehended for similar crimes. Since the nonchild offender group included adolescents referred for the commission of sexual assaults against peers or adults—behavior that typically assumes force, coercion, and/or violence—they may have been acting out anger, power, or control issues that generalize to much of their interpersonal behaviors. Hence they may be more likely than child molesters to have previous arrests for crimes against persons.

One section of the Confidential Family Questionnaire filled out by the parent(s) is a 39-item behavior problem checklist. The parents were asked to indicate whether the adolescent exhibited any of the listed problem behaviors. The results indicated that the sibling incest offenders, as a group, were significantly more likely than the other two groups to have exhibited a variety of behavior problems often associated with generalized conduct disorder.

The majority (55%) of the adolescents referred to PHASE had some previous involvement with psychotherapy or counseling. Incest offenders were the most likely to have been involved in therapy previously (60%), followed by the child molesters (54%) and the nonchild offenders (47%).

School performance, in general, appeared to be problematic for the adolescents in the sample. Some 60% of those interviewed had below-average school performance, 32% were average, and 8% were above average. Incest offenders showed only slightly more school performance problems than the other groups.

Social Adequacy and Blockage Theory

Another common assumption about sex offenders in general, and adolescent offenders in particular, is that they suffer various social deficits that predispose them to victimize others sexually (Fehrenbach et al., 1986; Groth, 1977). In summarizing theoretical concepts that attempt to explain why some people molest children, Finkelhor (1984) includes social skills deficits under the broad explanatory category of "blockage." Blockage theories suggest that sex offenders are somehow blocked in their ability to get their sexual and emotional needs met in appropriate peer relationships and therefore choose alternative victimizing avenues for need fulfillment.

The incest literature in particular has relied heavily on blockage explanations for father-daughter incest. Typically, the marital relationship is described as having broken down; the wife is alienated from the husband, sexually and emotionally rejecting him. The husband is described as being too inhibited (because of social inadequacy or moral rigidity) to pursue outside relationships, turning to his daughter as a substitute source of emotional and sexual gratification (De Young, 1982; Mieselman, 1978).

If the blockage theory has any power as an explanation for adolescent sex offenders, one would expect to find these teenagers to be

Table 5.7
Frequency of Nonexploitive Sexual Interactions (in percentages)

Offender Group	None	Low	Moderate	High
Incest offender	64	25	11	—
Child molester	72	17	8	4
Nonchild offender	48	21	17	14

much less sexually experienced than their peers and generally less well socialized. Of this study's total sample, 32% admitted having had sexual intercourse prior to their offenses. A comprehensive adolescent health survey of 36,000 young people conducted by the University of Minnesota found that 47% of ninth-grade metropolitan-area male youth had experienced sexual intercourse at least once (Resnick, 1987). Since the modal grade of the adolescent offenders was the ninth grade, it appears that, compared with normal peers, these adolescents were less sexually experienced. If the school performance findings are integrated, a significant portion of the offenders were a year older than most ninth graders, but still less sexually experienced.

The adolescents in the study sample appeared generally willing at intake to reveal nondeviant sexual behaviors that occurred prior to their sexual offenses. A total of 64% admitted masturbation, 22% reported fellatio with a peer, 12% reported cunnilingus with a peer, 46% reported petting, and 71% admitted to having kissed a peer-aged partner. Only 6% of the sample denied having engaged in any prior acts of sexual expression.

The sibling incest offenders were similar to the extrafamilial child molesters in their relatively low rate of prior sexual intercourse. Only 26% of both groups had ever had sexual intercourse prior to their offenses, compared with 45% of the nonchild sex offenders, whose rate closely matches the norm for metropolitan-area ninth-grade males.

Having had a prior sexual experience with a peer, of course, does not necessarily negate the blockage theory. One also must consider the frequency of nonexploitive sexual interactions with peers that were occurring at the time the sexual offenses were committed. Table 5.7 shows the relative rates of nonexploitive sexual interactions by offender group. The table reveals that child molesters were least likely to have been sexually active, followed by the sibling incest offenders and then the nonchild offenders. If *being sexually active* is defined as

Table 5.8
Level of Socialization (in percentages)

Offender Group	Under-socialized	Somewhat Socialized	Antisocialized
Incest offender	64	28	9
Child molester	57	34	10
Nonchild offender	37	48	14

having a moderate or high rate of frequency, only 12% of the adolescents who victimized children (Groups 1 and 2) could be so rated, compared with 31% of the nonchild offenders. Clearly, the child offenders were less likely to be engaged in sexual interactions with peers at the time they molested children.

One explanation for this may be the degree of social functioning among the adolescent sex offenders. On the whole, 54% of the sample adolescent offenders were evaluated as undersocialized, 36% as somewhat socialized, and 11% as antisocialized. *Undersocialized* was defined as having few if any peer-age friends and generally poor social skills. *Socialized* was defined as having some appropriate peer relationships and adequate social skills. *Antisocialized* meant the adolescent's affiliations were primarily with delinquent youth. Table 5.8 shows the percentages of each group by level of socialization. Adolescents who sexually abused children either within or outside the family were assessed as more undersocialized than those who committed sex offenses against peers or adults. The incest offenders were not significantly different from child molesters on this variable.

These data, taken together, suggest some support for blockage theories. Perhaps the incest offenders and child molesters chose child victims because their poor social skills militated against their having meaningful involvement with peers. They carried out sexual experimentation with younger children or siblings available to them who served as substitutes for more desired peer partners.

Offenders as Victims

A currently popular notion about sexual offending by adolescents is that the behavior is a direct result of the adolescents having been sexually victimized. This "vampire syndrome" hypothesis, that sex offenders are first sexual victims, is an appealing theory of causation because its explanatory logic is simple and because it facilitates empathy for the offenders. While sexual offenders have comparatively high rates of previous sexual victimization (Becker et al., 1986, 23%; Gomes-Schwartz 1984, 38%; Fehrenbach et al., 1986, 19%), they are not high enough to support the hypothesis as an all-encompassing causative explanation.

The rates and figures from the sample examined here do, however, support the recognition of prior sexual victimization as a significant contributing factor in the development of offending behaviors. More than 38% of the adolescents in this study disclosed that they had been sexually abused. The sibling incest offenders had the highest rate of prior sexual victimization (42%), followed by the extrafamilial child molesters (40%) and the nonchild offenders (29%).

These rates are particularly significant when compared with the incidence of sexual abuse among nonclinical samples of males. Finkelhor (1979) found an incidence rate of 9% for his sample of New England college men. Among Minnesota ninth-grade teenagers surveyed, 3% of the boys disclosed being victims of sexual abuse (Resnick, 1987). Given the comparative data, it appears reasonable to assume that having been sexually victimized is an important contributing factor in explaining sex offender behavior.

Another assumption of the vampire syndrome theory is that the gender of the victim will most likely mirror the gender of the victimizer—that is, an adolescent abused by a male will tend to abuse a boy. A psychodynamic explanation is that the offender may be trying to achieve symbolic mastery over his own victimization experience in identification with the aggressor. By reversing roles he becomes the powerful victimizer rather than the powerless victim, restoring in himself a feeling of being in control. To achieve this, the theory suggests, he needs to recreate the dynamics of his own victimization experience, hence the choice of a male victim.

The data show that adolescents who are victims of sexual abuse by males were more likely to abuse males than were adolescents who were victims of females. Most (68%) of the adolescents abused by males victimized boys, whereas only 7% of those who were victims of females chose boys as their victims.

Thus the data suggest a fairly strong association between choice of victim gender and the adolescent's own experience as a victim of sexual abuse. An adolescent who was a victim of sexual abuse by a male perpetrator and who later went on to victimize others sexually appeared predisposed to choose males as his victims or both males and females. This does not necessarily provide strong support for the psychodynamic explanation, however. An alternative explanation is

that the early sexual victimization of a boy by a man, even if traumatic, became associated with sexual arousal and sexual pleasure
through the process of conditioning. The adolescent boy abused by a
male may have incorporated features of the sexual victimization experience into fantasies of sex with males (boys) that are highly eroti-
cized. These fantasies may have become reinforced through masturbation and then acted out periodically. As a result of the reinforced eroti-
cization toward boys, the offender primarily or exclusively chooses
boys as victims.

Being a victim of sexual abuse certainly appears to play a role in the
development of deviant sexual behavior patterns in some boys; it may
also be a significant factor in choice of victims. However, it is only one
of many variables. By itself, it is not a sufficient explanation for adolescent male sexual offending in general or sibling incest in particular.

CONCLUSION

The results of this study challenge the commonly held belief that
the phenomenon of sibling incest is relatively benign or clinically
insignificant. There are instances of sibling sexual interactions that
might be properly regarded as sibling sex play when, for example, the
acts are mutually exploratory, limited in both type and duration, and
consistent with the peer-age siblings' developmental levels. However,
the data reveal that sibling incest may often represent significant individual and family pathology.

The sibling offenders in this sample went beyond sexual exploration. Compared with other adolescent sexual offenders referred to the
treatment program, they admitted committing more sexual crimes,
reported longer offending careers, and generally engaged in more
intrusive sexual behaviors (i.e., penetration) than either the nonfamilial child molesters or those offending against peers or adults.

It might be argued that the sibling incest offenders in this sample
represented a unique set of adolescents who were referred for treatment precisely because referral sources viewed the behavior as particularly serious and requiring intervention. While this argument has
merit, my clinical experience has been that in the majority of cases, it
was not until after the adolescent and his family were involved in the
program that the full extent of the abuse was revealed. Furthermore,
although they committed more sexual crimes of a more serious nature
over a longer duration, the sibling incest offenders were the least
likely of the offender types to be adjudicated for their offenses. Only

about one-third of the sibling offenders were court ordered to the program, while three-fourths of the comparison offenders came to the program through the courts.

This failure to treat sibling incest behavior as criminal may be sending the message that society views an adolescent's sexual victimization of his sibling as less serious than if he had chosen a victim from outside the family. One explanation for this failure may be that in certain communities, child protective services have traditionally maintained responsibility for intrafamilial sexual abuse, with the result that the criminal justice system chooses not to handle these cases. Nevertheless, the judicial process is generally regarded as the more potent intervention. Ideally, it holds the offender accountable; demonstrates that the behavior is serious (i.e., criminal) and will not be tolerated; ensures a comprehensive assessment to evaluate the need for treatment, type of treatment, and treatment setting; provides an initially strong external motivation for change; and maintains supervision over the offender to ensure that treatment will be successfully completed.

A stronger social response is required because resistance to viewing sibling incest as a serious matter is often strongest within the family itself. When the behavior is first disclosed, the family homeostasis is disrupted and the family experiences a crisis. Parents often attempt to reestablish family stability by denying that the abuse has occurred, by minimizing its seriousness or impact, or by making superficial and premature attempts at reconciliation in a quick-fix, forgive-and-forget approach that serves to mask the pathology.

If the family is allowed to prevail in these attempts, the dynamics that fostered the abuse will remain, the victim and the offender will go untreated, and ultimately the sibling incest may resume—if not between the current offender and victim, then perhaps between the offender and other siblings or children of the next generation.

Professionals in the criminal justice, child protection, and mental health systems have often reinforced the family's resistance to treatment by investigating inadequately, deciding not to prosecute, and failing to provide appropriate treatment. Clearly, a change in social policy regarding sibling sexual abuse is in order. Police should be involved, along with child protection services, in conducting thorough investigations. Prosecution should become standard operating procedure in all but clearly mutual, peer-age sex-play situations. The courts must order comprehensive family and individual assessments in order to determine risk factors and appropriateness for treatment.

In many cases it is advisable to remove the offending sibling from the home to provide psychological safety for the victim and the motivation to change for the offender and the family that is so important in the healing process.

This study also investigated a number of factors believed to have etiological significance: family environment, socialization, and sexual victimization. Generally, the sibling incest offenders were found to be from the most dysfunctional families, those having high rates of physical, sexual, and/or substance abuse. There was some evidence for the hypothesis of an intergenerational transmission of the incest dynamic: A significantly higher proportion of the sibling offenders' parents were themselves victims of sexual abuse. One might speculate that the interpersonal boundary problems of the parents' families of origin became replicated in their current families. Also, since few of the parents had ever received therapy regarding their own victimization, patterns of denial and minimization may have persisted and guarded against recognition of the sibling abuse.

The implications for treatment are clear. Family involvement in the treatment of the sibling offender is critical, because family system dynamics probably play a significant role in the development and maintenance of sibling abuse. Specific structural interventions to correct dysfunctional family patterns need to be explored. However, it is important that the offender also be required to work in individual and group therapy settings to complete sex offender-specific treatment goals. Viewing the problem only as a systems dysfunction dangerously minimizes the specific responsibility of the offender and fails to address the intrapsychic issues associated with the abusive behavior. Both the individual and system factors that contributed to the incestuous behavior must be addressed in treatment.

The literature on adolescent sexual offenders cites social inadequacy as a major factor predisposing offenders to victimize others sexually. They suffer deficits in social skills, according to this theory, that prevent them from establishing meaningful peer relationships, and they therefore turn to alternative avenues (i.e., sex with young children) as substitutes for more prosocial strategies. This study found that the sibling incest offenders did, in fact, have serious deficits in social skills compared with a nonclinical population of teens. The sibling offenders had low rates of prior sexual intercourse with peers and were not likely to have been sexually active with peers at the time of their offenses. This lends some support to the blockage theory. A comprehensive treatment program should help facilitate the development of adequate social skills for these teenagers so they can meet their needs in appropriate ways.

The vampire syndrome hypothesis, that sexual offenders learn their behavior through having been sexually victimized themselves, is not supported as an all-encompassing explanation by the study data. But prior sexual victimization is clearly a significant factor. Some 38% of the adolescent offenders were victims; this figure is much higher than has been found in nonclinical samples. The sibling incest offenders in our study had the highest rate of prior sexual victimization (42%) and were more likely to have been sexually abused by family members, especially fathers, than the other offender types. However, the majority of the adolescent sexual offenders (including the sibling incest offenders) did not report that they had been victims of sexual abuse.

Caution must be exercised in generalizing from this study to other adolescents involved in sibling sexual behaviors because this sample was specifically selected for evaluation and treatment by referral sources. While the inclusion of comparison groups improves upon the research to date, allowing discussion of unique features of the sibling incest offenders relative to other offender types, the study suffers from the lack of a control sample of adolescents with no sexual offense histories.

Comparisons of teenage sexual offenders to other delinquent teen groups and to normal adolescents would be interesting in that characteristics unique to sexual offenders might be discovered. Such comparisons were well beyond the scope of this study, but they remain an important research direction for the future. This preliminary investigation of the characteristics of sibling incest offenders suggests that the phenomenon of sibling incest is multidetermined and can be accounted for only through an investigation of contextual, intrapsychic, and family variables.

The topic of sibling incest has largely been neglected in the professional literature on family sexual abuse. It is my hope that these preliminary findings will serve to stimulate further empirical research into causes, dynamics, and effects of sibling incest so that more appropriate prevention, intervention, and treatment strategies can be developed and instituted.

REFERENCES

Beavers, W. R. (1977). *Psychotherapy and growth: A family system perspective*. New York: Brunner/Mazel.

Becker, J., Kaplan, M., Cunningham-Rathner, J., & Kavoussi, R. (1986). Characteristics of adolescent incest sexual perpetrators: Preliminary findings. *Journal of Family Violence, 1*(1), 85–97.

Cole A. (1990). *Brother-sister sexual abuse: Experiences, feelings, reactions and a comparison to father-daughter sexual abuse.* Unpublished doctoral dissertation, Union Institute.

De Young, M. (1982). *The sexual victimization of children.* Jefferson, NC: McFarland.

Fehrenbach, P. A., Smith, W., Monastersky, C., & Deisher, R. W. (1986). Adolescent sexual offenders: Offender and offense characteristics. *American Journal of Orthopsychiatry, 56,* 225–223.

Finkelhor, D. (1979). *Sexually victimized children.* New York: Free Press.

Finkelhor, D. (1980). Sex among siblings: A survey on prevalence, variety and effects. *Archives of Sexual Behaviors, 9*(3), 171–194.

Finkelhor, D. (1984). *Child sexual abuse: New theory and research.* New York: Free Press.

Gomes-Schwartz, B. (1984). Juvenile sex offenders. In U.S. Department of Justice, *Sexually exploited children: Service and research project.* Washington, DC: Government Printing Office.

Goodwin, T., McCarthy, T., & DiVasto, P. (1981). Prior incest in mothers of abused children. *Child Abuse and Neglect, 5,* 87–95.

Groth, A. N. (1977). The adolescent sexual offender and his prey. *International Journal of Offender Therapy and Comparative Criminology, 21,* 249–254.

Lindzey, G. (1967). Some remarks concerning incest, the incest taboo, and psychoanalytic theory. *American Psychologist, 22,* 1051–1059.

Magal, V., & Winnec, H. Z. (1968). Role of incest in family structure. *Israeli Annals of Psychiatry and Related Disciplines, 6,* 173–189.

Mieselman, K. (1978). *Incest: A psychological study of causes and effects with treatment recommendations.* San Francisco: Jossey-Bass.

Resnick, R. (1987). *Adolescent health survey.* Minneapolis: University of Minnesota.

Russell, D. E. H. (1986). *The secret trauma: Incest in the lives of girls and women.* New York: Basic Books.

Weinberg, S. K. (1955). *Incest behavior.* New York: Citadel.

6

Resilience and the Intergenerational Transmission of Child Sexual Abuse

JANE F. GILGUN

Why some people maltreated in childhood become perpetrators of child sexual abuse and others from similar backgrounds do not is a question with important theoretical and practical implications. This chapter is a report of research in progress. The research involves comparing developmental patterns of men known to have abused children sexually with others from similar backgrounds who are not known to have committed such acts. Such comparisons can help us to understand which factors might be specific to child molesters and which are not. Understanding such factors can contribute to prevention of abuse.

DEFINING CHILD SEXUAL ABUSE

For this research, child sexual abuse is defined in detail as follows:

Child sexual abuse is defined as non-consensual genital contact between a child who is 17 years old or younger and a person who manipulates, tricks, or forces the child into sexual behaviors. Non-consent is presumed when the child is 15 or younger and the other person is 19 or older, or when there is a 5-year or more age gap between the older person and the

AUTHORS' NOTE: This research was supported by The Saint Paul Foundation and the Minnesota Agricultural Experiment Station. The author would like to thank Caroline R. Weiss for her reading of an earlier draft of this chapter.

child victim. When there is less than a 5-year gap in age, non-consent is determined by the victim stating that the genital contact was not wanted.

Types of genital contact include penetration, attempted penetration, or stimulation of the vaginal or rectal area by a penis, finger, tongue, or any other part of the perpetrator's body, or by an object used by the perpetrator; and also includes any type of genital or anal contact of the perpetrator by the victim, such as fellatio, masturbation, and intromission of any kind. Unwanted touching of breasts is included in this definition.

No-contact sexualized behavior. The definition of child sexual abuse in this research also encompassed no-contact sexual behavior. This was operationalized as an adult sleeping in same bed with a child when either the child or the adult or both experiences sexual stimulation; seductive looks and talk to a child age 17 and younger by parents or other persons who have power over the child and such talk violates generational and/or personal boundaries; allowing or forcing others to witness sexual behavior such as intercourse, masturbation, and fellatio; allowing or forcing a child to observe pornographic pictures or films; inducing the child to pose for sexually explicit photographs; or inducing the child to perform sex on others. For the purposes of this research, a one- or two-time incidence of being a victim of exhibitionism and voyeurism by acts of a stranger is not included; but being victimized through exhibitionism or voyeurism within a family or intimate setting over time is included. (Gilgun, 1988)

Child sexual abuse then, as defined above, involves a misuse of power, where an older, stronger, and more sophisticated person takes advantage of a younger, smaller, and less sophisticated person in order to satisfy the wishes and feelings of the more powerful person without regard for the less powerful person.

TRANSMISSION AND SOCIALIZATION

The present research builds on theories of intergenerational transmission of child maltreatment and on differential sex role socialization to help explain the origins of sexually abusive behavior. Previous research has suggested that sexual abuse is frequently found in the backgrounds of men who become child sexual abusers (Ballard et al., 1990; Davis & Leitenberg, 1987; Groth, 1983). This supports the intergenerational transmission hypothesis. On the other hand, many abusers have had no known experiences of sexual abuse, although other forms of maltreatment are common in backgrounds of known perpetrators. This additional finding suggests that the transmission of maltreating behavior is not direct and other factors besides being abused are significant.

Research also has found that women are much less likely than men to become sexual abusers of children, although they are more likely to have been sexually abused. This finding provides a basis for arguing that sex role socialization may be an important factor in understanding why some persons become perpetrators of child sexual abuse while others from similar backgrounds do not.

With these general ideas in mind, I decided to take an in-depth look at individual lives, using open-ended interviews, in order to understand complex developmental pathways. My analytical approach to the masses of data that result from such interviewing is based on the grounded theory method of Glaser and Strauss (1967). The findings are data-based hypotheses, hence the term *grounded theory*.

In the course of data collection and analysis, I saw that some of my findings on sexual abuse were consistent with findings from research on the intergenerational transmission of child physical abuse (Egeland, Jacobvitz, & Sroufe, 1988; Fraiberg, Adelson, & Shapiro, 1975; Kaufman & Zigler, 1987) and research on resilience and vulnerability (Garmezy, 1987; Masten & Garmezy, 1985; Murphy, 1987; Rutter, 1987; Werner & Smith, 1982). Briefly, research on child physical abuse suggests that when parents who have been maltreated as children have the opportunity to work through the effects of their own maltreatment and are also able to find supportive relationships, they are much less likely to abuse their own children physically. Those who deny or are unaware that their own child maltreatment has affected them are more likely to perpetuate the cycle of abuse.

RESILIENCE

The resilience literature adds a wider perspective to the findings on the intergenerational transmission of maltreatment. Murphy (1987) defines resilience as recovery from adversity. Children who experience adversity are vulnerable to developing adverse outcomes. Growing up in poverty, living in institutional settings, and being a child of a mentally ill parent are examples of situations that are associated with vulnerability to negative developmental outcomes. When children overcome difficult childhoods and develop good peer relationships, respectable academic records, and success in their work, they are considered resilient.

Researchers have identified several protective mechanisms related to resilience: affection from at least one parent; harmonious relationships between parents; persons inside or outside of the family who encourage and facilitate the child's ability to cope and who foster positive values; and the personal qualities of the child, such as the ability to express internal states and to empathize with the internal states of others (Cicchetti, 1987; Garmezy, 1987; Rutter, 1987; Werner & Smith, 1982). Internal states include feelings, thoughts, wants, input from the five senses, physiological states, ability, and volition. Personal attributes are theorized to develop from secure attachments to parents and parental figures during infancy, early childhood, and/or across the life span (Bowlby, 1973; Cicchetti, 1987; Egeland et al., 1988).

Persons unable to overcome adversity are at risk of developing behavioral patterns that could be harmful to themselves or to others. They often have been unable to find supportive persons who could have helped them to overcome the effects of living under adversity. Sometimes their life circumstances curtailed the possibility that they might form relationships of trust with others, as in the case of children who have experienced many foster home placements. For others a biological predisposition can lead to vulnerability, as in some forms of mental illness, where environmental support was not sufficient or not able to overcome the effects of the vulnerability-inducing condition.

Such research and theory are integrated into the findings of the present study. I conceptualize child maltreatment as a vulnerability factor that places the maltreated individual at risk for committing sexually and physically violent acts. Whether the individual becomes violent depends on the presence or absence of protective mechanisms, the presence or absence of vulnerability factors, and the amount of stress the person perceives. These factors are in dynamic interaction. The particular type of maltreatment the individual perpetrates depends on many factors, such as gender, models of violence available to the person, and the type of sexual environment to which the person has been exposed. In the pages that follow I shall discuss the sample studied and further elaborate my findings.

METHOD

The findings are based on intensive life-history interviews with 48 adults (36 men and 12 women) maltreated as children, including physical and emotional abuse and neglect, sexual abuse, and neglect of sex education. (These terms are defined in Gilgun, 1988.) Each life history was based on extensive interviewing, with an average of 12 hours per person on six different occasions. I was the sole interviewer. Sources of subjects were a maximum-security prison (20 subjects), medium-security prisons (3 subjects), Sex Addicts Anonymous (11 subjects), and community-based treatment programs (14 subjects), all located in the Upper Midwest.

Of the 36 male subjects, 15 were perpetrators of child sexual abuse. The 19 men who were not perpetrators of child sexual abuse during adulthood included 12 convicted felons (8 for rape, 1 for armed robbery, 1 for attempted murder, and 2 for murder). An additional man was convicted of both rape and child molestation.

Also part of the study were 12 women, 8 of whom were married to male subjects. Of these, 7 were married to perpetrators of child sexual abuse and 1 was married to a man sexually abused as a child and who was not a perpetrator of child sexual abuse or a rapist. Of the women subjects, 2 had been convicted of felonies (larceny, prostitution, and aiding in the rape of an underage person) and 1 was sexually involved for two years with a girl who was under 16. She reported herself for child sexual abuse, but was not charged.

The subjects were ages 21 to 56, with an average age of 32. The sample was white except for five of the male convicted felons, four of whom were black and one of whom was American Indian. All subjects were volunteers, selected using the principles of theoretical sampling (Glaser & Strauss, 1967), in which subjects are chosen on the basis of whether their characteristics might challenge or add to the emerging findings (Gilgun, in press). The first subsample to be interviewed consisted of seven perpetrators and seven spouses of perpetrators. The patterns differentiating them were then compared to patterns in the lives of men from similar backgrounds not known to have abused children sexually.

An interview guide provided a structure for data collection. The general areas of inquiry were family history, history of friendships, forms of discipline within the family, history of abuse and neglect, and history of sex education and sexual behavior. (Details of the interview can be found in Gilgun & Connor, 1989.) Interviewing began in 1985. Interviews were tape-recorded, transcribed, and content analyzed.

Because this research is sensitive and involves persons who might feel obligated to share information they truly might not want to share, subjects were encouraged to have "freedom of choice" (Gilgun, 1989). Subjects were asked not to talk about anything they did not want to talk about and to stop talking about something if they began to feel uncomfortable. Not only did this approach help assure that coercion was minimized, but it appeared to have a paradoxical effect. Many subjects reported that having the freedom to choose whether to disclose or not helped them to feel freer to talk about sensitive issues.

RESULTS

The interviews showed that childhood maltreatment, no matter the type, was associated with intense emotional pain for the persons interviewed. Each subject attempted to cope with this pain, some in ways that harmed others and some in ways that did not. Those who were not convicted felons tended to confide in other persons, while the convicted felons isolated themselves emotionally from others over their lifetimes. Figure 6.1 shows the relationship of child maltreatment and outcomes.

The convicted felons reported that they never talked about their personal and painful feelings with others. Several said they tried when they were children, but they felt punished or betrayed because of their attempts and did not risk self-disclosure again. One convicted rapist said that when he was in the second grade he confided in a teacher at school about his mother's physical abuse of him. The school principal called the mother, who beat him when he got home from school and told him never to reveal anything about their family. There was no follow-up on his report of abuse, and he never told another person about his physical and emotional abuse.

Those subjects who did not harm others reported being able to tell other people they trusted about their personal and private thoughts and feelings. They were capable of self-disclosure, although they sometimes went through periods of intense isolation. As one woman subject said about her childhood: "I can remember being alone. I can more or less feel that overwhelm me. I seems like nobody felt exactly the way I felt or seemed to want to hear about it." When this woman was in high school, she met a few other "gals" who "told each other everything," and who became lifelong friends. For the subjects in this study, self-disclosure and feeling understood by at least one other person, a confidant, differentiated those who committed antisocial acts from those who did not.

Patterns of Early Sexual Experience

Men who committed sexual crimes not only did not have confidants, but they also learned to use masturbation and other forms of

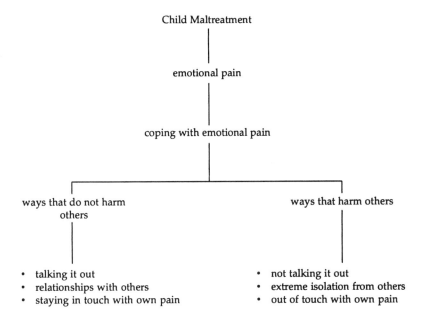

Figure 6.1 Outcomes of Child Maltreatment

sexual activity to make themselves feel better (Gilgun, 1988). Men who became child molesters and were not known to be rapists began their sexual careers (defined as age at first intercourse and age when masturbation began) earlier than the rapists and usually had other sexual outlets in addition to masturbation, such as exhibitionism, voyeurism, and bestiality, as means of giving themselves some emotional charge or release.

Of the 15 men convicted of child sexual abuse, 13 began abusing children in adolescence or at younger ages. Table 6.1 shows the age at first intercourse and age masturbation began for the convicted felons compared with the nonfelons. Although the 9 men who became rapists tended to begin their sexual careers later than the child molesters, once they began to masturbate they seemed to use masturbation as the molesters did—usually on a daily basis and not for the satisfaction of sexual desire but for the release of tension.

Some of the men who were convicted of rape only, however, had some characteristics in common with child molesters. One man, for

Table 6.1

Age at First Intercourse and Masturbation for Men Convicted of Rape or
Child Molestation, compared with Nonfelons

	N	Age at First Intercourse	Age Masturbation Began
Molesters	14	14.5	11.4
Rapists	9	16.6	15.4
Nonfelons	9	21.7	12.9

example, attempted to rape his younger sister several times during his adolescence, but he stated he did not molest children as an adult. A second convicted rapist was sexually active with an 8-year-old sister when he was 12, which he said involved bribes rather than physical force. Another man convicted of rape experienced his sexual milestones at about the same time as the molesters in this sample, but he stated that he had never molested children and had never been tempted to do so. These exceptions to the general pattern of sexual behavior found in this sample point out that there is not likely to be one pattern that will fit all rapists or molesters exactly.

The one man who was convicted of both rape and child sexual abuse began masturbating when he was almost 12, had intercourse at age 17, and was molesting other children from middle childhood on. He had a sexual history with aspects similar to those of convicted rapists and convicted child molesters in this sample.

Some of the men who did not commit antisocial acts had sexual profiles similar to those of child molesters. They, too, began their sexual careers earlier than rapists and often used masturbation, exhibitionism, voyeurism, and bestiality as a means of giving themselves some emotional release. As one man, a nonfelon, said of his daily masturbation: "I used masturbation instead of a drug or pill. . . . There wasn't much pleasure in it. I'd masturbate and go back to being miserable."

Of the 9 men who did not commit antisocial acts, 8 did not sexually abuse other children during childhood or adolescence. When one of these subjects was 12, he was sexual with his 6-year-old sister a few times. He told his mother, who did not punish him, but he said he felt ashamed and never was sexual with a younger person again.

A Critical Difference: Confiding in Others

What differentiated these nonfelons from the convicted child molesters was their ability to confide in others. They sometimes went for years without telling other people about personal feelings and intimate details of their lives until they found persons in whom they developed trust, then they disclosed their feelings. By adolescence, all of the male nonfelons had developed confidant relationships. They had deep and long talks with male peers, girlfriends, or adults whom they trusted. Often the relationships were typically adolescent, with one friend calling a subject a "pain in the ass," for example. Yet, in this relationship, the subject talked with his friend about "being horribly depressed and not being able to enjoy life," as well as about how to be popular with girls. None of the male nonfelons who had been sexually abused, however, told friends about this form of abuse. Almost all of the women who had been sexually abused in childhood told someone, usually a peer.

Of the 12 women in the sample, 4 never found someone in whom to confide. These women had far more chaotic lives than did the 8 women who found confidants. One of the women who did not confide in others sexually abused a 16-year-old girl when she was in her early 30s. She also was the only woman subject who admitted masturbating throughout her adolescence. A second subject was convicted of grand larceny when she was 20 years old. A third ran away from home during adolescence and married her high school sweetheart. He beat her, became a criminal, and deserted her. Between her first and second marriages, she, in her own words, "slept with just about anybody" and was gang raped when a man she met in a bar took her into the woods and then invited his friends to rape her. She married her second husband, who beat her, sexually molested her daughter, and was an undetected grand larcenist. A fourth subject became a prostitute, something she continued throughout her marriage, without her husband's knowledge. She had a middle-class life-style, a responsible job working with children, and was well respected in her community. She said she had kept a facade of middle-class respectability throughout her life.

Having the capacity to confide in other persons, however, is not an ironclad protection against victimizing oneself or others. Two women in the sample did confide in others while adolescents, but both had extremely harsh life circumstances. Both women were homeless juvenile prostitutes. One became a lifelong prostitute; the other did not.

The prostitute was convicted in her mid-20s of aiding her pimp in the rape of an underaged woman. The person in whom she confided—by telling her life story—was a counselor in a group home where she was a resident for about six months during adolescence. Her long-term homelessness and consequent lack of long-term confiding relationships probably overcame whatever protective mechanisms her ability to confide may have provided.

The second female subject who had been a homeless juvenile prostitute had no convictions, either as an adolescent or as an adult. She, too, confided in other persons while on the run. In early adulthood, she married and started a family. Her husband sexually abused their two children, and she and her husband voluntarily terminated their rights to one of their children.

This detailed look at the lives of persons abused as children suggests that the existence of confidant relationships may be the single most important factor associated with breaking the cycle of abuse. Replicated in the case of physical abuse (Egeland et al., 1988; Kaufman & Zigler, 1987), this finding also is linked to research and theory on resilience. When the intergenerational abuse cycle is not broken, the particular form of abuse appears to be associated with gender, type of sexual environment, and models of violence to which the subjects were exposed. Women may be less likely than men to act out in sexual or sexually violent ways because they have more exposure to models of nurturing and are given more permission than males to express personal and painful feelings.

DISCUSSION

The findings of this research are suggestive, and they cannot be applied uncritically to explain individual cases of abuse. Each case is idiosyncratic and may represent a major variation on the patterns described. The findings of this research, however, can be helpful in alerting practitioners to possible ways of assessing clients and developing treatment plans.

In interpreting these findings it also is important to think about opportunity. It could be that some of the subjects have not raped or molested children because they have not been in situations where this behavior could happen. Some of the subjects were fairly young, for example. It is possible that later in life those who have not been sexually abusive could become so.

Sex Role Socialization as an Abuse Factor

Since men abuse more often than women and women are more often abused, this research suggests that sex role socialization may play a role in the development of sexually abusive behavior toward children. Men might be more at risk for sexual problems than women as well as more at risk for acting-out behaviors. Men are taught to be aggressive, and a fairly consistent message that young men receive links sexual conquest with masculinity. When males are troubled and have been discouraged from talking things out, they may be susceptible to seeking sexual solutions to their problems, through either sexual aggression or masturbation (which may be an attempt at self-comfort).

Women are encouraged to confide, and, compared with men, they have few cultural images of female physical and sexual aggression. Most cultural images of women are in nurturing roles, such as breastfeeding, child care, and husband care. When troubled, women are more likely to try to work out their problems through talking or some other socially acceptable method. However, they are also exposed to images of women as sexual objects; for example, three women in the sample became prostitutes. One of these women felt she deserved the degradation of prostitution, and she also did not confide in other people. Women as well as men may be susceptible to acting out negative sex-typed images when their ability to confide in others is blocked.

Many factors undoubtedly contribute to the development of sexually abusive behaviors toward children, socialization being one of them. While men may be more at risk for this behavior than women, this does not mean that men are more innately abusive than women. What it does mean is that boys who have been abused are less likely to deal with the effects of the abuse through talking. They are more likely to seek mastery of painful feelings through avenues that are open to them, and these avenues are often sexual and sometimes violent.

Prevention

This research suggests potential directions for prevention programs. Such steps as providing more services to families in which abuse has occurred and to children who have been abused, not neglecting the effects of abuse on boys, providing boys and girls with a variety of images of what it means to be males and females all may help break the cycle of abuse. Information on how to talk about emotional pain, on how to recognize signs that suggest an individual may be in trouble emotionally, and on sexuality and on violence all would be important in prevention programs. Providing intervention to all children and their families at the time abuse is disclosed is likely to be a major factor in breaking the cycle of abuse.

This research also provides empirical support for resilience theory and protective mechanisms theory, which posit that the availability of supportive, confiding relationships is associated with overcoming adversity, while their absence is associated with problematic developmental outcomes.

Future Research

The present research is clearly exploratory and incomplete, given the small and selective sample. Some of the patterns I have been working with are not clear. For example, I do not include enough male subjects who are felons but not sexual offenders. I also need many more female subjects in order to begin to understand the effects on women of abuse and isolation. It is critical that research on these issues be continued and expanded if we are to prevent sexual abuse, develop effective treatments, and refine theory that will contribute to both treatment and prevention.

REFERENCES

Ballard, D. T., Blair, G. D., Devereaux, S., Valentine, L. K., Horton, A. L., & Johnson, B. L. (1990). A contemporary profile of the incest perpetrator: Background characteristics, abuse history, and use of social skills. In A. L. Horton, B. L. Johnson, L. M. Roundy, & D. Williams (Eds.), *The incest perpetrator: A family member no one wants to treat* (pp. 43–64). Newbury Park, CA: Sage.

Bowlby, J. (1973). *Attachment and loss: Separation, anxiety, and anger* (Vol. 2). New York: Basic Books.

Cicchetti, D. (1987). Developmental psychopathology in infancy: Illustrations from the study of maltreated youngsters. *Journal of Consulting and Clinical Psychology, 55,* 837–845.

Davis, G. E., & Leitenberg, H. (1987). Adolescent sex offenders. *Psychological Bulletin, 101,* 417–427.

Egeland, B., Jacobvitz, D., & Sroufe, A. L. (1988). Breaking the cycle of abuse. *Child Development, 59,* 1080–1088.

Fraiberg, S., Adelson, E., & Shapiro, V. (1975). Ghosts in the nursery: A psychoanalytic approach to the problems of impaired mother-child relationships. *Journal of the American Association of Child Psychiatry, 14,* 387–421.

Garmezy, N. (1987). Stress, competence, and development: Continuities in the study of schizophrenic adults, children vulnerable to psychopathology, and the search for stress-resistant children. *American Journal of Orthopsychiatry, 57,* 159–174.

Gilgun, J. F. (1988, October 27–28). *Factors which block the development of sexually abusive behaviors in adults abused and neglected in childhood.* Paper presented at the First National Conference on Male Victims and Offenders, Minneapolis, MN.

Gilgun, J. F. (1989). Freedom of choice and research interviewing in child sexual abuse. In B. R. Compton & B. Galaway (Eds.), *Social work processes* (4th ed., pp. 358–368). Homewood, IL: Dorsey.

Gilgun, J. F. (in press). Hypothesis generation in social work research. *Journal of Social Service Research.*

Gilgun, J. F., & Connor, T. M. (1989). How perpetrators view child sexual abuse. *Social Work, 34,* 249–251.

Glaser, B. G., & Strauss, A. L. (1967). *The discovery of gounded theory: Strategies for qualitative research.* New York: Aldine.

Groth, A. N. (1983). Treatment of the sexual offender in a correctional institution. In J. G. Greer & I. R. Stuart (Eds.), *The sexual aggressor: Current perspectives in treatment* (pp. 160–176). New York: Van Nostrand Reinhold.

Kaufman, J., & Zigler, E. (1987). Do abused children become abusive parents? *American Journal of Orthopsychiatry, 57,* 186–192.

Masten, A. S., & Garmezy, N. (1985). Risk, vulnerability, and protective factors in developmental psychopathology. In B. V. Lahey & A. E. Kazdin (Eds.), *Advances in clinical child psychology* (Vol. 8, pp. 1–52). New York: Plenum.

Murphy, L. (1987). Further reflections on resilience. In E. J. Anthony & B. J. Cohler (Eds.), *The invulnerable child* (pp. 84–105). New York: Guilford.

Rutter, M. (1987). Psychosocial resilience and protective mechanisms. *American Journal of Orthopsychiatry, 57,* 316–331.

Werner, E., & Smith, R. S. (1982). *Vulnerable but invincible.* New York: McGraw-Hill.

7

Intrafamilial Sexual Abuse in American Indian Families

IRL CARTER
LAWRENCE J. PARKER

Incest is increasingly recognized as a serious problem among American Indians. The National American Indian Court Judges Association (NAICJA, 1985) states:

> The [Indian] community must publicly admit that child sexual abuse does exist and can happen to its children. Statements by respected community members (elders, council members, religious leaders) providing personal testimony of abuse can be extremely effective in forcing a community to recognize that, yes, it does happen here. (p. 11)

In an informational brochure, the Division of Indian Work (DIW, 1987) states:

> Over the years, extreme deprivation, discrimination and victimization of Indian people by the dominant society that has rarely recognized or acknowledged the Indian way of life has led to a startling reality: approximately 80% of American Indian families in urban areas now have a history of family violence including incest, sexual abuse and battering; over 65% are unemployed, over 50% are chemically dependent and 65% are single parents, four times the state average.

In Hennepin County (Minneapolis), more than 12% of the children in foster care placement are American Indian, even though Indians make up only 1% of the county's population. Minnesota is one of the states that most frequently removes Indian children from their fami-

106

lies (Unger, 1977). Incest can be viewed as one symptom of the systemic deprivation of Indian families.

THE PURPOSES OF THIS RESEARCH

The purposes of this study were to investigate the nature and definition of incest among Minnesota Indians, establish some baseline data, suggest some further questions to be explored, and identify treatment models compatible with Indian culture. Relatively little research has been conducted on incest among Indians—in part, we think, because of a lack of interest among social scientists and professionals. Social scientists are interested in broader social and cultural issues, and professionals generally have infrequent contact with Indian clients or patients. Because of the lack of literature on incest among American Indians, the "knowledge" that exists is largely impressionistic.

We undertook this research with the belief that incest among Indian families has too long been ignored by both Indian families and service agencies. But the danger that Indian families will be misunderstood and maltreated by outsiders is real. In order to deal responsibly and intelligently with the problem, it is necessary to demystify it, identify ways to address it, and provide hope. It may also be helpful for Indian groups to be able to point to research that substantiates their concern for, and willingness to treat, all the victims of incest—victims, families, and perpetrators. This may provide a creative and helpful perspective for services to Indians—and to non-Indians as well.

METHODS

The researcher in Indian affairs, particularly one researching a topic as sensitive as incest, must bear in mind the admonition, "First, do no harm." Personnel who work with Indians must earn their trust. That trust and confidentiality is sometimes kept at the expense of full, detailed records. Further, there is knowledge within the Indian community that non-Indians may not (and sometimes should not) be trusted to have; it is "none of our business." Our methods and the limitations of this study must be understood in this context.

We conducted several lengthy interviews with the Division of Indian Work counselor, our key informant for this study. The taped interviews were transcribed, with both researchers independently analyzing the typed transcripts. These transcripts were also reviewed by two counselors in the community, both American Indian, who have experience with incest cases. Their reactions and insights were incorporated into the study.

In addition, we recorded client information system data from the files of the Division of Indian Work. Analysis of these data was confined to tabulation. No further statistical analysis was performed because of the limited number of subjects. We did not obtain data directly from Indian victims due to the confidentiality of files, limited time and resources, and the potential intrusiveness of such interviews. Thus we are limited in this exploratory study to data from key informants and files.

We compared and cross-checked sources of data and interpretations whenever possible. Thus we compared the DIW counselor's reports, the interpretations made by the two external Indian counselors, and our own interpretations. Our conclusion is that these methods were sufficiently rigorous for an exploratory study to offer reasonable assurance of consistent and fair interpretations. Nevertheless, it is clear that the scope and data base of this study are extremely limited. Their value is in direct proportion to the dearth of existing information.

DIVISION OF INDIAN WORK FILE CASES

Minnesota has 11 federally recognized Indian reservations; four Sioux (Dakota) in southern Minnesota and seven Chippewa (Ojibwa) in central and northern Minnesota. It is likely that the U.S. Census undercounts Indians even more than other minority groups, but a figure of 45,000 in Minnesota in 1980 seems to be a reasonable estimate. Of these, about half are urban residents in the Twin Cities area or Duluth; the other half are on reservations, in rural areas, or in small towns.

The Division of Indian Work serves primarily the Twin Cities metropolitan area. The south side of Minneapolis has the largest urban concentration of Indians in the United States (DIW, 1987). DIW also serves Indian clients from reservations who may be temporarily in the Twin Cities or who migrate between the reservation and the city.

The survey of DIW files revealed 41 clear cases of incest: 39 female victims and 2 male. This survey covered all case files from January 1986 to August 1988. Most of these cases involved women in their early 20s whose experiences with incest took place several years before. Many perpetrators were geographically distant or dead. The range in ages of the women when they first contacted DIW was from preschool age (up to 5 years old) to 40 years old.

Clients were of two types, primary and secondary victims, a common distinction in the literature of incest. Primary victims were those who themselves had been incest victims. Secondary victims were family members who suffered the effects of the incest. Counseling was available to both through DIW.

Perpetrators included fathers, stepfathers, uncles, brothers, and nonrelatives acting in a parental role as part of their relationship with the child's mother, such as the mother's boyfriend or partner. In the cases of the two boys who were incest victims, the perpetrators were older females. Fathers and persons in parental roles accounted for about 44% of incest incidents; other relatives, 34%; and siblings, about 22%.

Of 36 cases with available data, 25 victims were assaulted by two or more perpetrators; in addition, 8 other victims were assaulted multiple times by one perpetrator. Fathers and other persons in parental roles accounted for 40% of all cases regardless of number of incidents, but siblings were the sole perpetrators in 27% of the cases of a single perpetrator and 16% of the cases of multiple perpetrators. It appears that parental and sibling violations tended to occur as solo perpetrators, while abuse by other relatives tended to occur as part of a larger number of perpetrators.

PERSPECTIVES ON INDIAN INCEST

As the preceding data indicate, incest does exist in some American Indian families. One issue is whether definitions of incest in the Indian context are different from non-Indian definitions. This did not appear to be an issue in the cases examined in this study or among our Indian key informants.

In many tribes, including that of the DIW counselor, sexual relations or marriage within a clan (a subset of a tribe) is considered incestuous. NAICJA (1985) has commented as follows:

As with any population, the occurrence of child sexual abuse in American Indian communities does *not* indicate that it is culturally sanctioned. Native Americans place high value on children and find the occurrence of child sexual abuse to be damaging, disgraceful and frightening. (p. 5)

There is historical evidence that tribes were aware of incest and its dangers. Fischler (1985) has studied incest among American Indians, and concludes:

> All Indian cultures appear to have strong sanctions against incest, which includes sexual relations with the immediate family, as well as within the entire clan. A variety of physical and psychological symptoms, including suicide and psychotic behaviors and epilepsy, are attributed to incest. The victim as well as the perpetrator of sexual abuse may suffer symptoms and ostracism. (p. 102)

The tribal court judges have estimated that the incidence of incest in Indian families is about the same as that among non-Indian families (NAICJA, 1985, p. 5). But they also note that in geographically isolated communities, such as in Alaska, the risk may be significantly higher (Ashby, Gilchrist, & Miramontez, 1987, p. 27; NAICJA, 1985, p. 4). This study could not address the question of whether incest is more or less common among Indians or non-Indians. It seems likely, however, that geographic isolation is a factor regardless of ethnic background. The DIW counselor and one of the non-DIW Indian counselors did note that incest seems to persist through generations, and that perpetrators appear to be victims themselves.

Cultural Perspectives

From the perspective of our primary Indian key informant, the major difference between incest in the Indian context and incest in non-Indian contexts does not appear to be in definition or causation, but rather in reactions to and handling of incest. She views much Indian behavior in the context of survival in a hostile environment. As applied to incest, the DIW counselor stated that Indians learned abusive behavior from whites who were in authority over them. This is consistent with her view that sexual abuse, including incest, was not characteristic of Indian communities previous to contact with Europeans.

The same view applies to alcohol abuse. Alcohol abuse apparently was not a major problem among Indians before European introduction of alcohol in refined form. According to this explanation, Indians may have internalized cultural exploitation and denigration of Indian cultures, and the combination of alcohol and racism has led to lowered self-worth, in a downward spiral. Alcoholism, as discussed later, is related to family violence. Whether it is more of a problem for Indians or non-Indians is debatable. The counselors agreed that alcohol does not "cause" incest or other family abuse, but that abuse is more likely to occur in the presence of alcohol, by loosening the strength of the traditional taboo against incest.

It is the senior author's hypothesis that a victimization ideology pervades Indian cultures, an ideology of being victimized and existing in a hostile environment. It appears to be a powerful and pervasive ideology. The term *ideology* here is not meant to convey that the belief is untrue; there is ample support for the belief that victimization exists, historically and currently. If the ideology is as powerful as it appears, it requires our most serious attention, because it may underlie Indian behaviors in a way that is very difficult for non-Indians to understand, requiring the focusing of energies on basic "safety" and "security" needs as Maslow defines them.

The Indian Family

In attempting to understand incest in Indian families, it is important to understand Indian families more generally.

> Urban Indian families saw themselves as emotional, financial, strategic and geographical continuations of kin on home reservations. Many urban Indian domestic units were flexible, extended family groupings composed of a variable number of visiting or other kin in addition to a central core of kin. . . . Urban Indian children often circulated throughout extended kinship networks along the same lines of distribution as economic or other resources. Children were frequently subject to multiple parenting and to reciprocal rights and obligations spread over a wide range of kin. The movement of Indian children back and forth between domestic units located in both city and on home reservation encouraged strong emotional ties between geographically dispersed kin. [There was] extremely strong kinship affect. This strong affect represented an investment which ensured both the allegiance of individual kin, and solidarity of group of kin in the face of migration, geographic separation, and rapid social change. (Molohon, 1978; quoted in Manson, Dinges, Grounds, & Kallgren, 1984, p. 44)

Given this description of Indian families, it is possible to understand threats to Indian family integrity. Many families and communities are currently in a severe state of dysfunction. In many American Indian communities, for example, the extended family has broken down and traditional child-rearing practices no longer operate (NAICJA, 1985, p. 4).

Many in the Indian community attribute the breakdown of the Indian family, in part at least, to government boarding schools:

A substantial number of today's Indian parents were raised apart from their families in boarding schools, non-Indian foster and adoptive homes, where parental modeling may have been poor. . . . Children from dysfunctional families often fared poorly. Unprepared for separation, they were more vulnerable to identity confusion in placement and returned to the reservation alienated from their culture and maladjusted. Assessment of maltreatment in Indian families should include careful assessment of the early childhood experiences of parents, including details of placements. (Fischler, 1985, p. 100)

The connection with incest may be more explicit, following from sexual abuse of these parents during their boarding school years. This is, again, consistent with the rationale that assault and violence are the result of white influence.

Given these threats to family integrity, it is understandable that preservation of family would take precedence over one's own welfare. As the DIW counselor stated the client's view, it is "not taking care of number one but taking care of everyone else within that family system, the extended family system as well. And I'll sacrifice my needs for that entire family system."

In view of the environmental threat, the DIW counselor saw the perpetrator as a fellow victim. With this perception of the perpetrator as victim, it is not surprising that families would seek to protect perpetrators. A DIW (1987) pamphlet states:

Historical factors often magnify this situation. Since the pattern of violence begins with the historical oppression of the Indian man and ends with his oppression of the Indian woman or child, the cycle becomes a double one of oppression and violence. Often an Indian woman will choose to stay in a violent relationship out of loyalty to the companion because he is Indian and also oppressed, and because of her desire to remain in her own support system. . . . This cycle of violence is frequently passed on to their children.

Nondisclosure to outsiders is the norm. In his book on fetal alcohol syndrome among American Indians, Indian author Michael Dorris (1989) reports the opinion of one interviewee:

There really is a difference between Indian and non-Indian culture. . . . Family is important, even if you come from a drinking family. Family is number one. And people think you're helping if you don't tell the cops that they're drinking. You don't want to get them in trouble. You kind of cover up and hide for them. Because they're family. That's what families do. (p. 195)

Cultural Values and Nonreporting

Beyond protecting the family, our informants believed that other reasons incest behavior might go unreported include traditional Indian values of noninterference and nonassertiveness. One does not lightly interfere in others' affairs. During investigation or treatment an Indian tendency to talk little may be interpreted as resistance or non-cooperation.

In seeming contradiction to noninterference, however, is the high value placed on children in Indian cultures. Incest violates that norm. How can this seeming contradiction be resolved? As mentioned earlier, traditional communities reportedly had means of ostracizing the perpetrator, in typically indirect fashion. Again, such behavior cannot be generalized to all Indian cultures. Also, it might be very difficult for a small minority population to report situations of suspected or actual abuse without anticipating repercussions for themselves personally or professionally within the Indian community.

Delays in Seeking Treatment and Reporting Abuse

The DIW files revealed that women often delay treatment for several years, by which time the perpetrators are often geographically distant or dead. They deny or repress the experiences until an event or memory releases the emotions tied to it. An assault upon the woman or someone close to her might be the trigger, or an incident in a movie or television show, or an event in the news, such as the serial slaying of three Indian women in Minneapolis, for which a white man was subsequently convicted.

How long women wait to report perpetrators appears to vary according to the identity of the perpetrator. In the sample we studied, incidents involving stepfathers and other cohabiting adults were more readily reported. A third of the "other relatives" were reported relatively earlier, also. Fathers were typically not reported until the daughters were well into adulthood. There could be many reasons for this, among them that fathers were protected by mothers or daughters or both, that the shame or stigma was greater with fathers than with others, or that the victims were more likely to report after the incidents had ceased, and that this occurred earlier with others than with fathers. Of victims who reported the incidents themselves, their age at time of report was bimodal: They were either in age range 6–15 or in the range 26–30. This may be because they were either brought in as children or came in themselves when well into adulthood.

These women typically looked for help first from their immediate families and then from their extended families, such as aunts, uncles, or cousins. They were frequently accompanied to DIW by family members (secondary victims). They were more likely to come if family members, friends, or neighbors encouraged them to do so, and, conversely, were likely not to come if they were discouraged from it.

Nearly a third of the cases were referred to DIW by one alcohol and drug treatment center, the largest source of referrals. About 15% were self-referrals. A little more than a third were referred by a range of community agencies. Friends referred three cases, all age 26 or older. Children aged 5 or younger were referred by public agencies and one Indian agency.

"Revolving door" participation in treatment is also a problem. Indian women typically enter treatment several times, for a brief period each time, as they experience temporary relief of symptoms; a few women continued treatment for extended periods, up to two years.

Nonreporting and Prosecutions

A reason for nonreporting appears to be fear of public authorities, especially child protection services. When the client is the mother, she may already be involved with child protection and may not wish to lose custody of the abused children, or may fear intervention by other authorities such as police or the county attorney. As the DIW counselor stressed, the client's primary concern is likely to be survival of herself, her family, and even the perpetrator, in the face of external threats from white institutions and culture.

There were 23 referrals to police in the 41 cases studied. There were only two referrals to the county attorney, and in only one of these cases was the perpetrator charged. The fact that, in many cases, the incest events occurred several years before may have deterred some prosecution. The DIW counselor reported that police rarely take action in cases in which Indian women are assaulted; the same may be true of law enforcement regarding incest in Indian families.

Shame as an Issue

The DIW counselor and the junior author, himself an Indian, both stressed the powerful effect that shame has upon Indian clients and families. As opposed to internalized guilt, shame is responsive to negative judgments by others in the community or tribe. The client may report anger as an alternative to admitting shame for participation in incest. Indian clients may resort to chemical abuse to "medicate" or numb the feeling of shame. They report being "out of balance," using drugs. Many do not deal with these feelings until they are adults. In turn, failure to deal with feelings becomes reason for self-criticism. As noted, shame may lead to repetitive abusive relationships. Shame is reinforced by repeated experiences with white culture and institutions, in which Indians perceive that they are always receiving less than somebody else.

Spirituality as a Resource: Healing and Balance

This study included examination of Indian resources for dealing with incest. The ideology of healing was pronounced in the work of the Division of Indian Work and other counselors. Also, the traditional Indian concept of *balance* was seen as important; restoring a sense of balance and control is essential to recovery from the incest experience and the feelings and behaviors that follow from it. Balance was defined by the DIW counselor as

anything in terms of what good life talks about . . . feeling safe, feeling healthy . . . feeling happy, feeling safe, feeling protected, feeling nurtured, feeling all of those good things in terms of what a good life encompasses.

The sense of wholeness implied here can counteract the sense of loss, death, and violation that accompanies the incest experience. For Indian clients, traditional spirituality can be a powerful resource for achieving or recovering this sense of balance. Referral to spiritual leaders is routinely made by the DIW counselor, and clients often report that this is helpful. The use of a "talking circle" or the use of an eagle feather or other symbol of divine intervention can have great significance. The DIW counselor suggested that an encampment of Indian women who are incest victims might be helpful, also.

SUMMARY: PATTERNS

This study provides confirmation that incest does exist in some Indian families and tribes, that it is a serious problem, and that there are efforts by tribes and Indian agencies to treat the problem. We verified that Indians deplore incest, but some cultural values discourage reporting and intervention. We verified also that Indian families tend to retain the perpetrator in the family while seeking an improvement in the situation and restoration of "balance" and "wholeness" in the family.

Chemical dependency plays a definite, strong role in incest among American Indians, although it is not clear what that role is, whether as cause, effect, or both. It affects family members before and during incest events, and can affect the victim, who may resort to chemical dependency as a means of coping.

The effects of incest on victims can be devastating for Indians. The pressures upon Indian victims to protect their families and the perpetrators may be severe, and may force denial and inability to confront the perpetrator or attempt to reach a resolution until well into the victim's adulthood. Already members of a disadvantaged population, their adjustment as persons, as members of Indian cultures, and their identity as partners and parents may be made extremely difficult.

The picture is not entirely bleak, however. The tribal court judges and the DIW counselor noted that there are resources in the community, particularly spiritual resources, that can be brought to bear and have potent meaning for Indian victims and their families.

IMPLICATIONS FOR PRACTICE

Professionals working with Indian incest victims should enlist the help of family and support groups, whenever possible with the client's consent, particularly when these groups are culturally oriented to the Indian experience. Referral to culture-sensitive treatment personnel is very important. Such professionals recognize the inappropriateness of some therapies to Indian clients and the appropriateness of others. They are likely to employ a holistic approach, dealing with issues of culture and spirituality. The treatment person should be knowledgeable about Indian spirituality, at least in general, and should be able to assist the client in making interpretations based on understanding while validating the client's felt need for spiritual healing. The professional should also be able to make referrals to spiritual leaders who could be helpful to clients, and should have sufficient knowledge of ceremonies to discuss whether they might be of use.

Treatment personnel must, by means of the knowledge and skills just described, be able to establish acceptance and trust. While this is perhaps best done by Indian personnel, non-Indians can be helpful. In the long run, however, the best route would be to train more Indians and increase tribal services; the second best course is to train non-Indians who respect and understand Indian cultures.

There are resources in Indian communities. In the extreme, the tribal council could employ its traditional right to expel the incest offender from the community (NAICJA, 1985, p. 6). The following recommendations testify to the adaptability of Indian cultures:

> The community, or its monitoring representative, must be aware of what actions professionals should properly take in investigating, prosecuting and treating child abuse cases and must insist that these actions be taken. Adequate training for law enforcement, social service and court personnel should be demanded . . . according to the customs and values of the Indian community.
>
> . . . The community can provide public support to child victims through acknowledging the child's experience and reinforcing the message that the child is not to blame. Responsibility for the abuse should always be placed on the offender.
>
> . . . Indian communities may want to revitalize old traditions in dealing with sexual abuse. Banishment and various healing ceremonies can serve to protect the community's children . . . while giving the offender the message that what he/she has done will not be tolerated. (NAICJA, 1985, pp. 11–12)

REFERENCES

Ashby, M. R., Gilchrist, L. D., & Miramontez, A. (1987). Group treatment for sexually abused American Indian adolescents. *Social Work with Groups, 10*(4), 21–32.

Division of Indian Work (DIW). (1987). [Informational pamphlet.] Minneapolis: Author.

Dorris, M. (1989). *The broken cord.* New York: Harper & Row.

Fischler, R. S. (1985). Child abuse and neglect in American Indian communities. *Child Abuse and Neglect, 9,* 95–106.

Manson, S. M., Dinges, N. G., Grounds, L. M., & Kallgren, C. A. (1984). *Psychosocial research on American Indian and Alaska Native youth.* Westport, CT: Greenwood.

Molohon, K. T. (1978). *The adjustment of Native American students to public schools in the east San Francisco Bay Area.* Unpublished doctoral dissertation, University of California, Berkeley.

National American Indian Court Judges Association (NAICJA). (1985). *Child sexual abuse in Native American communities.* Washington, DC: Author.

Unger, S. (Ed.). (1977). *The destruction of American Indian families.* New York: American Association of Indian Affairs.

PART III
EVALUATING TREATMENTS AND INTERVENTIONS

8

Evaluation of a Multiple-Family Incest Treatment Program

DEBORAH L. WOODWORTH

When incest occurs, it affects every family member. Clinicians have increasingly incorporated this understanding into therapy programs designed to treat entire families, hoping to heal both individuals and their relationships with each other. This chapter presents an evaluation of one such program, the Family Project (described below), that includes multiple-family treatment groups.

The purpose of this study was to find out how incest victims have fared in various aspects of their lives since their treatment ended. All clients were female victims abused by fathers or stepfathers. Four outcome categories were examined: (a) recurrence of the abuse, (b) personal adjustment or functioning (psychological, educational, and job-related), (c) relationships within the family, and (d) friendships and cross-sex relationships. Also, former clients were asked for comments and suggestions for improving the program.

Studies of child sexual abuse have appeared with increasing frequency within the past decade (Finkelhor & Associates, 1986), and evaluations of treatment programs for victims and offenders are even more recent. In particular, the treatment of the incestuous family unit is receiving intensive clinical attention (see Friedman, 1988; McBean, 1984) and descriptions of various approaches to family treatment have begun to appear (see, for example, Burgoyne, 1985; Dovenberg, 1985; Herman, 1983; James & Nasjleti, 1983; MacFarlane, 1983; Sgroi, 1982). Many of these approaches assume that the family operates as a system within which incestuous behavior is allowed and, in many cases, learned by succeeding generations (James & Nasjleti, 1983; Lusk & Waterman, 1986). However, the literature contains little systematic follow-up research that examines outcomes for clients who have completed these programs or the success of multiple-family treatment programs.

THE FAMILY PROJECT

The Family Project was developed through the Amherst H. Wilder Foundation's Child Guidance Clinic and began treating its first clients in November 1980 (Dovenberg, 1985). The Family Project works only with entire families in order to effect lasting change in family systems that had previously supported incest. Moreover, the treatment model involves therapy in multiple-family groupings and with multiple therapists, thereby giving family members opportunities to experience both mutual support and challenge from others facing the same issues. Peer groups for men, women, couples, and children also meet regularly, and all family members have opportunities for individual therapy, couple therapy, and individual family therapy.

From its inception in November 1980 through September 1986, the period evaluated, the Family Project treated a total of 22 families. Of these, all but one completed therapy to the satisfaction of the program therapists. In other words, therapists judged that the incest had stopped, offenders had been able to establish sexual boundaries, the women were aware of their feelings and could protect their children, the parents were clearly in charge of the family unit, the children had developed healthier patterns of behavior and relationships, and the marital relationship had either improved or was being resolved in some way, such as through further therapy.

Staff at the Wilder Research Center, the foundation's research arm, conducted the study. An advisory committee offered expert advice and problem-solving assistance at each major stage of the research.

DATA COLLECTION STRATEGY

Initially, letters introducing the research were sent to every family selected for the study. Experienced interviewers, not connected with the Child Guidance Clinic, contacted potential respondents and conducted face-to-face interviews. In a few cases, clients preferred to complete the questionnaires privately and return them by mail. Others were more comfortable with telephone interviews. When the family was still intact, interviewers attempted to interview family members together. However, in most families at least one individual either was absent or declined to be interviewed.

Table 8.1
Response Rates

Interview Status	Victims		Mothers		Offending Fathers or Stepfathers		Siblings		Families	
	%	N	%	N	%	N	%	N	%	N
Agreed	42	13	65	13	63	12	8	2	73	16
Refused	52	16	30	6	32	6	88	23	23	5
Not Found	6	2	5	1	5	1	4	1	4	1
Total	100	31	100	20	100	19	100	26	100	22

SAMPLE

All 22 families who had completed treatment in the Family Project between November 1980 and September 1986 were eligible to participate in the study. The sample included offenders, mothers, siblings (if they participated in the treatment), and victims. The interview response rates are listed in Table 8.1. In 16 (73%) of the 22 families, at least one person agreed to be interviewed; 5 families refused the interview. Only one entire family could not be located by either clinic or research staff.

The sibling refusal rate was remarkably high—88%, or 23 out of 26 siblings. The number of refusals is probably due to at least two major factors: (a) Mothers often refused interviews for their nonvictim children, as well as for victims, and (b) according to program staff, siblings were hardest to reach clinically and also least convinced that they, too, might benefit from participation in therapy.

Table 8.2 shows background characteristics of the sample. At intake, the typical victim was 13.3 years old, white, female, living with a parent, and in a family with a median income of $19,000. Family Project parents were typically fairly well educated (an average of 12.2 years of education for fathers and 12.9 years for mothers) and employed. Only one family was on welfare. All families interviewed were white.

In addition, some background information was collected from clients who agreed to be interviewed (see Table 8.3). Again there is evidence of the higher-than-average socioeconomic status of Family Project clients, reflected in the average educational level of offenders (13

Table 8.2
Demographic Profile of Family Project Victims at Intake

Characteristic	Interviewed		Refused		Not Located	
	%	N	%	N	%	N
Race						
white	100	13	88	14	100	2
Hispanic	—	—	12	2	—	—
Income sources supporting client at intake						
employment	85	11	100	16	100	2
welfare	8	1	—	—	—	—
Client lived with parent at intake	92	12	94	15	100	2
Median family income at intake	$16,000 (N = 13)		$23,000 (N = 15)		$12,500 (N = 2)	
Mean age at intake (years)	14.5 (N = 13)		12.1 (N = 16)		15.0 (N = 2)	

Table 8.3
Respondent Demographics at the Time of the Interview

	Victims		Mothers		Offending Fathers or Stepfathers	
	%	N	%	N	%	N
Currently employed	46	6	92	12	100	12
Marital Status:						
married	—	—	46	6	50	6
never married	100	13	—	—	—	—
divorced	—	—	46	6	50	6
separated	—	—	8	1	—	—
Mean educational level (years)	12.5 (N = 13)		14.2 (N = 11)		13.0 (N = 12)	

years) and especially of mothers (14.2 years, or more than 2 years of college). Most victims were still in school. About half of the parents were divorced. All the offenders and all but one of the mothers were employed at the time of the interview.

During the research design stage, project therapists had mentioned their impression that their incest clients seemed very interested in having children and might be at risk for early pregnancy. Among the 13 victims who were interviewed, only 1 had a child. Since these respondents' ages ranged from 15 to 22, with an average age of nearly 18, the evidence indicates that therapists' fears have not been realized.

DATA COLLECTION INSTRUMENTS

The interview had two parts. The first involved a general family form, designed for a group interview, containing questions about background, needs, use of services, and a number of program evaluation questions. These questions were believed to be nonthreatening enough that respondents would answer them honestly in front of other family members. It was also hoped that the interviewer might observe interaction among family members and obtain some information about missing family members.

Second, respondents were asked to complete self-administered questionnaires that contained questions about employment, housing, more background information, relationships within the family and with others outside the family, mental and physical health, frequency of selected positive and negative feelings, recurrence of sexual abuse, and additional evaluation questions. The forms were varied slightly to allow for differences in family role. The instruments were pretested with an entire family that had recently completed treatment in the Family Project.

FINDINGS

A total of 40 interviews were completed with former Family Project clients—13 incest victims, 13 mothers, 12 offenders, and 2 siblings. In light of the small sample size, I will describe interview results, but will not attempt intensive statistical analysis.

Recurrence of Sexual Abuse

Project personnel were guardedly hopeful that abuse had not recurred at the time of the interview in at least 16 (73%) of the 22

Table 8.4

Responses to Question Measuring Assertiveness

Question: How true is the following statement for you: When a close friend wants to do something that I don't want to do, we usually end up doing what he or she wants to do

Responses	Victims		Mothers		Offending Fathers or Stepfather	
	%	N	%	N	%	N
Very true	—	—	16.7	2	—	—
Somewhat true	72.7	8	16.7	2	36.4	4
Not true	27.3	3	66.7	8	63.6	7
Total	100	11	100	12	100	11

Family Project families. While none of the 40 persons interviewed reported recurrence, several factors should be considered. First, all respondents were warned that the interviewer was required by law to report any new sexual abuse they might reveal. Second, there was no information available about recurrence in the 6 nonrespondent families.

Personal Adjustment

On the whole, former Family Project clients (abuse victims) expressed assertiveness, self-respect, and satisfaction with their lives. Victims said that they protected themselves from sexual pressure and felt happy and confident. Mothers were more inclined to express sadness.

Respondents were asked about several aspects of assertiveness and self-respect. For example, they were asked if they usually did what a close friend wanted, even if they did not wish to. Table 8.4 shows that mothers and offenders expressed the most assertiveness, since about two-thirds of both groups claimed that this never happened. Nearly three-fourths of the victims said that it sometimes happened, which may actually reflect the normally lower resistance of adolescents and young adults to peer pressure.

Victims were also asked about how they would handle being asked to be sexual when they did not want to be. Of 13 victims, 9 said they would "say no," while another said she would leave the situation; 3

Table 8.5
Responses to Life Satisfaction Question

Question: Overall how satisfied are you with your life these days?

Responses	Victims		Mothers		Offending Fathers or Stepfather	
	%	N	%	N	%	N
Extremely satisfied	30.8	4	7.7	1	8.3	1
Very satisfied	38.5	5	23.1	3	50.0	6
Satisfied	30.8	4	61.5	8	41.7	5
Dissatisfied	—	—	7.7	1	—	—
Total	100	15	100	13	100	12

did not respond to this question. Also, 8 said that they had said no to being sexual and that they did not end up being sexual when they did not wish to be. Whether these self-reports are manifested in actual behavior remains an open question.

In general, respondents were satisfied with their personal lives. As shown in Table 8.5, victims were most satisfied, while mothers were least. A total of 38% of the mothers said that they always or often felt "down" or "sad." Project clinicians confirmed that mothers were more depressed in general than were most other family members. Half the offenders reported being very satisfied with their lives, and none were dissatisfied.

Finally, victims were asked how frequently they thought about the incest, a measure of personal adjustment suggested by clinic staff. Presumably clients have recovered more thoroughly if they are not "obsessed" by thoughts of the sexual abuse. Table 8.6 shows little evidence of obsession among any of the respondent groups. Most victims said that they thought about the incest no more than occasionally, and two claimed never to think about it.

Family Adjustment

Of the 12 victims who still had contact with the offenders, 7 (58%) said they were either "pretty comfortable" or "very comfortable" around the person who abused them and 5 (42%) claimed that they never felt "creepy" around the abuser (see Tables 8.7 and 8.8). While

Table 8.6

Responses to Measure of Personal Adjustment

Question: How often do you think about the incest?

Responses	Victims		Mothers		Offending Fathers or Stepfather	
	%	N	%	N	%	N
Never	15.4	2	—	—	8.3	1
Seldom	61.5	8	30.8	4	58.3	7
Occasionally	23.1	3	53.8	7	25.0	3
Often	—	—	7.7	1	—	—
All the time	—	—	7.7	1	8.3	1
Total	100	13	100	13	100	12

these findings are encouraging, the 58% who still felt "creepy" may exemplify the difficulty of completely healing a father-daughter relationship once sexual abuse has occurred. Even if the victims no longer fear recurrence, the presence of the father may trigger memories of the abuse.

Some victims still hesitated about expressing feelings toward the offender. Half claimed to express anger whenever they felt it, while only three said they could express good feelings toward the offender at least sometimes. However, many of these victims were still teenagers, so their reticence may, in part, have been developmental in origin. Virtually all the parents reported being able to express both their good feelings and their anger to each other.

Friendships and Cross-Sex Relationships

Most respondents reported having close friends and were able, at least sometimes, to express good feelings toward these friends. However, victims were more likely to report that they could express anger most or all of the time to friends (73%) than were mothers (50%) or offenders (50%).

All respondents were asked a series of questions about their marriages or "love" relationships. When possible, their relationships were compared with relationships that several studies have found in both nonabused and other abused populations. Overall, Family Project

Table 8.7
Responses to One Measure of Family Adjustment

Question: How comfortable are you around the person who abused you?

Responses	Victims	
	%	N
Very comfortable	16.7	2
Pretty comfortable	41.7	5
Pretty uncomfortable	16.7	2
Very uncomfortable	25.0	3
Total	100	12

Table 8.8
Responses to Second Measure of Family Adjustment

Question: Do you ever feel "creepy" around the person who abused you?

Responses	Victims	
	%	N
Yes	58.3%	7
No	41.7%	5
Total	100%	12

respondents matched more closely the nonvictim populations, with the exception of relationships involving alcohol or drug abuse.

Nearly half the respondents (primarily victims and mothers) reported relationships in which there were some drug or alcohol problems, and 25% reported more-than-rare involvement with persons who had drug or alcohol problems. A community study of families in a Minnesota metropolitan county found drug or alcohol problems in only 12% (weighted) of parents (Mueller & Cooper, 1987). Future research should examine the extent of and reasons for such involvement in populations similar to this sample.

Approximately one-fourth of victims reported some violence in their relationships. Parents reported virtually none. This proportion compares favorably with a community study by Russell (1986), who found that between 38% and 48% of adult female child abuse victims had physically violent husbands, compared with 17% of the non-victims.

A total of 15% of the victims reported some fear of the persons with whom they formed relationships. Again, the sample matched more closely the nonvictims in a study by Briere (1984), who found that 48% of the incest victims in his sample feared men, compared with 15% of the nonvictims.

More than half of the mothers reported that they were sexual when they did not want to be, while only 20% of the victims (who were in relationships) did so. Finkelhor and Associates (1986) cite evidence that incest victims may be more prone than nonvictims to later sexual revictimization. Though most of these studies dealt with subsequent rape of incest victims, they do indicate victims' vulnerability to revictimization. It is interesting that, in this sample, the victims reported much less vulnerability on this measure than did their mothers.

Education and Employment Outcomes

On the whole, former Family Project clients reported that they were doing well in the areas of education and employment. The parents who responded to the questionnaire were well educated (an average of some college for both men and women), and about three-quarters of the victims were still in school, completing their education. Moreover, the fathers were fully employed, as were most of the mothers.

Current Needs of Respondents

Fewer than 12% of former clients interviewed reported having unmet needs for medical care, housing, education, job training, or further counseling. Some reported improvements in problems such as alcoholism. While two mothers and one father admitted to difficulties with drugs or alcohol prior to treatment at Wilder, only one mother reported problems with alcohol after treatment. Of parents who were not currently receiving counseling, only one mother and one father felt they needed to talk to a counselor. However, 25% of victims felt this way.

Use of Other Services

Clients were also asked about their use of services relating to sexual abuse and other mental health issues, aside from the treatment for sexual abuse that they received at Wilder. A continued use of such services may indicate that some clients need more help to resolve personal problems related to the abuse. Many of the former clients reported continuing some form of therapy, though not necessarily related to sexual abuse, after finishing Family Project treatment.

The foundation's client record system, which contains reentry information for Wilder programs, showed that only 10% of the entire Family Project sample had reentered any form of treatment by the end of the study. On the other hand, only one person, a mother, reported taking part in any treatment program for sexual abuse problems, other than treatment at Wilder, indicating that the personal problems were beyond the incest.

During treatment, very few respondents were involved in other programs or were seeing other clinicians. However, nearly half the mothers and victims and a third of the fathers began seeing private clinicians after leaving the Family Project. Some respondents said that they continued to discuss sexual abuse issues informally with mutual support groups (23% of victims and mothers), friends (half of the parents), and relatives (about one-third of the parents).

Former Clients' Satisfaction with Family Project Treatment

Former Family Project clients were asked to discuss the helpfulness of the project as a whole, as well as project components, such as the multiple-family and peer groups. Offenders were by far the most positive in their responses: 88% were strongly satisfied with the help they received, and 83% felt that the therapy was very helpful to them personally. Only one offender expressed any dissatisfaction with the program.

Mothers and victims were favorable overall, though 31% of the victims and 30% of the mothers were dissatisfied with the help they received in treatment at Wilder. However, 75% of the Family Project victims and 83% of the mothers felt the therapy to have been personally helpful.

As shown in Table 8.9, respondents most frequently mentioned that the therapy (a) helped them to learn about themselves, the abuser, and why the abuse happened; (b) gave them emotional support; and (c) helped them to gain self-respect. Four of the offenders (36%) felt that the program helped to bring their families closer together. The two most frequently mentioned suggestions for program change were more direct confrontation of perpetrators, favored primarily by mothers, and more use of smaller groups.

Table 8.9
Responses to Question Measuring Client Satisfaction

Question: In what way was the therapy at Wilder helpful to you?

Responses	Victims (N = 13)		Mothers (N = 13)		Offending Fathers or Stepfathers (N = 11)	
	%	N	%	N	%	N
Learned about myself	8	1	15	2	27	3
Learned about the abuser and why abuse happened	23	3	38	5	18	2
Learned to deal with the abuse problem	15	2	15	2	27	3
Gained support	46	6	54	7	36	4
Brought family closer	8	1	8	1	36	4
Gained self-respect	31	4	23	3	37	4

NOTE: This table contains the most frequently mentioned comments from responses to an open-ended question.

On the whole, clients' ratings of the peer groups constituting Family Project treatment were quite positive. By far the most commonly appreciated aspect of all the groups was the support that clients received from each other and from counselors. Also, respondents valued having the freedom to express themselves openly. Their few suggestions indicated some desire for more focus and direction. Two clients complained that counselors (usually interns) left the project too soon.

A total of 75% considered the multiple-family group (several families meeting together for therapy) to have been helpful. Comments indicated that some respondents thought the group needed more guidance from the facilitators, that offenders should have been confronted more, and that the group was too large.

Effects of Evaluation Findings on Program Structure

In February 1990, I interviewed the chief therapist for the Family Project, who reported several responses to the evaluation findings. First, program leaders tried to help mothers better overcome their depression and heal their relationships with their daughters by establishing an optional mother-daughter group, but they found that the group was not well attended over time. Therapists also tried to lessen the emphasis, perceived by mothers, on the behavior and support of the offenders. Program leaders have observed that the mothers currently in the program seem less discontented. Project leaders also increased the frequency of couples groups to twice a month and found that parents took advantage of the opportunity.

Some problems remain. Siblings still are least involved in treatment, particularly the males. The father-son relationship continues to be difficult to improve. However, staff report that many siblings enjoy and participate in the sibling groups.

The staff still struggle with the problem of interns leaving the program after forming emotional bonds with children, whose therapy groups they staff. At present, this problem is inevitable since the expense of such a staff-intensive program requires the use of interns. However, some clients still complain about the negative effect the interns' leaving has on the children.

Leaders said that they hear fewer complaints about the lack of structure and control in groups. Staff think some improvement has resulted from having the children's group leaders involved in the multiple-family group and having leaders talk to parents before and after multiple-family group sessions.

In general, the project leaders believe the multiple-family approach to incest treatment offers distinct advantages to the therapists involved. Staff say that they feel less overwhelmed and suffer less burnout in this multiple-therapist approach because they share the load. Three of the five permanent staff members have been involved in the project for ten years, one for nine years, and another staff member for five years. Moreover, staff report that by participating in multiple-family and other groups, they are forced to see each family member's point of view and are better able to maintain their objectivity.

SUMMARY

In general, the majority of former Family Project clients interviewed appear to be doing well. Most of the family members reported improved and relatively healthy relationships within and outside the family. Some former incest victims reported comfortable relationships with their fathers, the offenders. Most former clients praised the mutual support they had experienced through group participation. However, victims' siblings often declined to be interviewed; according to project staff, this reflects their relative lack of involvement in family treatment. Since an important Family Project aim is to stop the intergenerational transmission of incest, involvement of siblings in treatment is critical and must be addressed.

NOTE

1. The Amherst H. Wilder Foundation is an operating foundation located in Saint Paul, Minnesota. Foundation staff offer human services related to the elderly, children, corrections, and housing.

REFERENCES

Briere, J. (1984). *The long-term effects of childhood sexual abuse: Defining a post-sexual-abuse syndrome.* Paper presented at the Third National Conference on Sexual Victimization of Children, Washington, DC.
Burgoyne, M. A. (1985). Treatment of child sexual abuse. In C. M. Mouzakitis & R. Varghese (Eds.), *Social work treatment with abused and neglected children* (pp. 297–319). Springfield, IL: Charles C Thomas.
Dovenberg, D. C. (1985). *The Family Project: Multiple family/multiple therapist treatment of incest.* Saint Paul, MN: Amherst H. Wilder Foundation, Wilder Child Guidance Clinic.
Finkelhor, D., & Associates. (1986). *A sourcebook on child sexual abuse.* Beverly Hills, CA: Sage.
Friedman, S. (1988). A family systems approach to treatment. In L. E. Auerback Walker (Ed.), *Handbook on sexual abuse of children* (pp. 326–349). New York: Springer.
Herman, J. (1983). Recognition and treatment of incestuous families. *International Journal of Family Therapy, 5,* 81–91.
James, B., & Nasjleti, M. (1983). *Treating sexually abused children and their families.* Palo Alto, CA: Consulting Psychologists Press.
Lusk, R., & Waterman, J. (1986). Effects of sexual abuse on children. In K. MacFarlane & J. Waterman (Eds.), *Sexual abuse of young children: Evaluation and treatment* (pp. 101–118). New York: Guilford.
MacFarlane, K. (1983). Program considerations in the treatment of incest offenders. In J. G. Greer & I. R. Stuart (Eds.), *The sexual aggressor: Current perspectives on treatment* (pp. 62–79). New York: Van Nostrand Reinhold.
McBean, A. J. (1984). *Intrafamilial sexual abuse: Considering the next steps.* Saint Paul, MN: F. R. Bigelow Foundation.
Mueller, D. P., & Cooper, P. W. (1987). *Caring for children: Family change, parent-child relations and child care* (report from a needs assessment of children in Ramsey County). Saint Paul, MN: Amherst H. Wilder Foundation, Wilder Research Center.
Russell, D. E. H. (1986). *The secret trauma: Incest in the lives of girls and women.* New York: Basic Books.
Sgroi, S. M. (1982). Family treatment of child sexual abuse. *Journal of Social Work and Human Sexuality, 1,* 109–128.

9

Family Effects of Offender Removal from the Home

SARA WRIGHT

What is it like for the victim, the offender, the nonoffending partner, and the family as a whole when the offender is removed from the home during family sexual abuse treatment (FSAT)? How does each family member experience this intervention? What kinds of effects does offender removal have on the process of therapy? These are some of the questions that Dakota Mental Health Center's FSAT team struggled with as we began our new treatment program in January 1987. As we developed the philosophy and program statement that would guide our treatment, we found ourselves increasingly concerned about questions of offender removal. We did not doubt that the intervention would be useful in many ways, but we also had questions about what *else* it would do. If systems thinking has taught no other lessons, it has taught us that an intervention can have varied and unexpected repercussions for different subjects.

Turning to the literature in the field, we found opinions about the usefulness of the intervention, but no reports of research about the actual effects. With no substantive guidance, we decided to begin by simply asking our clients and their family members for their ideas, feelings, and beliefs about the experience of offender removal. This chapter describes some of what we learned from them.

METHODS

We interviewed 27 clients from DMHC's FSAT program: 8 male offenders, 10 nonoffending female partners, and 9 victims· (3 young children and 6 adolescents). Whenever possible, we talked individually to two or three people from the same family. We interviewed most of these people twice—once early in their treatment and then again 6–8 months later.

We used a structured interview schedule consisting of 17 questions grouped to cover feelings, power issues, perceived costs and benefits, effects on treatment, and the helping systems' responses to the family. We asked questions about how offender removal affected each person's feelings of safety. We asked how family members influenced one another or used power, and how this was different from when the offender was in the home. We asked what they thought the costs and benefits of offender removal were for each person in the family. We asked how they thought offender removal affected each person's progress in treatment. And we asked how they felt about the way social service, police, court, and mental health systems had responded to their families.

In addition to talking to two or three people from the same family, we got a richer picture of the family system by asking each respondent to talk about each other member of the family. In other words, we asked all interviewees to answer every question not only for themselves, but also to answer as they believed each other family member would answer. For example, we asked, "What do you think it has cost each member of your family to have [offender's name] out of the home? Start with [offender's name]. What do you think it has cost him to be out of the home?" Then the interviewer would ask about the next family member, and on down the line. This procedure was followed for each of the 17 questions.

It is extremely important to keep in mind the type of people we interviewed when considering the findings of this study. Our sample consisted of white, middle-class, mostly blue-collar Minnesotans living in the suburbs or rural communities surrounding a large metropolitan area. Clients for the treatment program are screened carefully before being admitted, and those who do not seem appropriate for a weekly outpatient program are referred elsewhere. This means that offenders must admit at least some responsibility for the abuse, must not be seriously mentally ill, and must not be dangerous to others. Persons with chemical dependency issues are sent through chemical dependency treatment before formal admission into the FSAT program. Most of the families in the program had experienced sexual abuse in the mild to moderate range of severity and frequency.

MAJOR FINDINGS

It would be nice if offender removal were an isolated intervention—something that primarily affects offenders, with perhaps mild consequences for other family members. But our interviews with offenders, nonoffending partners, and victims gave us a powerful picture of the emotional, structural, and financial changes in the lives of *all* family members when the offender is removed.

This report emphasizes the negative aspects of offender removal because that is what the people we interviewed talked about most. It may be that they focused on the negative aspects because that is where they were hurting the most, or because that is what they most wanted those in charge of decisions about such things to understand. In any case, in spite of efforts to ask people equally about the perceived costs and the benefits of offender removal, we heard far more about the costs.

Two main themes pervaded the interviews: financial effects and structural effects. These themes came up again and again, scattered throughout the interviews, at times in response to seemingly unconnected questions. In contrast, issues of safety, treatment effects, expression of power, and so on did not pervade the interviews—they came up only in response to explicit questions about those areas. In other words, the implications of financial changes and family structure changes seemed to cut across many aspects of the lives of these families. Therefore, these two areas are the focus of this chapter.

Financial Effects

> Financially, it has almost destroyed the family. It completely drained all the bank accounts. (OFF, 003)

Throughout their interviews with us, family members expressed desperation, fear, anger, and hopelessness about their financial condition. It is important to remember that much of the financial stress families face in the aftermath of sexual abuse reporting is not due to offender removal from the home. Many families face financial stress as a precursor of sexual abuse. Treatment costs and legal fees are high whether or not the offender lives at home. However, when the offender is removed from the home, the family income must stretch to cover living expenses in two households at a time when they are facing other extraordinary expenses:

It's putting a big strain on us trying to pay rent at two places and keep up two places. It's breaking us up, you know, money wise. (NOP, 027)

It is clear that the effects of this financial drain are borne by every member of the family, not just the offender. As one victim facing the loss of her family home and a move away from her friends put it:

All this [financial cost] is part of the punishment. But it's supposed to be punishment for *him*, but it's us, too. (VIC, 024)

Fighting for Fiscal Survival

Parents went to extraordinary lengths to remain financially solvent. Both offenders and nonoffending partners took on extra jobs and worked long hours of overtime:

For a while I had a second job, word processing for a law student and I just in the last couple of weeks gave that up because I couldn't keep my nose above water. I was working 20 hours a day and it finally took it's toll on me and I got really sick before Christmas. (NOP, 007)

Earlier in the interview this woman had described the work life of the offender since removal:

He starts work at 3:30 in the afternoon and he works until 4:00 in the morning. . . . For him it's been work, sleep, and little time in between. (NOP, 007)

An offender explained:

Me, I just try to keep up with the budget, and end up taking the extra time—second job, working as much as I can. I've been averaging any-where from 70 to 85 hours a week now just to keep up . . . it's a drain. (OFF, 013)

Another nonoffending partner spoke of her life:

I'm working a full-time and a part-time job and trying to keep every-thing up and it's not always real easy. . . . I could barely go to work, on the verge tears all the time, just barely holding together. The financial problems have been devastating. (NOP, 020)

Financial Effects on Children

Victims and nonvictim children were affected by changes in their family's financial standing. Two mothers mentioned that there was now no longer any money for hoped-for college educations (one was concerned about the victim's education, the other about a nonvictim daughter). One mother expressed her pain about the impending loss of the family home:

> I'm scared to death that I'm going to lose the house—the one thing that I've loved. It's not so much the house per se, but it's the only thing left of the family to me, and it's the same with [victim]. . . . she would probably have to go to another school. At this point in time I don't know if she can emotionally handle that. (NOP, 020)

A marital separation under any circumstances is often enough to drive people, especially women and children, into a transitional state of poverty that can last for several years (Duncan, 1984). The marital separations in these offender-removed families were also accompanied by overwhelming treatment and legal expenses, making the burden of sustaining an extra household almost unbearable.

In short, financial costs of offender removal affect the whole family, not just the offender. Most offenders in our study made credible efforts to stay financially responsible for their families. In spite of their efforts, both offenders and nonoffending partners reported working long hours at multiple jobs, just to make ends meet. Older children took jobs of their own and helped out financially. Some children lost their college education money, access to after-school activities, and access to the nonoffending parent due to her longer working hours. No bankruptcies were reported by the time of the second interview, but some previously middle-class families were forced onto welfare.

Conclusion: Treatment Needs to Address Financial Issues

Money problems are not the traditional province of mental health services. There are both pragmatic and psychological reasons, however, for explicitly addressing financial issues in family sexual abuse treatment programs.

Our findings suggest that financial problems become a major concern that cuts across the boundaries of many other issues for these families. We know that financial problems are one of the major causes of divorce in the population at large. We also know that financial stress can be a risk factor for incest (Jason, Williams, Burton, & Rochat, 1982; Paveza, 1988; Vander Mey & Neff, 1986). Presumably, it may be a factor in recidivism as well. It is important, then, that financial concerns be considered as a legitimate province of therapy, worthy of significant amounts of time in treatment sessions. The practical aspects of financial trauma should be handled as any other crisis situation, allowing clients to express their feelings and helping them to make a survival plan.

The ongoing psychological aspects of financial trauma should also be handled as any other major therapeutic issue. Clients may need to be asked from time to time where they are in the adjustment process; they may need help in exploring some of the identity and self-esteem issues involved; they may need help in legitimating the grief they feel at the loss of their previous life-style and in overcoming shame they might feel at finding themselves in the "underclass" of a materialistic society after working hard for years as part of the middle class.

Effects on Family Structure

> All it does is tear the family apart even more. That's all it does. I think removing people from the home is just really stupid. It's just gonna tear apart the family. (17-year-old victim, VIC, 040)

Marital Relationships and Systemic Factors

Although no one was asked directly whether offender removal had contributed to a marital breakup, 40% of the adults we interviewed volunteered comments to the effect that they believed offender removal had contributed to marital dissolution. For these people, and perhaps for others who did not think to mention it, there was the enduring sense that the original relationship could have been saved.

> The feeling is, or I have perceived from conversations with my wife . . . that if I hadn't been yanked out of the family during the first six months to the first year, the family could have rebuilt. But right now, emotionally, it destroyed the cohesiveness of the family. Because she could have built the trust back up. . . . the trust level could have been built back. (OFF, 003)

> It cost me a partner in a relationship that I thought was salvageable. If the system had handled it differently, we wouldn't have divorced. (NOP, 007/028)

Family sexual abuse couples are almost universally couples with marital dysfunction that preceded the sexual abuse (Giaretto, 1982; Justice & Justice, 1979; Sgroi, 1982). It seems likely that many of the marriages were already beyond repair. Rather than seeing these couples simply as being in bad marriages that need to end anyway, it may be important to consider whether systemic factors created by offender removal may be contributing to marital dissolution.

The interview data suggest that one such systemic factor is the kind of boundary ambiguity (Boss & Greenberg, 1984) situation into which these couples are thrust. Just when clinicians are trying to teach families about appropriate boundaries, couples are forced to experience a major boundary ambiguity situation—is the offender "in" or "out"? Are we married or not? A family or not? One nonoffending partner talked about the ambiguity of whether she was single or part of a couple:

> I guess it has forced me to spend more time with women who are divorced. . . . a lot of my friends are, uh, socially, you know, you don't want to feel like a fifth wheel to a wagon and so, uh, I tend to distance myself when I know there are going to be couples around. . . . seeing all the couples sitting in church together. I absolutely couldn't tolerate it. (NOP, 007)

An offender expressed similar confusion:

> Well, I'm normal and I know sometimes you want to do stuff and you can't and you need a partner to do it with. I enjoy going to dances, I enjoy it a lot. . . . Now that I am out of home, I could do it if I could find a companion that would do these activities with me. But I don't feel right about that either because I am still married. (OFF, 004)

In addition to boundary ambiguity, couples faced the reality of very little time to work toward reconciliation. They felt that their contact was being monitored, that their working hours allowed them little free time, and that they could not afford to pay babysitters so they could have privacy:

> It's very difficult to maintain contact and really get inside one another's heads when the contact you have, the only contact you have is maybe a phone call and then it's necessities you talk about. (NOP, 007)

Another major systemic factor that may contribute to marital dissolution is the structure of the treatment program. Many family sexual abuse treatment programs call for a logical, linear progression in therapy. First, the offenders, nonoffending partners, and victims focus on their own individual issues in groups with their peers. Then, if all goes well, they may progress to some parent-child dyadic treatment— for example, as mothers and daughters have special time together and fathers and victims have the opportunity for an "amends" session. Next, couple and family therapy may occur after clients have had the opportunity to individuate from their enmeshed system. The disadvantage of this orderly progression is that people do not live their lives linearly. Relationships do not remain static or "on hold" while individual issues are sorted through.

In this system, marital therapy is given low priority. Other components of therapy are required, so that even when therapists encourage couples' sessions, clients with very strained financial, time, and energy resources are unlikely to participate.

Finally, clients we interviewed reported the sense that the people who were controlling their lives, the experts on what was healthy and okay, just did not think they should stay married. Couples who wanted to stay together felt as if they were fighting an uphill battle against the system:

> It's extremely difficult having him out—we sort of get mixed messages. We're told it's okay if what we want to do is reestablish this relationship, but it's very hard. I mean, you can't have contact with that person on a day-to-day basis. (NOP, 007)

> [My wife] loves me still and we have, I believe, a good marriage, but she has influence from outside sources . . . that I think are advocating that she not see me. (OFF, 019)

After having her husband out of the home for over a year, one nonoffending partner finally refused to continue participating in the women's group because she felt the program was doing too little to help couples reunite. (She and her husband eventually became involved in a newly formed multifamily group.) Another woman stated in her interview that she would continue coming to group only because she did not want to risk having reunification delayed any further, but that she was too "fed up" to participate. One couple simply cheated. They lived together surreptitiously until they were caught and the husband was removed from the treatment program.

There was no apparent malevolence on the part of the treatment team, no deliberate attempts to impede marital reunion, just the systemic pressures cited above, along with a culturally pervasive bias toward autonomy over relatedness (see Hare-Mustin & Maracek, 1986, for a discussion of this bias in therapy).

Impact on Relationships

Offender removal from the home also had impacts on various family members and relationships: mother-child, father-child, parent-child generally, and siblings. These are discussed in turn below.

The Goal of Closer Mother-Child Relationships

One justification for removing the offender from the home is the hope that this will allow weak mother-child bonds to become stronger. This did in fact happen in some cases. Some comments about mother-child relationships showed more warmth and closeness at the second interview than during the first.

> [Mother speaking about daughter, second interview] I think she and I are closer than we've been. I think she was termed Daddy's girl from the time she was born and think it's been a real change for her to have spent as much time with me as she has—for me to be the primary parent. . . . she's my delight. (NOP, 028)

But not all mothers and children became closer when the offender was removed:

> The only thing [having Dad out of the home] really changed is my Mom's never home anymore. (VIC, 040)

In addition to our interviews, we had access to rating scales that clinicians filled out quarterly on each client in the program to measure progress toward treatment goals. One item on the Victim Scale reads, "Attempts to establish healthy relationship with mother." (The four subgoals under this item go on to define various areas of mother-child communication.) Only 4 of the 11 victims who were rated on this scale showed an improvement on this item. The remaining 7 victims showed a decline in their relationships with their mothers.

Children Out of Mother's Control

Another change in mother-child relationships was the lack of control mothers experienced over their children. While a certain amount of this is reported following most divorces (Heatherington, Cox, & Cox, 1976), the problems of the people in our study seemed to be compounded by the family dynamics and history of abuse. In families where mothers and daughters had a history of strained or remote relationships and where mothers sometimes felt they had something to make up to the daughters, maintaining effective parental control was difficult. In some cases fathers and stepfathers had been the disciplinarians in the family; in some cases, mothers simply were too overwhelmed with financial and emotional stress to be firm; in some cases, mothers were stronger than ever before and children were reacting to this new strength. For many reasons, some children were perceived to be out of control by their mothers:

Question: What do you do differently with [offender] out of the home that you would not do with him still at home?

Stay out later, go out whenever I want, go out every night, go out every day, come and go as I want, don't clean my room, don't make my bed . . . . I don't eat meals home. I do whatever I want—totally outrageous things like whatever I want. (VIC, 024/033)

Some Children Taking on the Parent Role

While there were some indications of children being out of control, there were also some indications of children taking on a parent role when the father was removed from the home—that is, being "parentified."

[Mother talking about 13-year-old nonvictim daughter] She's trying to be the second mother. She's trying to be the other parent. She'll try to take over my role in disciplining the children and making decisions. (NOP, 001)

Almost every family represented in the study had some similar examples of mild or moderate parentification of children. However, there were no examples of extreme parentification, where parents had completely abdicated their adult roles and children were responsible for the emotional or physical survival of the family.

Father-Child Relationships

Relationships between fathers and their children generally became distant. Sometimes the distance was externally imposed, as when fathers were denied any access at all to their children, or were allowed only extremely limited visitation. These limits were sometimes imposed by the legal system, as when fathers were incarcerated for long periods of time. Sometimes the limits came from treatment program restrictions or from the custodial parent's insistence.

Often the distance between fathers and children came from more subtle barriers to contact. The literature on noncustodial parenting talks about the psychological and emotional barriers to maintaining contact with children through visitation, including the constant reopening of wounds with each visit, feelings of guilt about not being a full-time parent, and eventually the desire to start fresh in life, leaving old mistakes behind. Fathers in this study faced similar feelings, exacerbated by the guilt of having abused their children.

Nonvictim Children (Siblings of Victims)

Relationships among victims and their nonvictim siblings for the most part seemed unaffected by offender removal; that is, the effects were essentially neutral. In fact, siblings seemed peripheral to the family as a whole. When they were mentioned as an important piece of the picture, it was as the favorite confidant of the mother, the child the father hoped would someday come to live with him, or the father figure chosen by a young victim to replace her absent dad. In other words, when siblings were talked about as important people, they were cherished for the roles they could fill, not for themselves. For the most part, they were pictured as peripheral, doing fine or not, but not really part of the big family drama.

The importance of involving siblings is apparent to most people at face value—these are children whose families are undergoing enormous change and stress. They are losing their fathers, their mothers are changing, the whole world seems suddenly to be involved in the private lives of their families. One nonoffending partner talked about her nonvictim child as follows:

> I think she feels kind of lost. She's watching all the family change and seeing the difference and hearing all of this and I think she's a little confused. . . . She needs as much help as [victim] does. She really does. (NOP, 011)

In addition to alleviating the current pain, stress, and confusion of these children, there is a compelling preventive reason to involve them in therapy. We know that a large percentage of offenders come from families where sexual abuse occurred, that is, current offenders were often nonvictim siblings in their families of origin. If we hope to break the cycle of sexual abuse in families, nonvictim siblings should be a major concern.

Summary of Effects on Family Structure

A sizable number of adults in our study felt that offender removal had contributed to the breakup of their marriages and that their marriages could have been salvaged if the offenders had not been removed from home. The interviews suggested several systemic factors that could, indeed, contribute to marital dissolution, including boundary ambiguity, structural constraints on togetherness, structural bias of treatment programs, and perceived attitudes of helpers. Other effects on family structure included some, but not most, mothers becoming closer to their children and all fathers becoming more distant from their children.

CONCLUSION

The people interviewed for this study gave us their view of a system that profoundly affected their lives. As the interviews progressed, it became increasingly apparent that the respondents were participating at no small personal sacrifice. Almost every person interviewed was struggling with long working hours, heavy child-care demands, and the scheduling demands and emotional work of family sexual abuse treatment. These people came into our office on their own time, with no financial reimbursement, and with no expectation that the findings of the study would improve their own personal situations. Again and again we were told in various ways, "I just hope this study can help other people."

I hope that I have kept faith with these respondents, and that the time, energy, and personal sharing that they offered have been accurately and adequately represented here. They gave us important new pieces of information. It is our job as clinicians and researchers to pick up these new pieces and fit them into the complex puzzle of family sexual abuse treatment.

REFERENCES

Boss, P., & Greenberg, J. (1984). Family boundary ambiguity: A new variable in family stress theory. *Family Process, 23*, 535–546.

Duncan, G. J. (1984). *Years of poverty, years of plenty: The changing economic fortunes of American workers and families.* Ann Arbor: University of Michigan, Institute for Social Research, Survey Research Center.

Giaretto, H. (1982). *Integrated treatment of child sexual abuse: A treatment and training manual.* Palo Alto, CA: Science and Behavior.

Hare-Mustin, R. T., & Maracek, J. (1986). Autonomy and gender: Some questions for therapists. *Psychotherapy, 23*, 205–212.

Heatherington, M., Cox, M., & Cox, R. (1976, October). Divorced fathers. *Family Coordinator*, pp. 417–428.

Jason, J., Williams, S. L., Burton, A., & Rochat, R. (1982). Epidemiologic differences between sexual and physical child abuse. *Journal of the American Medical Association, 247*, 3344–3348.

Justice, B., & Justice, R. (1979). *The broken taboo: Sex in the family.* New York: Human Sciences.

Paveza, M. (1988). Father-daughter child sexual abuse. *Journal of Interpersonal Violence, 3*, 292–305.

Sgroi, S. M. (Ed.). (1982). *Handbook of clinical intervention in child sexual abuse.* Lexington, MA: Lexington.

Vander Mey, B. J., & Neff, R. L. (1986). *Incest as child abuse: Research and applications.* New York: Praeger.

10

Effects of Reunification on Sexually Abusive Families

JANE KINDER MATTHEWS

JODIE RAYMAKER

KATHLEEN SPELTZ

This study focused on the impact of reunification on sexually abusive families. A project of this nature seems warranted since our review of the literature indicated very little research to date that examines the functioning of reunited families. Trepper and Traicoff (1985) studied the effects of a specific treatment modality on incest families. O'Connell (1986) formulated a step-by-step procedure for reuniting incest families.

This research moves beyond previous studies and focuses on the functioning of reunited families—specifically on how reunification was perceived and experienced by each family member. The study also identifies what intervention and treatment had occurred and was further needed. By studying reunification from this perspective, we hoped to identify factors that could give professionals in the field early warning that reunification would be either detrimental or constructive for individual family members or for the family as a whole.

What follows is a description of the background and limits of this study, discussion of the research methodology, the foundation for defining a "good enough" family, and findings on the experience of reunification as described by the perpetrators, spouses, and victims of a limited sample of five families. This research is continuing, with the goal of studying at least 15 families, including additional data on levels of family functioning.

DEFINING REUNITED FAMILIES: THE SAMPLE

For the purpose of this study, the definition of a reunified family is one in which child sexual abuse has taken place, the abuse has been disclosed, family members have been separated (i.e., the perpetrator has been removed or the child/victim has been placed in foster care), the family members have had therapy as individuals and/or as a family, a reunification plan has been established and implemented, and the family has been physically reunited, assuming the same living arrangements that they had prior to the disclosure of the sexual abuse. The research has been limited to only those families in which the sexual abuse has been perpetrated by a parent, stepparent, or a person who functions in the capacity of a parent. Sibling incest and sexual abuse perpetrated by someone outside the family exceed the scope of this study.

For the purpose of this study, data are being collected on only three members of each reunited family: the perpetrator, the spouse, and the victim. By design, siblings and other extended family members are not being interviewed. Additionally, the sample is limited to families in which the victim was between the ages of 5 and 16 at the time of the disclosure. Children under 5 years old present unique interviewing problems, and children over 16 may, for other reasons, not be reunited with their families. The research seeks to collect data on 15 families who have been reunited for not less than 8 months and not more than 24.

Defining a "Good Enough" Family

In the absence of literature defining "good enough" functioning for a family to be reunited, we invited 20 professionals to meet and help define these factors. The professionals were drawn from three major groups involved in reunification: social service workers (including child protection and social workers), criminal justice system representatives (attorneys, probation officers, judges), and therapists (for the victim, offender, and family). The professionals, in a workshop setting, were asked to write about the "process" and "critical factors" they looked for in determining if a family was "good enough" for reunification. Following this, the professionals had a discussion in which they shared their responses, concerns, and insights regarding reunification decisions. This information was used to develop the data collection instruments described in the methodology section that follows.

There was strong consensus among the professionals regarding necessary preconditions for each family member before the reunification

Table 10.1
Desirable Preconditions for Family Reunification

Victim

    able to acknowledge and discuss the sexual abuse

    does not blame self for the abuse

    willing to be reunited with entire family

    confident about ability to report any further abuse

    feels safe and protected in the home if the perpetrator is to be returned

Perpetrator

    accepts full responsibility for the sexual abuse

    shows empathy for the victim

    shows remorse for the offense

    willing to talk with the victim about the abuse, making appropriate apologies

    demonstrates understanding about the motivation for the abuse

    resolves family-of-origin issues

Spouse

    able to put victim's need for protection first

    able to confront the offender and express anger

    able to discuss the abuse openly

    holds offender responsible for the abuse

    does not blame the victim

The Family

    desire to reunify

    completed treatment

    openly discussed the sexual abuse together

    potentially risky situations identified and a protection plan formulated

    involved in a family support system; not isolated

    demonstrates healthy ways of interacting

    makes concrete changes in the home

should occur. Table 10.1 summarizes the professionals' prescriptions and criteria. We shall return to these criteria to interpret the five case studies on reunification presented in this chapter.

STUDYING REUNIFICATION: METHODS

Both quantitative and qualitative data are being collected on reunited families, taking into account the small participant sample targeted and available (15 families, 45 individuals) and the emergent nature of this research area. The qualitative data consist of in-depth interviews in which the participants are asked to describe their families and asked how, from their perspectives, their families are doing. This is intentionally open-ended so that the participants may report their experiences in their own terms. This approach follows the work of Perry (1970), Gilligan (1982), and Frost (1987) and is consistent with the work on qualitative methodology by Lofland (1971), Bogdan and Taylor (1975), and Patton (1990).

Following completely open-ended, in-depth questions on the overall family experience, participants are asked standardized open-ended questions that focus on participants' perceptions about intervention, treatment, and current family functioning. During the final phase of the interview, participants are asked Likert-type scale questions related to their current evaluation of their functioning, according to the requirements formulated by the professionals.

PRELIMINARY FINDINGS

The preliminary status of this research is due to the difficulty in securing a full sample of 15 families. The initial barrier to securing participant families rested with the referring clinicians. At the onset of the project over a dozen clinicians expressed willingness to cooperate with the research project. In actuality, when faced with reviewing their files to identify families, contacting those individuals, and securing a release of information for researchers to contact them, many clinicians were hard-pressed to find the time.

The second barrier was the families themselves. In four cases the perpetrator, who was the contact person, expressed willingness to participate in the research but the spouse refused to go forward based on either her own resistance or her belief that it would be detrimental to the victim. In an attempt to overcome what we speculated was a lack of trust, we offered, in these cases, to have the referring clinician conduct the interviews. This did not help.

It is important to note that the five families who to date have participated have all been involved in therapy in some capacity with one of the researchers. We believe that over time we will secure the cooperation of at least 15 families, but in all likelihood they will come solely from the client base of the research team.

The five families on which this chapter is based were from the metropolitan area of Minneapolis/Saint Paul: two urban families, two suburban families, and one exurban family. Socioeconomic status varied, including welfare recipient, blue-collar, white-collar, and business owner statuses. All but one of the women in the two-parent families worked outside the home. Four of the perpetrators were male, two fathers and two stepfathers of the victims, all of whom were female. The fifth perpetrator was female and the mother of her male victims. All of the perpetrators were convicted of criminal sexual conduct of varying degrees and court ordered to participate in sex offender treatment. The circumstances of separation varied from family to family; these are indicated in the brief descriptions of the families that follow.

Family A: The Andersons

This is a blended family consisting of Dave, the father; his son from a previous marriage; June, the mother; her daughter, also from a previous marriage; and Dave and June's two daughters. Dave physically and sexually abused his stepdaughter and Sarah, the older of his and June's daughters. The stepdaughter was out of the home and not available for interviewing. As members of a rigid, fundamentalist religious group, they accepted corporal punishment and male dominance as part of family life. The sexual abuse occurred over a period of about seven years, ending when Sarah was 14. The abuse was revealed when Sarah told a friend at school that her sister was being abused. The friend told school authorities, and when they questioned Sarah she additionally disclosed her own abuse. Dave was immediately removed from the home and the family was separated for almost three years.

The Andersons participated in a family sexual abuse treatment program that included group and individual counseling for the perpetrator, spouse, and victims. Dave was expelled from this program after two years when he made what the primary therapist deemed inappropriate contact (not involving sexual abuse) with his family. He sought treatment elsewhere and eventually successfully completed an outpatient sex offender program. The mother and victims simultaneously participated in and completed treatment at both centers.

The Andersons were interviewed approximately eight months after reunification. At this time Sarah, an 18-year-old single mother, was living at home with her daughter, but contemplating moving out on her own. Her older half sister, age 22, unmarried and pregnant with twins, was living independently, but contemplating moving home. The son was estranged from the family, apparently choosing to have little contact with his father in particular. The youngest daughter, age 12 and not victimized, was living at home.

Family B: The Browns

This family consists of the father, Fred; the mother, Marla; and three children—Pamela, the oldest; a younger sister; and a brother. Fred sexually abused Pamela over a five-year period until she was 16. Pamela disclosed the sexual abuse when a girlfriend confronted her. The friend reported it to the school counselor, who in turn questioned Pamela. Fred was removed from the home and the family was separated for approximately nine months. Fred completed outpatient sex offender treatment consisting of group and individual counseling. Marla participated sporadically in a spouses' group primarily when crisis ridden. She later participated in family counseling with Pamela. Approximately four months after the sexual abuse was disclosed, Pamela attempted suicide and was placed in inpatient mental health treatment for three weeks. Following this, she reluctantly participated in both individual and group victim therapy. Eventually all three (the perpetrator, spouse, and victim) participated in family therapy.

The family was interviewed approximately 12 months after reunification. Pamela, a senior in high school, stated her intention to move out following graduation. Her parents, concerned about her marijuana and alcohol abuse, had placed sharp restrictions on her independence. The two younger children, who were in elementary school and junior high, were living at home.

Family C: The Carters

This family consists of the stepfather, Floyd; mother, Harriet; and her daughter, Melody, from a previous marriage. Floyd's two children from a previous marriage live with their mother. Floyd sexually abused his stepdaughter for six years until she was 15. Melody eventually ran away from home and disclosed the abuse in a shelter. Her stepfather denied the abuse and her mother believed and defended him. Because of Melody's acting-out behavior and the unprotective stance of her mother, she was placed in foster care. Floyd and Harriet remained together in the family home. Only after Floyd admitted the abuse in court did Harriet believe her daughter. Floyd successfully completed outpatient sex offender treatment that included group and individual counseling. Harriet participated in a spouses' group and in joint sessions with both her husband and daughter. Melody was a reluctant participant in individual therapy as well as in counseling sessions with her mother. No information is available about family therapy for this family. Melody was returned to the home after about 10 months in foster care.

The Carters were interviewed approximately eight months after reunification. Melody, a senior in high school at the time, was threatening to move out and in fact had run away from home on several occasions. Although the parents expressed concern about Melody's associates, they doubted they could influence her decisions and expected she would indeed leave home as soon as she turned 18.

Family D: The DuPonts

Ashley is a single mother of three children, a daughter and two sons, Phillip and Brent. Ashley had attempted to abuse her daughter sexually, but the child refused. She sexually abused her two sons over a period of about seven years until Phillip was 14 and Brent was 11. She disclosed the abuse herself when she was in treatment for chemical dependency. Her children were placed in the care of their maternal grandmother for a period of approximately 18 months. Ashley participated in a community corrections day treatment program for women and an outpatient sex offender treatment program with individual and group therapy for female sex offenders. Phillip and Brent participated in individual therapy and eventually in family therapy with their mother.

The DuPonts were interviewed approximately 10 months after reunification. Phillip, a junior in high school, recently transferred to a small private school in hopes of improving his grades and his associates. Brent, in junior high, was experiencing academic and athletic success. The daughter and her three children had recently returned to live at home. The DuPonts were on welfare despite Ashley's entry-level income. The family was experiencing the stress of the working poor.

Family E: The Emersons

This family consists of the stepfather, Harvey; mother, Betty; and her three children, two daughters and a son from a previous marriage. At the time of the abuse Harvey was living with Betty and the children but the couple were not married. Harvey sexually abused the older child, Samantha, over a period of about four years until she was

12. Samantha disclosed the abuse when she was confronted by her school social worker. Harvey admitted the abuse, left the home, and the family was separated for approximately 10 months. Harvey participated in outpatient sex offender treatment that consisted of individual and group therapy. Samantha was a reluctant participant in individual and group therapy. Betty participated in couples counseling and, after reunification, the entire family participated in family therapy. After reunification the couple married, believing this would add to family stability.

The Emersons were interviewed approximately 24 months after reunification. Samantha refused to be interviewed, not wanting to talk about the sexual abuse. She was 16, had quit school, and, although she was living at home, she was threatening to move in with her 20-year-old boyfriend.

PATTERNS

In reporting our preliminary results we shall confine our discussion to the reported experiences of each of the groups under study: the victims, the perpetrators, and the spouses. Individual responses will be assessed against the framework set forth by the professional "definers" who formulated what they would require before reuniting a family. A summary of those requirements was presented earlier in Table 10.1.

The Victims' Experiences

Most of the victims stated that they could, if they chose, talk about their sexual abuse. However, most of them expressed some reluctance to do so.

> It's not something we would talk about over dinner every night. If it comes up, or we hear about somebody being too flirtatious or being overly aggressive or something, we'll talk about it. . . . It could come up but we don't talk about that. (Sarah)

> There's not a real rush occasion for it. If anything we would probably just try to live our lives around it. . . . We're trying to eat away at it little by little, but until it's all gone, we're going to be going around it and around it and around it. (Melody)

All of the victims could acknowledge that the sexual abuse was not their fault.

Oh, my dad, my dad's responsible for the sexual abuse. (Pamela)

My dad. I mean, it's like, if I was in the shower and had the door wide open, I never blame myself for it at all. I do blame myself for the physical abuse because I thought, well, I was talking back to him. (Sarah)

When it came to considering the victims' feelings in planning for the reunification of their families, only two reported that their wishes were taken into account.

My parents are sitting there going, "Melody, you do want to come home, DON'T YOU? YES, you DO want to come home DON'T YOU?" I think now, when I look at it, I think it's more of they were embarrassed to keep having to make excuses for me not being home. (Melody)

And my mom said that dad's coming home, and she said, "You can come home if you want, if you don't want to, if you don't feel comfortable, you can go to the children's home in St. Cloud." Back then I was totally into my friends. . . . Yeah, I wasn't comfortable with it, but I didn't feel like I had much of a choice. (Pamela)

All the victims stated that they would report to someone if they felt threatened by sexual abuse again.

I would just say, talk to somebody they trust, even though they might lose their mom and dad for a while. (Brent)

I'm just ready to slough it off or feed it back to him. Cause I'm not going to take shit from him in any way, shape, or form anymore. I'm sick of that. I've had it up to here. (Melody)

One of the victims was frightened that the sexual abuse was about to recur and related how she managed to tell her therapist but could not tell her mother.

You'd think like if it ever happened again I could just tell my mom, or something, but it's not like that. . . . I don't know, it just doesn't feel right. I don't have the closeness to talk to my mom. My parents don't even know who I am. . . . I don't know if she'd understand it. I didn't want her to be hurt by it. (Pamela)

In four of the five families the victims' statements indicate that they suffered continued emotional pain after reunification. In all these cases the offender, spouse, and victim had received therapy and were seen by professionals to be functioning at a higher level than before the abuse. In four of the five cases, the victims were seen as happier and better adjusted by their parents than the victims themselves reported.

In two of the five cases the victims believed that their negative feelings about reunification would be ignored if they voiced them. They chose to "go along" with the decision to reunify and kept silent about their reservations. In a third case the victim insisted that she wanted her father home, but later admitted that she was still harboring feelings of anger and betrayal that had never been addressed. In the other two cases the victims' wishes were taken into consideration regarding when and how to reunify. The reunification itself was fairly positive for one family and marked by some difficulties for the other. It is interesting to note that the victims cited many instances in which they sacrificed their own feelings for fear of hurting other family members, apparently still placing themselves in the victim role, even after therapy and reunification.

The Experiences of the Perpetrators

All of the perpetrators accepted full responsibility for the sexual abuse.

> The whole thing. My idea, my doing it. . . . I made the decisions, how often. Guess I wasn't feeling guilty at first. It was me. I was totally responsible for the whole thing. (Ashley)

> [What was your responsibility?] Total. . . . Everything, everything that happened is my responsibility. (Floyd)

All the abusers showed an intellectual understanding of the impact of the sexual abuse on the victim. However, only the female perpetrator seemed to have deep emotional empathy for the pain of the victims.

> I wish I had never done it. Didn't realize at the time that what I was doing could be so damaging. (Floyd)

> I think a real devastating [effect], real hard on the children, especially those I abused, and real difficult on my wife. (Dave)

> It's like the way I feel now. I want them to be mothered the way they's supposed to be. How come I couldn't do that then, [during] the sexual

abuse. It's like when I look at them I picture myself being in they shoes and, and, when I was doing it. . . . I feel like if I can't be a mother like I'm supposed to, they belong in a foster home somewhere having the life they should have. (Ashley)

In regard to talking freely about the sexual abuse, the perpetrators stated that it was possible to discuss the abuse in their families, but that in reality open discussion was not frequent.

It's very rarely brought up anymore. (Fred)

Not very often. I think there's been a couple of times when there's been something on television, something we've been watching. And we all kind of look at each other like, "Boy, do we remember that," or "We can relate to that." And sometimes we will bring that up. I think what we do talk about more is the therapy issues and the communication issues, and not the actual abuse. (Dave)

I don't, not at this stage. With Betty, yes. Betty and I talk about it freely. It's always hard for me to talk about it because it's such a sick thing anyway. Between Betty and I there's no problem. . . . As far as Samantha, it'd be great if we could talk about it. Then I know there'd be a lot of progress made, because, yeah we acknowledge it, but we were able to overcome it, but we're not right now, we're not at that stage. I don't think we'll ever be. Never know. (Harvey)

All of the perpetrators made statements that indicated that they had an understanding of the factors that motivated their sexual abuse.

I think a lot of it, as far as how I set myself up maybe was my having a lot of pressure, not knowing how to deal with it, having a lot of feelings, not being able to understand them. One of the outlets was to seek comfort from my kids. And comfort was sexual comfort. (Dave)

It was again, my way of showing control. I justified it by telling myself I was showing her the real world. . . . My abuse [as a victim] was frightening and scary. I couldn't talk to anybody about it. I thought I was going to end by being gay. . . . I had to be in control. I had to be the guy hurting someone instead of being hurt. I know now that it's wrong, but it was what I'd learned. . . . I don't know if it was so much for sexual satisfaction as it was for a feeling of power. (Fred)

They also all successfully completed treatment and confronted family-of-origin issues.

I had been kind of depressed for many years back in my teens, late teens and early twenties. And I never knew why. I went into what I consider a pretty severe depression where I didn't want to do anything. I'd lay in my bed at my parents' house and do nothin'. And that might last a couple of weeks. Of course, smoking pot didn't help. . . . I was an alone person. I had a hard time relating to people. (Harvey)

Then I end up growing up and when my kids are about, oh, anywhere from the range 5 to 7 years old, my past life as a child started coming back, rolling and rolling around in my mind. And I [started to need] getting around people and talking about these things, possibly get some help, therapy and counseling over these things in my mind. I let them bother me and ended up drinking real heavy. (Ashley)

Improved family interactions and more appropriate ways of parenting were noted by most of the perpetrators.

And basically, our family is one that expresses themselves and communicates well, to a certain extent. Not that we're perfect, but we do talk. And I do owe that to the counseling. (Harvey)

As far as the kids' mommy leading a sober life and that's me. I see the difference in their faces and in they eyes. They around now. I see them relaxed and not tense. Around me they're comfortable. I feel like that, they comes to me now and allow me a lot of talking on one thing or another, about different conversations or about things that go on in they lives. . . . And I guess my not drinking anymore has made a big difference. . . . I like that. (Ashley)

While all of the perpetrators met the criteria for reunification, it was obvious from some of their statements and from some of the victims' statements that they felt reunification had come too soon. Even though they may have lobbied hard to be reunified, they may not have given enough thought and consideration to the full impact of reunification.

The Spouses' Experiences

In talking about what they have learned from dealing with the sexual abuse the women discussed the importance of placing the needs of the child above the needs of the perpetrator.

Sarah sometimes will make comments about being the one who told about the abuse, and she is reassured by us. In the beginning she was real strong and angry. In the middle she needed me to reassure her that she DID the right thing. That the family had to get that out. And right now we tell her, "You did the right thing Sarah." We're a much better family now. (June)

First off, we're honest. Melody feels safe where she can tell us anything, especially tell me, and she knows that I'm not going to deny, that things will be taken care of immediately. And she feels that safety. I made certain that Melody had some more privacy, that she could have a place to go where it was private. (Harriet)

Another important issue was the ability of the women to confront the offender.

I feel I'm stronger, and when he falls into old patterns, I'm strong enough to stand up and say, "Hey, wait a minute. This isn't going to work. This isn't right." Or, "I don't like it." Whereas before I would have sat there quietly and let him go on and on and on. I don't do that anymore. (Marla)

Sometimes he falls into his old controlling, manipulating procedures where the sarcasm's out and tries to whittle away at your ego. I can see it. Sometimes it's frustrating for him, but I say to him, "Hey, I'm not playing into your controlling mood. The only one you can control is yourself, and I wish you would." (Harriet)

The women spoke of having a family atmosphere in which it was acceptable to express anger.

Or, if someone is showing some anger, we say, "Wait a minute, if you're angry, talk about what you're angry about. You're going about it this way, and you're taking it out on her. You're angry about something over here, talk about it. What is it?" And then it'll come out. Now it can be handled. Now we can take care of it. (June)

And then we have a good argument. He gets his feelings out and he feels better. I feel better and we go out or make love. We have a much deeper love for ourselves now and for each other. I love loving. It's nice. (Harriet)

Most of the women felt free to discuss the sexual abuse openly.

It isn't now. It was before, but not with the two younger kids. It was talked about with Samantha to a certain extent. We would talk about it, trying to get her to open up. We wanted her to tell us how she felt, to accept Harvey's apology for what he had done. He had told her how he felt, that he was sorry for what he had done, that he knew he was wrong, that he still loved her. . . . Then she came right out and told both of us that she hated us both and she told me that she would never be able to forgive me for taking him back. (Betty)

We do talk about it. Perhaps not as frequently as in the past. Melody is not comfortable with it. Even now, I don't think she wants to discuss it. So we just kind of let that go. Maybe sometime she'll be more open. . . . For me when I bring it up it is how hurt, how sad I feel. It's usually when I'm especially down. (Harriet)

All of the women eventually held the perpetrator responsible for the abuse.

And the sexual abuse was a complete surprise for me. Shock that Floyd could do that. Certainly he was a manipulator, certainly he was a controller, but to do something so despicable, that wasn't him. He couldn't do something like that. And poor Melody. Here's this kid, and I thought she was just into teenage rebellion. . . . The denial was so strong, was just so strong. To accept that, and accept me allowing that to happen was real, real tough. . . . Ashamed. Letting my own daughter down so badly, it was real hard for me to accept. And then to forgive myself—real tough to do. (Harriet)

Harvey is [responsible]. And he's admitted to it. And we talked. I told him how I felt, that I felt I was betrayed. I was hurt, but I loved him enough to stand by him and go through it. (Betty)

All of the interviews took place after the families had been reunited for quite some time. In spite of the amount of time that had passed, it seemed that many of the spouses were still very ambivalent about themselves and about their relationships. Some were more jealous of their daughters than they anticipated they would be, and forgetting the abuse proved to be more of a task than they had anticipated.

SUMMARY

Given the small number of cases involved thus far in this study, definitive conclusions certainly cannot be drawn. However, we believe the interview responses and reunited family patterns are worthy of reflection. More extensive research is certainly needed, and it will be interesting to see how the next 10 families differ from or are similar to these first cases. The results to date show that this kind of research is possible and important.

In every case, from the standpoints of the perpetrator, the victim, and the spouse, everyone was glad that the abuse had been reported. All saw the intervention of the system as a good thing, even if they had complaints about specific decisions or individuals. The main concern of the professionals who were consulted was that the sexual abuse not recur. The actual threat of repeated abuse seems, at this juncture, to be less an issue than the continued emotional pain that many of the victims endured after reunification.

REFERENCES

Bogdan, R., & Taylor, S. J. (1975). *Introduction to qualitative methods*. New York: John Wiley.

Frost, M. R. (1987). *Life decision making: A study of decisional structure and processes in young adults*. San Francisco: Saybrook Institute.

Gilligan, C. (1982). *In a different voice*. Cambridge, MA: Harvard University Press.

Lofland, J. (1971). *Analyzing social settings*. Belmont, CA: Wadsworth.

—O'Connell, M. A. (1986). Reuniting incest offenders with their families. *Journal of Interpersonal Violence, 1*, 374–386.

Patton, M. Q. (1990). *Qualitative evaluation and research methods* (2nd ed.). Newbury Park, CA: Sage.

Perry, W. G. (1970). *Forms of intellectual and ethical development in the college years*. New York: Holt, Rinehart & Winston.

—Trepper, T. S., & Traicoff, M. E. (1985). Treatment of intrafamily sexuality: Conceptual rationale and model for family therapy. *Journal of Sex Education and Therapy, 11*(2), 18–23.

11

An Evaluation Protocol for Incest Family Functioning

JAMES W. MADDOCK

PAMELA R. LARSON

CATHERINE F. LALLY

The study described here is part of a long-range research project on family sexual health that seeks to identify principles that facilitate *positive* expressions of intimacy and sexuality within the family. The overall project assumes that sexuality (both gender and erotic components) is a fundamental dimension of family experience that can contribute positively or negatively to the development and well-being of family members.

Our ecosystemic perspective on family sexual abuse concerns itself not only with the possible psychopathology of the perpetrator or the effects of abuse on the victim. We are also interested in disturbances in parent-child relationships, malfunctions among various family dyads (particularly the spouses), family role performance difficulties, interactions of the family with the community, and even the overall societal context that shapes family members' attitudes and behaviors related to sexuality, intimacy, and child socialization (Alexander, 1985; Bronfenbrenner, 1979; Garbarino, 1977; Gelles, 1979; Larson & Maddock, 1986; Trepper & Barrett, 1986, 1989).

This study had two primary objectives: to identify distinguishing characteristics of incest families, and to develop an evaluation protocol and criteria for assessing family functioning in the context of intervention and treatment of family sexual abuse. The study was conducted under the auspices of the Department of Family Social Science, an interdisciplinary unit at the University of Minnesota. A number of community clinics, both public and private, collaborated on the project, recruiting families as research participants and filling out treatment assessment forms.

FAMILY FUNCTIONING AND INCEST

Few studies of family-based incest treatment have been reported, and the effects of intervention on family functioning have rarely been systematically examined (Daro, 1988; Finkelhor, 1984; Sgroi, 1988; Trepper & Barrett, 1986). Disagreement exists regarding the degree to which incest is a form of *family* dysfunction rather than a direct result of individual psychopathology (Faller, 1981; Garbarino, 1977; Salter, 1988; Sgroi, 1988; Tierney & Corwin, 1983; Trepper & Barrett, 1986). The extent to which certain attitudes or behaviors characterize incest family members other than the perpetrator or the victim is unclear. Do all family members somehow participate in interaction patterns that accompany sexual abuse, thereby setting the stage for its transmission to future generations?

Even among family professionals, simplistic generalizations about incest families are common (e.g., all incest families are "enmeshed"; all mothers somehow "collude" in the incest). In reality, incest family dynamics are varied and complex. At the same time, clinical experience and subjective reports by victims suggest that some incestuous family dynamics may be predictable and that sexual abuse may reflect more general disturbances in family interaction patterns (Alexander, 1985; Finkelhor & Associates, 1986; Gelinas, 1988; Russell, 1986; Tierney & Corwin, 1983). However, just which family dynamics, if any, contribute most substantially to the occurrence of incest is unclear. Certain family characteristics, such as "boundary problems," are frequently cited (Bass & Davis, 1988; Gelinas, 1988; Larson & Maddock, 1986; MacFarlane & Waterman, 1986). Yet nonincest families demonstrate many of these same characteristics without evidence of social dysfunction.

TREATMENT AND EVALUATION ISSUES

Similar uncertainties exist in relation to intervention and therapeutic treatment of incest families. Missing from most family sexual abuse treatment programs are criteria for evaluating *family functioning* and member interaction. Professionals dealing with incest families—psychological evaluators, treatment staff, legal and criminal justice personnel, and even social policymakers—have few agreed-upon standards for judging the effects of intervention. The major criterion, nonrecurrence of the abuse, may be only an artifact of the absence of the perpetrator from the home or the current age of the victim. Objectively confirming program effectiveness or comparing several treatment approaches is therefore difficult (Daro, 1988; Finkelhor, 1984; Finkelhor & Associates, 1986).

Even the concept of "success" is disputed. Some view successful intervention as separating family members and enhancing their self-differentiation; others advocate keeping family members together and improving interaction (Conte, 1986; MacFarlane & Waterman, 1986; Trepper & Barrett, 1989). Meaningful evaluation requires outcome criteria and a method of assessment that can be shared and repeated in a variety of treatment settings. Since sexuality is a major dimension of family life and the symptomatic behavior in incest families is sexual in nature, distortions in sex-related attitudes and interactions seem likely contributors to family sexual abuse. Our ecosystemic model suggests that the following may be important—though not necessarily exclusive—variables influencing the occurrence of incest: sex-typed gender orientation; gender and generational imbalances in family structure; distortions in power and control; communication deficits (both general and sexual); and discrepancies in sexual meanings and attitudes, particularly between spouses.

METHODS

The study addresses these issues by examining sex-related aspects of family experience in samples drawn from three populations: incest families before treatment, incest families after treatment, and non-incestuous families. The families in which incest had not occurred consisted of a nonrandom sample solicited via posters and newspaper ads from the general population of the Twin Cities metropolitan area. Untreated incest families were drawn from the waiting lists or assessment rosters of the cooperating clinics. Treated incest families were obtained from the posttreatment populations of these and other clinical programs.

Although our goal was a total of 10 to 20 families in each of the three samples, in just over a year of effort we recruited only 8 pretreatment, 7 posttreatment, and 15 comparison families. Marital status varied. In the pretreatment group, only 1 couple was currently married, 4 were separated, 2 were divorced, and 1 mother had never married. The posttreatment group consisted of 3 current marriages and 4 divorced couples. Of the comparison couples, 12 were married, 2 were divorced, and 1 was cohabiting. Perpetrators in the incest families were predominantly fathers and stepfathers (6 and 5, respectively). The remaining perpetrators were 2 teenaged siblings, 1 uncle, and 1 whose relationship to the victim was not clear. Ethnic minorities were not well represented in the samples (one American Indian family in the clinical sample, one African-American and two racially mixed families in the comparison group). Family income ranged widely in all three samples, from less than $10,000 to over $100,000. Religious preferences were similar across the groups.

INSTRUMENTATION

Data were collected in a one-time sampling procedure via a combination of questionnaires and interviews. Questionnaire data were obtained from all family members age 12 or older who agreed to participate. In addition, all participating family members, including younger children, were interviewed together by two members of the research team. Families were paid up to $100 for about two hours of their time, with the exact amount proportional to the number of members participating. If all family members consented, interviews were also audiotaped and transcribed.

The instruments used in the study were as follows:

- *Family Adaptability and Cohesion Scales III* (FACES III; Olson et al., 1985): This is a measure that reflects family processes in terms of "balanced" versus "extreme" scores on two widely recognized dimensions of family functioning.
- *Bem Sex Role Inventory* (BSRI; Bem, 1974): This is a questionnaire assessing the degree of behavioral sex typing internalized by individuals in a culture. Family members rate themselves in relation to idealized standards of "masculinity" and "femininity."
- *Primary Communication Inventory* (PCI; Locke, Sabaugh, & Thomas, 1956; described and reproduced in Beach & Arias, 1983): Though not widely used in family research, this instrument has been established as valid and reliable in the study of marital communication processes. We adapted the inventory to examine gender-linked and generational communication patterns.
- *Index of Sexual Satisfaction* (ISS; Hudson, 1982): This is a brief questionnaire about sexual interaction between spouses that yields an overall measure of satisfaction with the sexual relationship.

- *Power/Control Survey* (P/C-S; Maddock, 1989): This is a new instrument that measures perceptions of spouses regarding the distribution of power and control in the marital relationship.
- *Sexual Meaning Scales* (SMS; Maddock, 1988): This is a recently developed instrument providing information on aspects of meaning that underlie subjects' attitudes toward sex. The questionnaire is a semantic differential consisting of 50 bipolar adjective scales (e.g., close/distant).

A 25-question semistructured interview schedule was devised to examine general family interaction patterns around gender and erotic aspects of sexuality, sex-related attitudes, sexual communication, and the like. The interviews were conducted informally, encouraging contributions from all members present and allowing individuals to elaborate in any direction that might be important to them. The interview did *not* include any direct questions about family sexual abuse, although some family members responded to general questions by talking about incest.

In addition to the written measures filled out by family members, therapists in the participating clinics completed brief checklists focusing on perceptions of prognosis (for pretreatment families) or outcome (for posttreatment families). Following the interviews, both researchers filled out rating scales identifying their impressions of family interactions around each of the major issues addressed.

RESULTS

This section further describes the process of gathering data on incest family functioning and summarizes overall similarities and differences among families in the three groups.

The Evaluation Process

The structure of funding required that we work within a limited time frame. Since incest treatment is typically a lengthy process, we were unable to use the same subjects for pretreatment and posttreatment assessment, which would have made possible an actual evaluation process. Referrals of clinical families occurred very slowly, necessitating contact with additional treatment agencies beyond those that originally agreed to participate. Our greatest difficulty was recruiting posttreatment incest families, a category we originally expected to be the easiest due to the presumed benefits of treatment and better relationships with service agencies. Instead, many families were no longer in contact with their treatment programs. They had moved, "dropped out of sight," or, if contacted, often refused to participate. Their alienation from the community and from their "helpers" was still readily apparent.

Virtually all clinic administrators we approached were interested in the project. However, numerous staff members hesitated to involve their "difficult" clients in research. Some therapists directly acknowledged their resistance, fearing it would create a "hassle" for their clients or would be problematic and time-consuming for the staff. A few clinicians expressed open concern about potential legal complications that might result from client involvement in research, even though all of the safeguards were identified. The current social climate of litigation has clearly produced anxiety among clinicians and agency personnel. This conscious and unconscious resistance by therapists is an important factor to consider when implementing evaluation research in clinical programs treating involuntary clientele.

In addition, a number of clinics were unable to refer families in which the offender was available to participate in the research. Relatively few agencies treat the entire incest family unit (Daro, 1988; Larson & Maddock, 1984; Trepper & Barrett, 1989). Those that work with individuals actually involved in the incest—usually the perpetrator *or* the victim—often have no contact, or a hostile relationship, with other family members. Therefore, we encountered some situations in which clinicians worked hard to recruit subjects but important family members declined to participate.

Our efforts to secure subject families taught us an important lesson: Make formal agreements with treatment programs to solicit client participation in the research as a *routine* part of their own intake/assessment process. This procedure requires greater initial effort, including extensive discussions with governing boards, administrators, and entire clinic staffs. However, it builds stronger support for the project, regularizes the recruitment process, and provides better feedback to the participating clinics.

The data gathering process proved quite manageable. We concluded that the most desirable location for interviewing a family was the family's own home. A fuller picture of the home environment enriched the sense of understanding reported by members of the research team. Questionnaire packets were filled out individually by family members, usually with everyone gathered in the same room. After completing questionnaires, all participating family members were assembled for a group interview. Interviewers made efforts to involve all members as fully as possible. The most verbal family member was often the original contact person who had agreed to partici-pate in the project. Aided by preproject training, interviewers worked to maintain a positive, open, and supportive atmosphere for the entire family while remaining psychologically equidistant from individual family members. Sometimes this was difficult. Some interviews were characterized by chaotic activity, others by passivity or anxious inhibi-tion, and still others by extremely uneven participation.

The research payment undoubtedly played a role in the self-selec-tion of subjects and in the interview process. Several families from the clinical samples indicated that payment was a major incentive, and they talked about how it would be used.

Questionnaire Results Across the Three Samples

This study was based on the assumption that the variables directly measured by our instruments reflect underlying family characteristics and patterns of interaction. The results presented here are intended to be helpful in understanding the attitudes and interaction patterns of incest families and in assessing changes that might be connected with treatment. An important caveat: Since all clinical families were inter-viewed *after* incest had been reported, their behaviors probably reflected the influences of social intervention as much as the effects of the incest itself—one of the inevitable limitations of clinical research in the area of child abuse.

Cohesion and adaptability scores on FACES III (Table 11.1) show no significant differences among families in the three groups. The major-ity of families in each sample clustered in the midrange, while a few were more extreme (unbalanced). Though not statistically significant, family discrepancy and distance-from-center scores disclosed patterns that we had anticipated: highest in the untreated incest families and lower in comparison families, with posttreatment families scoring as low as or lower than the comparison group. Although incest families are commonly characterized by clinicians as "enmeshed," the families in our study had scores more representative of moderate to extreme "disengagement." While these findings might be interpreted as dis-proving clinical opinion, three alternative explanations are possible: (a) the reporting of incest and subsequent social intervention might create a reactive pattern of disengagement in incest family members whose emotional connections are rather fragile; (b) family members' defensive denial may prevent them from recognizing the actual extent of their psychological enmeshment; or (c) the FACES cohesion scale

Table 11.1

Family Mean FACES III Scores by Group: Analysis of Variance Results

	Pre (N = 8)	Post (N = 7)	Comparison (N = 15)	F	p
Family cohesion	33.49	32.67	36.90	.192	ns
Family adaptability	24.49	26.31	28.03	.156	ns
Family discrepancy	11.24	10.08	8.69	.356	ns
Family distance from center	6.53	9.08	6.36	.256	ns

Table 11.2

Family Mean BSRI Scores by Group: Analysis of Variance Results

	Pre[a]	Post[b]	Comparison[c]	F	p
Male feminine	46.17	49.31	46.10	0.363	ns
Female feminine	49.71	56.43	52.49	1.475	ns
Male masculine	50.83	50.58	50.07	0.018	ns
Female masculine	42.79	48.14	46.06	1.049	ns

a. N = 6 for male, 8 for female.
b. N = 6 for male, 7 for female.
c. N = 14 for male, 15 for female.

may not measure the phenomenon that clinicians refer to as "enmeshment."

Male and female family members' scores on the BSRI (Table 11.2) show no significant differences across the three samples, although female scores reflect a pattern that suggests treatment might be influential. When all subjects in the three samples are grouped according to Bem's four sex role categories (Table 11.3), a clearer pattern emerges. Posttreatment family members are less sex-typed than either pretreatment or comparison families. However, our hypothesis that incest families reflect greater sex role typing than nonincest families is not strongly supported by these data.

On the P/C-S, separate power and control scores were derived for each partner, with scores ranging from −100 (low power or control) to +100 (high power or control). Midrange scores (those close to zero) indicate balances between males and females on power and on con-

Table 11.3
Frequency of BSRI Sex Typing by Treatment Group (in percentages)

	Pre (N = 25)	Post (N = 26)	Comparison (N = 56)
Same sex typed	48.00	30.77	39.30
Undifferentiated	20.00	30.77	35.71
Androgynous	20.99	30.77	10.71
Reverse sex typed	12.00	7.70	14.29

Table 11.4
Family Mean P/C-S Scores by Group: Analysis of Variance Results

	Pre^a	Post (N = 4)	Comparison (N = 13)	F	p
Male power	12.75	6.75	−3.31	2.99	<.10
Male control	0.00	−.25	−2.62	0.346	ns
Female power	−12.50	−7.25	6.08	6.211	<.05
Female control	−12.33	−3.25	5.23	7.13	<.01

a. $N = 4$ for male power and male control, $N = 6$ for female power and female control.

trol. Here we found significant differences across the three samples on three out of four measures (Table 11.4). Husbands were perceived as most powerful in pretreatment incest families, less so in the posttreatment sample. Correspondingly, wives in the posttreatment sample were higher on both power and control. Incest couples contrasted with comparison couples, whose power and control scores were more balanced. The small number of couples in the incest samples dictates caution when interpreting these results.

Via the PCI, we measured the perceptions of family members regarding general communication across gender and generational lines. Table 11.5 indicates that overall communication was more effective in posttreatment than in pretreatment incest families, and better still in comparison families. In addition, our results tend to confirm the widely held clinical belief that incest families are characterized by cross-generational, within-gender alignments that contribute to the parent-child role confusion that seems to accompany intrafamilial abuse.

Table 11.5
Family Mean PCI Scores by Group: Analysis of Variance Results

	Pre (N = 8)	Post (N = 7)	Comparison (N = 15)	F	p
Within sex	72.93	80.11	80.9	3.017	<.10
Across sex	64.85	74.00	78.08	7.538	<.01
Within generation	63.65	77.49	83.85	10.919	<.01
Across generation	69.83	76.74	76.63	3.808	<.05

Table 11.6
Couple Mean ISS Scores by Group: Analysis of Variance Results

	Pre (N = 8)	Post (N = 7)	Comparison (N = 15)	F	p
Female sexual satisfaction	20.67	39.00	25.00	0.943	ns
Male sexual satisfaction	18.67	44.67	18.54	3.067	<.10
Couple sexual satisfaction	19.67	41.83	21.77	2.464	ns

The ISS was given only to spouses to assess their satisfaction with their erotic interaction. According to Hudson (1982), scores higher than 30 indicate difficulties in a sexual relationship that might lead the partners to seek sex therapy. In our findings (Table 11.6), pretreatment satisfaction scores approximated, and even exceeded, those of couples in the comparison group—a surprising finding except when viewed in light of the idealization and denial that typically characterizes untreated incest families. The high levels of sexual dissatisfaction may also reflect the failure of treatment programs to address problems of the marital relationship adequately. However, our conclusions are once again limited by the small number of couples reporting in the clinical samples.

On the SMS, a discrepancy score among members was computed for each family on each of the 50 adjective scales and these scores compared across the three samples (Table 11.7). As predicted, the discrepancies are greater in the incest groups than in the comparison group, with group difference scores approaching statistical signifi-

Table 11.7

Mean SMS Family Discrepancy Scores by Group: Analysis of Variance Results

Pre (N = 8)	Post (N = 7)	Comparison (N = 15)	F	p
15.374	14.774	13.396	2.748	<.10

cance. Differences would likely be greater on the meaning clusters derived for each sample; however, these factor scores have not yet been fully validated and are too complex to be reported here (Maddock, 1988).

As we continue to gather information from families involved with child sexual abuse and with other sex-related problems, more elaborate data analyses are planned. Family data will be organized in a variety of ways: individual family member scores, aggregate family scores, and sum of difference scores among family members. Data will be examined by utilizing more complex statistical methods and modes of depiction permitted by computer simulation, cluster analysis, and factor analysis. Validity and reliability studies of the instruments under development will continue, and their results will be fitted to the theoretical model from which the variables are derived.

Interview Findings

The transcripts, notes, and ratings from family interviews were examined to identify overall patterns and to gather impressionistic data. A more thorough content analysis is planned, using coding schemes and computerized methods of pattern analysis tied to our ecosystemic model (e.g., Leik, Roberts, Caron, Mangen, & Leik, 1990). Currently, we can only compare the narrative notes and impressionistic ratings of therapists and research interviewers. Interrater reliability on the interview checklists was adequate on most items. Consensus between therapists and researchers on overall family ratings was also acceptable. Therapists rated posttreatment families more positively than did researchers, perhaps because of the clinicians' unconscious investment in the families' success or a tendency to establish a lower baseline at the beginning of therapy when families were functioning poorly following disclosure.

Incest families were definitely more difficult to interview than comparison families. In particular, pretreatment families appeared most chaotic. Conflict between the perpetrator and the victim seemed to predominate, and family members often took sides with one or the other. By contrast, posttreatment families emphasized the similarities and positive relationship of the perpetrator and victim, while expressing more marital alienation. Overall, pretreatment incestuous couples presented their marriages in a more positive light than did either posttreatment or comparison couples. As one wife put it, "If I'm with someone I love and I'm married to him, it's sacred. . . . It should be a perfect union, with much eye contact and oneness like you might feel when meditating."

Comparison couples seemed more willing to reveal conflicts, particularly around gender issues. Perhaps this only indicates the greater constraints on clinical families, whose contacts with social and legal agencies might have motivated them toward more socially approved responses. However, clinical families appeared to the interviewers to be more traditional in structure, with husband domination accepted by both spouses. At the same time, interviews with incest families were sometimes characterized by subtle and not-so-subtle "male bashing." For example, one pretreatment mother stated, "[My daughter] feels I pay more attention to [my son] than the girls. I told her he's a boy—he needs that extra push." No clear instances of categorical derogating of females were noted. Perhaps this phenomenon would have differed had not both interviewers been female, thereby encouraging the subjects (who were predominantly female) to align themselves with the researchers around the theme "You know how men are."

Boundary difficulties in incest families were clearly evident in the interviews. One pretreatment mother described her relationship with her young daughter as "more like a friendship," saying, "I'm not too good at being a parent." Another stated, "We're more like friends than mother and daughter." A posttreatment mother observed, "[My daughter and I] really have a bond. I was good at telling the bad things. I overdid it—told her my problems. We're trying to undo that—let her be a little girl." As we had anticipated, signs of anxiety often became more noticeable as the interview progressed toward more specific questions about sex—although no one was asked to report or describe sexual behavior per se. A key question about the nature of sex-related communication in the family was sometimes a turning point in the interview. Family conversation either opened up or shut down. Merely asking the question probably constituted rule-breaking behavior in most families.

IMPLICATIONS

Clinical Practice

This project's greatest clinical significance is its progress toward a protocol for evaluating *family* outcomes as well as individual outcomes of incest treatment. Our findings support a concern that current treatment efforts may neglect and/or have a negative impact upon families as a unit. Identifying patterns of family sexual interaction has practical significance for clinical programs, including (a) providing methods and criteria by which families can be assessed prior to treatment, in order to differentiate high-risk from low-risk family units; (b) serving as a basis for setting treatment goals; (c) specifying standards for evaluating the effects of treatment; and (d) facilitating comparisons among various treatment modalities (individual versus family versus group) or differing theoretical approaches.

In addition, uniform standards for assessing family functioning can serve as a basis for designing policies to aid decisions such as removal of children from the home, sentencing guidelines for perpetrators, and selection of treatment options. Criteria of family functioning can also be used to evaluate various treatment efforts in order to make judgments about agency structure, funding priorities, and the like. Even far-reaching issues, such as the relative merits of individual versus family treatment programs, can be debated more fruitfully when empirical data are available to use as a basis for drawing conclusions.

Research

Evaluation of family functioning requires a multimethod approach, combining quantitative and qualitative data gathering procedures (Bryman, 1988; Gilgun & Allen, 1987; Nye, 1988; Olson, 1977; Rank, 1988). This study's use of information from multiple respondents, both inside and outside the family, permitted valuable triangulation of data that can improve validity and reliability when measuring complex underlying variables like those derived from our theoretical model (Fox & Long, 1990; Larsen & Olson, 1990). Interactive research interviews with whole families are themselves an important methodological step in family research—often advocated, but seldom utilized. They permit researchers a more in-depth understanding of a family's interactive processes and provide access to the unique *meaning* of shared experiences for members of a particular family.

The limitations of this study are numerous, among them a one-time sampling procedure rather than multioccasion sampling over the course of treatment and beyond, self-selection biases in sampling (families who voluntarily respond to research solicitations are unlikely to represent a "normal" cross section of a heterogeneous population, perhaps differing on the very issues—such as boundaries—that are of major concern), lack of matched subject families across samples, and data gathering procedures favoring adult respondents. Additional methods of data gathering and analysis might also have been used, such as videotaping interviews for later analysis by independent raters or involving families in structured experiences that could facilitate later behavioral analysis and comparison. We are currently considering the use of temporal mapping methods to analyze further the family communication processes reflected in the audiotaped interviews (Leik et al., 1990).

CONCLUSION

Based upon differences found among the families in the three samples, we have tentatively concluded that there are indeed family as well as individual characteristics that influence the occurrence of incest, and that measuring these characteristics can contribute to an evaluation protocol for family sexual abuse treatment programs as well as to a broader understanding of family sexual dynamics. Our results also appear to indicate that incest families are "out of balance" on a number of measures of internal family functioning—in addition to the violation of broader community mores that creates the need for social intervention. Based upon restricted sampling and other methodological limitations, few solid conclusions can as yet be drawn regarding the distinguishing characteristics of families in which incest occurs. Nevertheless, we believe that we have demonstrated the value of an approach to studying whole families in a clinical context and of assessing the systemic effects of social intervention on an abusive family. Equally important, in our view, is the momentum gained for a longer-term exploration of the dynamic processes of "ecological balancing" in the maintenance of healthy family sexuality, with the goal of *preventing* sexual abuse in the future.

REFERENCES

Alexander, P. (1985). A systems theory conceptualization of incest. *Family Process, 24,* 79–88.
Bass, E., & Davis, L. (1988). *The courage to heal.* New York: Harper & Row.

Beach, S., & Arias, I. (1983). Assessment of perceptual discrepancy: Utility of the PCI. *Family Process, 22,* 309–316.

Bem, S. (1974). The measurement of psychological androgyny. *Journal of Consulting and Clinical Psychology, 42,* 155–162.

Bronfenbrenner, U. (1979). *The ecology of human development: Experiments by nature and design.* Cambridge, MA: Harvard University Press.

Bryman, A. (1988). *Quantity and quality in social research.* London: Unwin Hyman.

Conte, J. (1986). Sexual abuse and the family: A critical analysis. In T. Trepper & M. J. Barrett (Eds.), *Treating incest: A multiple systems perspective.* New York: Haworth.

Daro, D. (1988). *Confronting child abuse: Research for effective program design.* New York: Free Press.

Faller, K. (Ed.). (1981). *Social work with abused and neglected children.* New York: Free Press.

Finkelhor, D. (1984). *Child sexual abuse: New theory and research.* New York: Free Press.

Finkelhor, D., & Associates. (1986). *A sourcebook on child sexual abuse.* Beverly Hills, CA: Sage.

Fox, J., & Long, J. S. (Eds.). (1990). *Modern methods of data analysis.* Newbury Park, CA: Sage.

Garbarino, J. (1977). The human ecology of child maltreatment. *Journal of Marriage and the Family, 39,* 721–735.

Gelinas, D. (1988). Unexpected resources in treating incest families. In M. Karpel (Ed.), *Family resources: The hidden partner in family therapy.* New York: Guilford.

Gelles, R. (1979). *Family violence.* Beverly Hills, CA: Sage.

Gilgun, J., & Allen, K. (1987). *Qualitative research methods and the development of family theory.* Paper presented at the Theory Construction and Research Methodology Workshop, at the annual conference of the National Council on Family Relations, Atlanta, GA.

Hudson, W. (1982). *The clinical measurement package: A field manual.* Homewood, IL: Dorsey.

Larsen, A., & Olson, D. (1990). Capturing the complexity of family systems: Integrating theory, family scores, and family analysis. In T. Draper & A. Marcos (Eds.), *Family variables: Conceptualization, measurement, and use.* Newbury Park, CA: Sage.

Larson, N., & Maddock, J. (1984). *Incest management and treatment: Family systems versus victim advocacy.* Paper presented at the annual meeting of the American Association for Marriage and Family Therapy, San Francisco.

Larson, N., & Maddock, J. (1986). Structural and functional variables in incest family systems: Implications for assessment and treatment. In T. Trepper & M. J. Barrett (Eds.), *Treating incest: A multiple systems perspective.* New York: Haworth.

Leik, R., Roberts, C., Caron, W., Mangen, D., & Leik, S. (1990). Temporal mapping: A method for analyzing process. In T. Draper & A. Marcos (Eds.), *Family variables: Conceptualization, measurement, and use.* Newbury Park, CA: Sage.

MacFarlane, K., & Waterman, J. (Eds.). (1986). *Sexual abuse of young children: Evaluation and treatment.* New York: Guilford.

Maddock, J. (1988). *The Sexual Meaning Scales I: Development of a semantic differential.* Unpublished manuscript, University of Minnesota, Department of Family Social Science.

Maddock, J. (1989). *Power/Control Survey.* Unpublished manuscript, University of Minnesota, Department of Family Social Science.

Nye, F. I. (1988). Fifty years of family research (1937–1987). *Journal of Marriage and the Family, 50,* 569–584.

Olson, D. (1977). Insiders' and outsiders' views of relationships: Research strategies. In G. Levinger & R. Rausch (Eds.), *Close relationships*. Amherst: University of Massachusetts Press.

Olson, D., McCubbin, H., Barnes, H., Larsen, A., Muxen, M., & Wilson, M. (1985). *Family Inventories*. Saint Paul: University of Minnesota, Department of Family Social Science.

Rank, M. (1988). *The blending of quantitative and qualitative data in family research.* Paper presented at the Workshop on Theory Construction and Research Methodology, at the annual conference of the National Council on Family Relations, Philadelphia.

Russell, D. (1986). *The secret trauma: Incest in the lives of girls and women*. New York: Basic Books.

Salter, A. (1988). *Treating child sex offenders and their victims.* Newbury Park, CA: Sage.

Sgroi, S. (Ed.). (1988). *Vulnerable populations: Evaluation and treatment of sexually abused children and adult survivors*. Lexington, MA: Lexington.

Tierney, K., & Corwin, D. (1983). Exploring intrafamily child sexual abuse: A systems approach. In D. Finkelhor, R. J. Gelles, G. Hotaling, & M. A. Straus (Eds.), *The dark side of families*. Beverly Hills, CA: Sage.

Trepper T., & Barrett, M. J. (Eds.). (1986). *Treating incest: A multiple systems perspective.* New York: Haworth.

Trepper, T., & Barrett, M. J. (1989). *Systemic treatment of incest: A therapeutic handbook.* New York: Haworth.

12

Incest Offenders After Treatment

GREG OWEN

NANCY M. STEELE

The purpose of this study was to examine the social histories, treatment, and parole experiences of 110 men incarcerated for incest. The study was designed (a) to describe the family characteristics of convicted incest offenders prior to and following their release from a prison treatment program, (b) to examine the opinions of offenders regarding the treatment and parole experiences of men treated in the Transitional Sex Offenders Program (TSOP), and (c) to review the reconviction patterns of incest offenders treated in the program.

THE TREATMENT PROGRAM

The prison-based Transitional Sex Offenders Program was started in 1978 by the Minnesota Department of Corrections with assistance from an LEAA grant. This study includes incest offenders served by the treatment program from 1979 to 1988.

TSOP begins inside Lino Lakes Correctional Facility, a medium-security prison about 20 miles north of the Twin Cities of Minneapolis and Saint Paul. The inmates in the program live in one cottage that houses 30 men. Inmates accepted into the program have asked for treatment as part of their prison sentence, have reasonably good behavior records in prison, and are able to work in the prison industry program for 40 hours each week. Treatment activities, except during the first 30 days of the program, take place in the evenings and on weekends.

The men spend about 10 months in the program prior to their release from prison. The prison treatment staff provide aftercare service while offenders are living in a halfway house located in the community. Staff of the prison treatment program help the men to make reasonable transitions back to their lives in the community. The staff have generally tried to involve wives and other family members in the treatment process as much as possible. However, more than half of the families are located outside the metropolitan area, and many families are reluctant to participate in treatment activities with these offenders, making it difficult to conduct family treatment.

When men enter TSOP, they are not required to work during their first 30 days in the program. During this time they complete five standard psychological tests, write autobiographies, and watch films and read books on the causes of sexual abuse and the impact abuse has upon victims. During the orientation phase, offenders attend daily group discussions with staff during which any minimization or denial of their crimes is confronted directly by both staff and other offenders. This is a training phase for treatment designed to orient the men to the program and describe the expectations staff have for each offender during treatment. It is also a diagnostic phase in which both inmates and staff assess what changes each man needs to make while in treatment.

Following the orientation phase, men typically go to work in the prison and attend 90-minute therapy groups three evenings a week. In this phase men are encouraged to come to grips with their behavior and to attempt to understand and change those factors that have contributed to their sexual offenses. Men are helped to overcome shame, develop self-understanding, and recognize the danger signs that may lead to new offenses. Group therapy attempts to help the men identify child-focused sexual feelings and develop ways of managing their behavior.

Men in the program also attend weekend educational groups led by inmates. They are required to read articles on social skills and answer questions about them as part of weekly lessons. Lessons dealing with assertiveness, anger control, social roles, and sex education are discussed as part of the weekend groups.

Once every nine months the program conducts a Sexual Attitude Reassessment. During this phase of treatment, offenders watch sexually explicit movies and discuss with staff their beliefs, feelings, and values about sexuality. In general, the reassessment part of the program is meant to teach the men how to express sexuality in healthier ways than they have in the past. Once every other month or so the program is visited by sexual assault advocates. These are usually volunteers being trained to counsel victims of incest and rape. In many cases these advocates are victims themselves who have powerful stories to share with the offenders. These meetings serve to confront offenders with the consequences of their acts.

During the transitional phase of treatment, offenders begin to attend the outpatient group that meets once a week in the 180 Degree Halfway House program. Staff transport offenders from prison to the group in preparation for their release to the halfway house. Following release, offenders are seen once a week in individual therapy and once a week in group counseling for four months while they live at the halfway house. Cooperation is encouraged among men while adjusting to life in the community. After moving out of the halfway house offenders typically attend group for up to another two months while living in the community.

Family treatment depends on the cooperation of the spouse and other family members. It is a goal of the program for each offender to have at least one family session with those family members closest to him. This could include parents, siblings, children, wives, or former wives. Generally the program has tried to promote ongoing couple sessions with wives or girlfriends who are willing to come to the institution or halfway house on a weekly or biweekly basis. Typically, however, this has included only a small number of wives.

RESEARCH METHODS

The investigation included four separate data collection procedures. The first involved extracting information from prison files maintained on each incest offender. Since the program also treats rapists and other types of convicted sex offenders, it was necessary to identify which of the 300 men served by the program had committed incest. Staff were able to identify 110 men who had committed crimes of incest and were treated in the Transitional Sex Offenders Program from 1979 to 1988. The second procedure was a telephone follow-up survey of parole officers who had supervised incest offenders following release. (Details of this component of the study are available in the full report; see Owen and Williams, 1989.) The third data collection activity was a follow-up of offenders through confidential telephone interviews. Finally, reconviction information was obtained through a computerized search of arrest records on offenders. (See Table 12.1.)

Table 12.1
Data Collection Outcomes

	Number
Offender Sample[a]	
failed in the institution phase of treatment	10
failed in the community phase of treatment	3
released to other locations without the program's aftercare	7
died prior to completing the program	2
completed both phases of the program	88
located and asked to be interviewed for the study	56
agreed to be interviewed	43
Parole officer sample[b]	
offenders whose parole officer agreed to be interviewed	80
not found	10
refused	6

a. The offender sample was made up of 110 male incest offenders treated in prison from 1979 to 1988. All files reviewed.
b. The parole officer sample was made up of 96 male incest offenders assigned to parole officers. Interviews were completed with 83.3% of the sample.

What Is Incestuous Abuse?

Incestuous abuse is defined as "any kind of exploitive sexual contact or attempt at contact that occurs between relatives no matter how distant the relationship before the victim turned 18 years old" (Russell, Schurman, & Trocki, 1988, p. 120). The legal definition of incest in the state of Minnesota is described in the Intrafamilial Sexual Abuse Law as sexual penetration or contact with a child under the age of 18. Sexual contact is defined as "a wide range of acts, if acts can reasonably be construed as being for the purpose of satisfying the actor's sexual or aggressive impulses." By statute, the offender may be related to the child by blood, marriage, or adoption, or may be someone responsible for the child's care. In fact, it can include an adult who simply resides in the same household with the victim on a regular or occasional basis. Consent is not an issue with this law. In the report prepared for the Bigelow Foundation by Anne McBean (1984), she notes, "In the eyes of the law, a relationship of authority and trust that is 'like family' is more pertinent than merely the biological relationship" (p. 5).

The following case examples are presented in order to provide the reader with an understanding of the type of acts subsumed under this law.[2]

> At the time of his arrest, Arthur was a 34-year-old married man with three stepchildren and two biological children. He was originally arrested for fondling the 12-year-old friend of his stepdaughter in a car. The girl told police this was the third such incident, and on previous occasions Arthur had put her hand into his pants and made her fondle his penis. In the course of the investigation, it was discovered that he had been having sexual intercourse with his 14-year-old stepdaughter every two or three weeks for nearly four years. His stepdaughter had reported it to school officials two years earlier, but then denied it to the police and no further investigation or physical examination was done at that time.

> Carl, a 41-year-old divorced male, was arrested for abusing three of his four stepsons, whom he had continued to see after his divorce from their mother. The oldest victim, age 15, reported having anal intercourse performed on him, as well as being forced to perform oral sex on the stepfather "at least weekly" for a period of more than seven years.

> When arrested, David had been divorced three times and was living with his fiancee and her daughters by a previous marriage. The girls, ages 5 and 9, described how David had involved them several times in sexual activity that included digital penetration (both vaginal and anal) as well as their genital fondling of him.

CHARACTERISTICS OF OFFENDERS

Minnesota places fewer convicted offenders in the state prison system than all but one other state in the nation (*Corrections Digest*, September 20, 1989, p. 3). For that reason those offenders who do end up in prison have usually committed serious crimes, in many cases over a long period of time. Unfortunately, the social history files were not always clear about how long the abuse had gone on. For the majority of victims, however, the abuse went on for more than one year. The type of sexual abuse in 83% of the cases included vaginal or anal penetration or oral sex. Only 25% of these men were known or suspected to have had only one victim; 45% had two or three known victims and 30% had four or more victims, including one man who was known to have had at least 12 victims in his lifetime. In about

85% of the cases the offender lived with the victim during the time the abuse occurred.

Aside from the seriousness of the crimes, these men, like many men in prison, were not well-off financially. Some 45% were working in semiskilled or unskilled jobs at or near minimum wage. Another 21% were unemployed at the time of arrest. Although Minnesota has a number of good quality outpatient treatment programs for incest offenders, they are generally available only to men who can pay for them or have employment with very good medical coverage. These same outpatient treatment programs are generally available only in the large metropolitan area of the Twin Cities. Half of the men in this study came from rural areas of the state, although one-fourth of the men in the prison system as a whole come from the rural areas. It is the impression of the treatment staff that there are many incest offenders from rural areas who would be good candidates for outpatient treatment if it were available in their home areas. Since the programs are not available and the offenders are sent to prison, a disproportionate number of men from rural areas do seek out and take advantage of the treatment resources available in prison.

The incest offenders who volunteered for treatment were primarily white (92%). Many (61%) had fewer than 12 years of education, although most of them had completed a General Equivalence Diploma. The men ranged in age from 19 to 64, with the average age being 38 years at the time of incarceration, which is older than the average age of inmates in general. Most of the men (54%) had been married more than once prior to entering the program. The typical offender had three children, although some had as many as nine children. Two-thirds were found to have had significant problems with drug or alcohol addiction as identified in their social history records. The 110 incest offenders identified and included in this study were treated, released, and in the community for at least one year prior to January 1, 1989.

Data on the family backgrounds of the offenders as they relate specifically to families of origin (the families in which the offenders were raised) are not gathered systematically in prison files. Nonetheless, we were able to document that at least 29% had divorced parents, and 15% did not know their fathers' identities; 28% of the men were raised by someone other than a parent. The typical offender came from a family with more than five children.

Some form of violence was present in the offender's family of origin in 37% of the cases. There was clear evidence to suggest that 14% were sexually abused by at least one parent, 17% were victims of sexual abuse perpetrated by a sibling, 9% were sexually abused by another relative, and 17% were victimized by someone outside of the family. At least 21% of the offenders were perpetrators of sexual abuse in the families in which they grew up. In total, 57% showed evidence of incest in the family of origin. The actual amount is probably under-stated, given that this information was not always recorded in therapists' treatment narratives.

Background information on the families formed by offenders prior to incarceration suggests that these families are often characterized by unstable marriages and the use of alcohol or other drugs. In addition, 42% of the men were known to have exhibited violent behavior in their own marital relationships.

The criminal conviction of an incest offender in the Lino Lakes pro-gram is seldom based on his full sexual offense history. For example, 49% of the convictions were based on information regarding only one victim, 36% on two victims, 12% on three victims, and 4% on four victims. However, when we look at the total number of known and suspected victims identified in the prison files, evidence is compelling that there are many more victims than are represented in specific con-victions.

With regard to how convictions were obtained, 22% pled guilty to the original charge (incest, sodomy, intrafamilial sexual abuse, or criminal sexual conduct); following plea bargaining, 64% pled guilty to a lesser charge than originally filed; and 14% pled not guilty and were convicted at trial. The average length of prison time for incest offenders in this program was 29 months.

About half of the men in the program (52%) did not have previous felony convictions; 27% had one previous felony conviction, 10% had two, 6% had three, and 5% had four or more previous felony convic-tions. Also, 24% of the men in this sample had previous sex-related felony convictions, and 18% had previous assaultive felony convic-tions.

Although there is not a great deal of systematic information pro-vided on victims of crimes in the prison records, we do know that most of the victims on which convictions were based were children over the age of 5. Only 19% of the victims were age 8 or younger at the time abuse was disclosed, and 81% of the convictions were based on disclosures by children ages 9 to 18. The vast majority of the vic-tims on which convictions were based were female (90%), 38% of these being daughters of the offenders and 30% stepdaughters. Other categories of victims included daughters of the perpetrator's girlfriend, 9%; other related females, such as a nieces or cousins, 10%;

and unrelated females who resided in the perpetrator's household, 3%. The 10% of victims who were male were stepsons, 6%, and sons of perpetrators, 4%.

With regard to family involvement in treatment, 35% of the men participated in at least one treatment session with their spouses and 30% participated in one or more treatment sessions with at least one of their children present. About 15% of the men had girlfriends who participated in counseling sessions in prison.

INTERVIEWS WITH OFFENDERS

Research staff were able to contact and interview by telephone 43 of the 108 offenders (40%) known to be alive at the time of follow-up. The relatively low response rate resulted from our inability to locate offenders who had been out of prison for longer periods of time. Table 12.2 provides comparisons to allow the reader to judge the representativeness of the offender follow-up sample. Offenders in the follow-up sample are in most ways similar to those we could not contact and have provided useful information on the perceived value of treatment as well as suggestions regarding program emphasis and direction.

Family Living Arrangements After Release

One of the most important aims of the study was to identify how many offenders again form families with young children. Most men we interviewed did not reunite with the same families they were living with prior to incarceration. Of the 43 men who participated in the follow-up study, 32 (74%) were married prior to the disclosure of abuse and lived with minor children. Following release, 11 of the 32 who were married (34%) reestablished families with the same spouses they had lived with prior to their arrests, and 9 of these men (28%) lived with one or more of the minor children they had lived with prior to their convictions. In all, 21 of the 43 respondents (49%) were married at the time of follow-up and 6 more were living with women in some type of ongoing relationship. Thus 27 (63%) were living in households with female partners. Of this group, 41% were also living with minor children. These percentages should be considered underestimates, since in nearly all cases living with minor children required approval from the parole officer. (Four of the men—9%—had been reincarcerated by the time of follow-up.)

Table 12.2

Comparison of Offenders Interviewed and Offenders Not Interviewed on Selected Characteristics from Prison Files

Variable	Mean Sample Score or Percentage of Offenders Interviewed (N = 43)	Mean Sample Score or Percentage of Offenders Not Interviewed (N = 65)	Significance Test Value	Degrees of Freedom	p
Average age of offender	41.9 years	44.9 years	$t = 1.89$	105	.062
Proportion nonwhite (%)	0	13.8	$\chi^2 = 4.81$	1	.028
Average number of prior felonies	0.67	1.26	$t = 1.82$	90	.072
Proportion with female victim	86.0	92.3	$\chi^2 = .53$	1	.467
Average age of primary victim	10.4 years	11.8	$t = 2.11$	106	.037
Spouse involved in treatment with offender while in prison	44.2	30.8	$\chi^2 = 2.02$	1	.155

These data suggest that family formation among convicted incest offenders is common following release from prison and that living arrangements involving minor children occur relatively often. For more than 70% of the follow-up sample, however, these arrangements did not involve family members with whom the offender lived prior to incarceration.

Activities After Release

Some 74% of the follow-up sample indicated involvement in some type of counseling, support, or self-help activity since their completion of Transitional Sex Offenders Program. They reported involvement in Sex Addicts Anonymous (20%), Alcoholics Anonymous (40%), some type of individual counseling (16%), or some type of family counseling (21%). Involvement in these activities, however, was not necessarily continued over time. For those who said they had not been involved in any type of counseling, support, or self-help activity (26%), only 5% felt that they needed some type of support activity.

At the time of the interviews, 74% of the offenders were employed. Most (42%) were employed in semiskilled or unskilled laborer positions; 21% had some type of technical training and were employed as skilled workers; and 12% were involved in work that required at least two years of college or the completion of a vocational or technical training experience. At the time of the follow-up, 23% of the men were not employed. The average hourly wage for those employed was approximately $7.00. These figures showed no significant change from the preincarceration employment characteristics described in the prison files.

The study also examined offenders' experiences with parole and halfway houses. Some 58% indicated they had benefited from the halfway house experience, and 65% thought they had benefited from contacts with their parole officers. (The full study includes a more detailed analysis of halfway house and parole experiences as well as interviews with parole officers; see Owen and Williams, 1989.)

Offenders' Views on Treatment

A total of 91% of the offenders interviewed felt they had benefited from participation in TSOP, 2% reported they did not benefit, and 7% were unsure. Offenders were asked to describe the most and least useful aspects of the program; their comments are summarized in Table 12.3. Overall, these comments suggest that group experiences

Table 12.3
Offender's Opinions Regarding the Most Useful and Least Useful Aspects of
Transitional Sex Offenders Program

	N	%
Most useful (N = 41)		
The group experience, group therapy sessions	23	53
Learning about myself, my behavior, and my family	11	26
Education in sexuality, and how it applies to people's lives	9	21
Least Useful (N = 25)		
films of sex among adults	6	24
weekend lessons reading, and answering questions on paper	5	20
being grouped with and treated the same as rapists, etc.	4	16
feeling discouraged and isolated	4	16
lack of emphasis on restoring the family	3	12
trivial rules and meaningless meetings	3	12

involving other offenders and family members were perceived as a valuable component of therapy. Moreover, activities designed to help the offender understand the reasons for his behavior and its impact on victims were also seen as useful. The group experiences provided opportunities for confrontation, understanding, and support. It is noteworthy that 74% of the offenders interviewed have had some contact following release with one or more of the men they met while in the Transitional Sex Offenders Program.

Offenders were also asked for any suggestions they might have regarding ways to improve the program. The following comments illustrate the range of suggestions offered.

There should be more contact in group settings with victims. . . . It helps you to understand how victims of incest feel.

There should be more incentives for people who really want to change to enter the program.

Smaller groups would be better . . . using ex-offenders as facilitators.

I had to push for couples counseling. There is a need for at least bimonthly counseling for couples.

Bring guys to the Sex Addicts Anonymous groups sooner.

There is a problem in releasing confidential information. If we talk about something we have done in the group sessions, that stuff can be held against us.

They need to teach a guy to deal with the pain he has to go through and how to deal with his kids again.

Perceived Benefits of Treatment

During the offender interviews, respondents were asked if they could identify any specific benefits of participation in the treatment program. All but one of the respondents identified at least one benefit that they could attribute to their experiences in the program. The following comments are illustrative:

The role playing helped me to understand my childhood victimization. It helped me to understand that I am a person with rights and responsibilities.

The program taught me that it was okay for men to ask for and receive affection, helped me show my feelings.

Basically it helped me understand that other people have their own sexuality and that I have been selfish about a lot of things.

It helped me to see the damage I had caused and the roots of the problem. I learned to be honest about myself and accept myself as a good person.

I learned what happens to victims and I learned technical terms for anatomy and sexual behaviors. I met with others and learned that I was not alone in my feelings.

The program gave me direction on what I wanted to do. But if I hadn't been ready the program couldn't have helped me.

Offenders were also asked whether their ability to control their sexual behavior was any different at the present time than it was before they entered the treatment program. Again, only one of the offenders interviewed indicated that there had been no change in his ability to control his sexual behavior. The following comments show the range of responses to this question:

Now I don't have a need for revenge.

I worked out the problem of being sexually abused by my brother and now I don't drink or take drugs anymore.

I don't have the same sexual feelings now, I can make choices. I'm not denying there is temptation, but I can and I have changed.

I learned how to deal appropriately with my fantasies, and to control my behavior and attitudes. I'm not using alcohol anymore.

Now I can look at children and realize they are just children. I have no fantasies about them, I no longer see them as sexual objects.

I have been able to change my fantasies. I now look for what needs aren't being met and it usually comes down to communicating with my wife. We talk, we work out things, and we compromise. We do whatever it takes.

I've got stop signs and new ways of thinking that the program provided. I play the history of the crime through in my head and that stops me.

I have tools to keep track of myself, signals that lead to the addictive cycle and acting out that I can recognize.

I don't think of women as sex objects or dwell on sex the way I used to. The feelings toward children are still there but I can control them. Now I can talk to my wife about how I feel, process my fantasies, and deal with them.

Finally, offenders were asked to indicate whether they felt that life was better, worse, or about the same compared to before they entered the correctional facility. Of the 43 men, 39 indicated that life was better for them now. Examples of their responses are presented below:

I was heading for death before, I was a suicidal drunkard. Now I go to church, I participate in SAA, and I have a good business. I pinch myself to make sure it's all true.

There's a great deal more communication with my wife. I'm emotionally better off, but financially things are worse.

I'm more conservative now and I look forward to the future with more optimism. I figure I've got a second chance to raise my kids right.

I know myself better and I recognize problems and do something about them right away. I communicate with my lady friend and she goes to the SAA meetings with me. I'm more active, I go more places and I relate to people a lot better.

My relationship with my wife is a lot closer and I stay on top of my anger and my stress. I let people in and before I didn't.

While my health is bad and I have a certain amount of depression, my living situation is better. I've personally come a long way in dealing with anger, sexuality, honesty, and my own self-confidence.

I've got a woman now that cares, and my financial situation is not as good, but we're working on that. I have a 16-year-old stepson who is affectionate but we have appropriate barriers.

RECIDIVISM

Data for the 110 men included show that 18% were convicted of new felonies prior to January 1, 1989. Table 12.4 provides more detail on subsequent offenses. Those men who completed both the inpatient and aftercare phases of treatment were compared with the men who failed to complete both phases of the program. Of the 20 men who failed to complete the program, 3 failed in the community and were returned to prison and released a few months later, 10 failed during the inpatient phase because they either quit or were removed by staff for breaking institution rules or being nonresponsive to treatment, and 7 were released to other places outside the Twin Cities area and thus were unable to complete the aftercare.

A total of 88 men completed both phases of the program. The time elapsed between release from prison and rearrest varied from one year to nine years at the time the rearrest records were checked. The greater reconviction rate for noncompleters was significant at the .013 level using a chi-square test of significance.

Recidivism rates are not readily available in published literature. It is generally agreed that reconviction rates are an underestimate of the

Table 12.4
Reconviction Rates for TSOP Participants[a] (Offenses Prior to January 1, 1989)
(N = 108)

	Completed Program		Did Not Complete Program		Total	
	N	%	N	%	N	%
New sex offenses	6	6.8	5	25.0	11	10.2
New other offenses (not sex related)	5	5.7	3	15.0	8	7.4
No new felony offenses	77	87.5	12	60.0	89	82.4
Total	88	100.0	20	100.0	108	100.0

a. Chi-square = 8.70, p. = .013.

amount of reoffending that really happens. Given this limitation it is still important to compare reconviction rates in this study with what is known from the few other studies available. The U.S. Department of Justice has published a report based on 108,000 offenders released in 11 states in 1983 and followed for three years after release (Beck & Shipley, 1989, pp. 134–135). Sex offenders, other than rapists, have a reconviction rate of 33% for any type of crime. Overall, the incest offenders in this study had a reconviction rate of 18% for all types of crimes. The incest offenders in this study who completed both phases of the program had a reconviction rate of 12.5%, which is significantly better than the 40% reconviction rate for the noncompleters. The lower overall rate of 18% is probably due to the fact that incest offenders generally have a lower rate of reconviction than other types of child offenders and exhibitionists who are included in the Bureau of Justice Report.

Finkelhor and Associates (1986, p. 135) report on three studies of incest offenders that show recidivism rates of 10%, 11%, and 12%. Such rates are very similar to reconvictions for new sex offenses in our study: 10% for both completers and noncompleters combined. Finkelhor et al. go on to cite other studies indicating that some types of child abusers, especially those who abuse boys, have higher rates of recidivism (p. 134).

Characteristics of Recidivists

An important issue related to the treatment of incest offenders concerns the characteristics of those men who commit subsequent crimes. Are there any factors that predict which men are most likely to commit additional sex offenses following treatment?

Based on information available in the prison records for all offenders who committed new sex offenses, several characteristics were found to be associated in a statistically significant way (using a chi-square test of significance) with the commission of additional sex crimes following treatment in the Transitional Sex Offenders Program. Men who committed additional sex crimes following treatment for incest in TSOP were more likely to have the following characteristics:

1. lived in a different household from the victim ($p = .016$)
2. had chemical dependency problems ($p = .021$)
3. offended against multiple victims prior to first incarceration ($p = .015$)
4. had a lower score on the A scale of the Clinical Analysis Questionnaire (i.e., are more introverted as measured at the time of release from prison) ($p = .05$)

Those offenders who lived in a household different from that of the victim were much more likely to reoffend. This included uncles, grandparents, and people who were somehow part of the extended family and so related to but not residing with the victim. These offenders are probably more like habitual child abusers, who also abuse outside of the home and so tend to have a higher recidivism rate. Some of them were known to have abused children both inside and outside of the family. Offenders who were known to have had three or more victims also had a much higher rate of reoffending. This is not surprising, since many studies show that the more a person has done something, the more he or she is likely to repeat that same behavior. It is of interest to note that length of time over which the abuse occurred did not seem to be related to reoffending. Again, offenders with three or more victims may be more like the child abuser who offends against children outside the home.

Having chemical dependency problems was found to be significantly related to reoffense rates. This finding is also consistent with other studies of recidivism. A return to drug or alcohol abuse seems to lower the inhibitions against sexual offending that treatment may have put in place.

The most unusual finding in this study, and one that may be of greatest interest, relates to the introversion score at the time of release from prison. Those men who were still very introverted when they finished treatment showed the highest tendency to repeat their crimes. Since we know that the introversion scores of many offenders changed over the course of treatment, this finding may give treatment staff a way to find out if the treatment approach is working. Introversion was measured on the A scale of the Clinical Analysis Questionnaire, and was defined as being reserved, detached, critical, and aloof. For group therapy to have a beneficial effect, there must be an emotional bonding among members of the therapy group. Without this connection there is little likelihood that other changes will or can happen. Effective therapy groups seek to draw in those individuals who are most isolated and distrustful of others. Obviously, they do not always succeed with every individual. This finding points directly to an important goal for future treatment with incest offenders. It would be of interest to see if this finding would hold up when applied to other types of sex offenders.

The commission of subsequent sex-related crimes was not found to be related to race, education, general intelligence level, duration of abuse, type of sexual acts committed, relationship to victim, violence in marital relationships, the presence of a diagnosable mental disorder, or exposure to incest in the family of origin.

SUMMARY

Our study of incest offenders treated in the Transitional Sex Offenders Program at Lino Lakes Correctional Facility suggests a number of conclusions, several of which are discussed below.

(1) Many offenders, when released, return to some form of family life. One-third of the men returned to the families in which their offenses occurred, and nearly half (49%) were married at the time of follow-up. Approximately 40% of the men who were married or living with partners were residing in households with minor children. One man in our study was working as a day-care provider at the time of the follow-up interview. This suggests that there is a need to extend supervision time in the community following release from prison.

(2) In the opinion of parole officers, at least one-third of all incest offenders who participated in the program were not supervised for an adequate length of time in the community. Moreover, nearly half (45%) needed additional services in order to solve personal problems and reduce the risk of reoffending. Parole officers identified those men

with low incomes and those who had abused biological children as the offenders most likely to need additional help.

(3) In the opinion of both parole officers and offenders, more attention should be given to the resolution of family problems, even in cases where offenders do not expect to return to their original families. This is important both while offenders are in prison and following release. In fact, the act of putting a man in prison severely limits the possibility of family therapy. This needs to be weighed carefully against the need for protecting the community and families.

(4) None of the parole officers suggested lengthening the period of incarceration for offenders. In fact, their comments would suggest that a greater portion of an offender's sentence should be spent in a supervised release program that provides treatment rather than in a prison setting.

(5) The majority of offenders reported that group therapy work involving other incest offenders was the most useful part of the treatment experience. Offenders recommended more contact with incest victims during the period of treatment.

(6) Many incest offenders thought that treatment efforts should be more specialized and tailored more closely to the problems and needs of incest offenders. Many men find that Sex Addicts Anonymous (a 12-step program similar in philosophy to AA) is a useful support group following release.

(7) About 18% of all program participants are returned to prison following release. However, men who complete all phases of the program are less likely to commit additional crimes than those who do not complete the program.

(8) Incest offenders who commit additional sex crimes following treatment in the Transitional Sex Offenders Program are more likely than those who are not convicted of subsequent offenses (a) to have lived in a different household from the victim, (b) to have chemical dependency problems, (c) to have had multiple victims prior to first incarceration, and (d) to score as more introverted at the time of release from prison as measured on the Clinical Analysis Questionnaire.

DISCUSSION

Limitations of the Study

It is important to recognize that incarcerated incest offenders are not the same as all incest offenders. In fact, as Finkelhor and Associates (1986) note, "we know from many other sources of evidence that the vast majority of sexual offenses never are reported, never come to the attention of the authorities, and, even when they do, the probability of conviction is still low" (p. 132). In general, perpetrators with younger victims (under the age of 5) are less likely to be prosecuted because of the difficulty in gathering convincing testimony from the child. Therefore, we would not generalize our findings to men who abuse very young children.

Second, it appears from our profile of offenders that the perpetrators in our sample represent a segment of the offender population with the fewest resources and the most extensive criminal histories. Although we note from other studies that incest offenders are found in all social strata, the men in our sample are predominantly poor, with limited education and marginal work histories. In other words, they are more like the rest of the prison population rather than a cross section of all incest offenders. In addition, 48% of all incest offenders in this program population have previous criminal convictions and at least 21% had tried and failed in a previous community-based treatment program. Thus our data support Finkelhor and Associates' (1986) conclusion that men who are sent to prison for sexually abusing children "have patterns of repetitive offending and . . . often have been convicted of previous offenses. Moreover, they are also men who have committed other kinds of nonsexual criminal acts along with their child molesting" (pp. 132–133).

Problems for Those Who Wish to Change

One of difficulties imposed by incarceration is separation from family members. Of course, separation from the family is seen as extremely important from the point of view of social service professionals who are attempting to prevent abuse from reoccurring. Nonetheless, the initial separation, and particularly the desire to keep the offender separated from his family, may result in additional problems not only for the offender but for other family members as well. Sara Wright's study in this book explores this issue in depth (see Chapter 9).

One respondent gave the following description of growing up in a family where his mother had herself been a victim of sexual abuse and what he saw as "the extremely dysfunctional family" his children live in now:

> My mother did not know how to give us kids a hug because she was still trying to deal with what she went through during most of her life. My

household as a kid was filled with sexual activity. My granddad molested most of my sisters and my mother.

Today my 17-year-old daughter is still in eighth grade, she goes to school filthy dirty. She might comb her hair once a week, but basically she doesn't give a damn. These kids aren't getting any help. My kids are afraid to write to me because they are afraid that they will get in trouble. We need to deal with this incest problem as a whole family. Now everybody sits with their pain alone. They haven't helped my kids one bit. My 7-year-old son will still piss in his pants in the living room because he doesn't care. They were given well-intentioned therapy but it was designed primarily to keep them away from me. While the courts agreed that County Services would provide reports to me on how the children were doing in counseling, they have not followed through on this at all.

Before I had no feelings. I was in torment with no place to turn and I was living like an animal . . . my whole family lived like animals. Now I still have a lot of pain but I can share my pain and my feelings with somebody. I used to have a fantasy world that I came from another place and another planet. Now I have some hope for the future, but I don't feel that my family has any hope. They are still functioning in pretty much the same way that we were functioning as a family when I lived with them. Incest is a family problem and you need to deal with it as a family. We could not get the county officials to help us set up a family counseling session while I was at Lino. If my children aren't helped they can't deal effectively with their problems and they are going to be bad parents like I was.

This interview points out some of the difficulties associated with the treatment of incest offenders. On the one hand, incest offenders who are convicted and sent to prison may have the opportunity to receive more treatment and more intensive treatment than the family members who are left behind. As a result of incarceration, the offender is the focus of attention, and it becomes a goal of the state to change the offender's behavior in order to prevent future sexual crimes against children. It is likely that some attempt to bring family members together with the offender may be beneficial, not only to identify the pain of the victim for the offender but also to encourage some healing that might not take place without face-to-face contact among family members. The offender quoted above concluded by saying:

Sometimes they treat this as more of a physical illness rather than a spiritual one. They view it sometimes as something that can't change, but you can make choices. I'm not denying that there might not be temptation, but you can decide to change. For me this was a learned behavior, it was passed from parent to child. Now I have the ability to choose. I haven't had a drink in five years and I have learned to avoid sexual behavior with children.

NOTES

1. Bruce McManus and others at the Minnesota Department of Corrections provided access to necessary records and other information about men treated in the program. Judith Williams, a research associate at Wilder Research Center, also helped to develop the design, examine the prison records, develop coding schemes, and code information for the analyses. Jane Frost, also of Wilder Research Center, assisted with much of the coding. An Advisory Board was assembled to develop procedures, review data, and discuss study issues as they arose. The board included Bruce McManus, Gail Wik, and Dottie Bellinger, all with the Minnesota Department of Corrections, and Paul Mattessich, the director of Wilder Research Center.

2. Case examples were prepared by Judith Williams (1989) of Wilder Research Center, Saint Paul. Names are fictitious.

REFERENCES

Beck, A. J., & Shipley, B. (1989). *Recidivism of prisoners.* Rockville, MD: U.S. Department of Justice.

Finkelhor, D., & Associates. (1986). *A sourcebook on child sexual abuse.* Beverly Hills, CA: Sage.

McBean, A. (1984). *Intrafamilial sexual abuse: Considering the next steps.* Saint Paul, MN: F. R. Bigelow Foundation.

Owen, G., & Williams, J. (1989). *Incest offenders after treatment: A follow-up study of men released from the Transitional Sex Offenders Program at Lino Lakes Correctional Facility.* Saint Paul, MN: Wilder Foundation.

Russell, D. E. H., Schurman, R., & Trocki, K. (1988). The long-term effects of incestuous abuse: A comparison of Afro-American and white American victims. In G. E. Wyatt & G. J. Powell (Eds.), *Lasting effects of child sexual abuse* (pp. 119–134). Newbury Park, CA: Sage.

13

Female Sexual Offenders: A Typology

JANE KINDER MATTHEWS

RUTH MATHEWS

KATHLEEN SPELTZ

This research focuses on a sample of adult female sex offenders involved with Genesis II for Women, a private, nonprofit community corrections/treatment agency located in Minneapolis, Minnesota, that provides services for adult females and their children. In 1985, when the need for treatment of female sex offenders became apparent, Genesis II established an outpatient adult female sex offender program designed to serve as an alternative to long-term incarceration. Jane Kinder Matthews and Ruth Mathews, both licensed psychologists, developed the Genesis II Female Sexual Offenders Treatment Program. They previously had extensive experience in working with adolescent and adult male sex offenders and nonoffending females.

Although social awareness of sexual abuse has greatly increased over the last decade, the female sexual offender has been virtually invisible. Viewing females as perpetrators of sexual abuse, perhaps parallel to viewing males as victims, challenges traditional cultural stereotypes. Since very little was known about female sexual offenders and their response to treatment, the intent of this study was exploratory. We set out to study variations in female sexual abuse, female offenders, their experiences with criminal justice and child protection services, their reactions to treatment, and the outcomes of treatment.

Professionals who deal with sexual abuse cases may find this information helpful in dispelling stereotypes that can lead to ignoring sexual abuse by a female and overreacting when such abuse is substantiated. A more realistic picture of the kinds of things that women do and their responses to treatment can aid in the effective disposition of these cases.

THE EXISTING KNOWLEDGE BASE

Primarily within the last 10 years, studies and papers have begun to identify and describe incidents of sexual abuse perpetrated by females (Brown, Hull, & Panesis, 1984; Faller, 1987; Mathews, Matthews, & Speltz, 1989; D. McCarty, 1981; L. McCarty, 1986; Wolfe, 1985). Finkelhor and Russell (1984) found that approximately 24% of sexually abused males and 13% of sexually abused females had been victimized by females, either acting alone or with an accomplice. In approximately 42% of the cases of male sexual victimization and 54% of female victimization by females, the female offender was acting in the company of others.

Early research on female sexual offenders was conducted on small samples of women incarcerated for rape (Brown et al., 1984; D. McCarty, 1981). This was followed by studies of females involved in treatment centers for sexually abusing children, usually their own (Marvasti, 1986; L. McCarty, 1986). Most of this research focused on describing the females' offenses and summarizing some psychological and background characteristics. Most recently, typologies of female offenders and treatment strategies specific to working with female offenders have appeared (Faller, 1987; Mathews, 1987; Mathews et al., 1989).

This study went beyond merely identifying female offenders and outlining the kinds of offenses they commit by studying women who were in treatment. We were able to analyze the changes that were apparent as a result of treatment and to assess what kind of threat these women represented to the community, whether they could function in the parental role after treatment, and whether reunification with their children was a viable option.

METHODOLOGY

Recent works have discussed differences between the sexes and have cautioned against assuming that male-derived models apply to females (see, e.g., Belenky, Clinchy, Goldberger, & Tarule, 1986; Gilligan, 1982; Keller, 1985; McCormack, 1987). To avoid adapting existing models for male sexual offenders to females or structuring specific questions that might be irrelevant (since no supporting research base on females exists), a "holistic-inductive" approach to inquiry (Patton, 1990) was chosen, using qualitative methods. This approach assumes that the researcher wishes to understand the totality and gestalt of the phenomenon under investigation and is open to whatever emerges from the data (Patton, 1990).

Our search for in-depth understanding of a limited sample ($N = 16$) of females who had sexually abused made qualitative inquiry particularly appropriate. We supplemented the qualitative data from interviews and case records with quantitative data from psychological testing. Information gathered for clinical purposes included an Intake Interview, Confidential Family History Questionnaire, case notes, assignments, progress reports, and testing (MMPI, Tennessee Self-Concept Scale, and FACES). Three additional interviews were conducted with the women who had entered treatment and remained in the group.

Data were analyzed using qualitative strategies. Case studies were constructed for inductive content analysis. The cross-case analysis focused on patterns, categories, and themes from which an analyst-constructed typology could be generated (Patton, 1990). In addition, interviews were initially coded into broad emerging categories (e.g., offense, child protection, treatment) and then further analyzed for emerging themes.

The sample consisted of 16 females referred to the Genesis II Female Sexual Offenders Treatment Program from May 1985 to December 1987, who formally consented to participate in the research. Referrals originated from three sources: the criminal justice system (10), child protection (5), and a psychiatrist (1). Most of the women (15) were residents of Minnesota; 1 was a resident of Michigan. Two of the females were women of color; the remainder were Caucasian. Each woman was given a fictitious alphabetized research name (Ann through Patti); the first letters of these names are used throughout this chapter to refer to the subjects (e.g., F and G were women of color).

The victims included 1 vulnerable adult and 44 children ranging from infants to adolescents. Of the victims, 28 were female (64%) and 16 were male (36%).

RESULTS

Commonalities and Differences Among Offenses

Table 13.1 summarizes the sexual abuse committed by the women participating in this study. Several differences and similarities in the offenses are noteworthy. First, Ann's offenses differ from those of the

Table 13.1

Sexual Abuse Data

Client	Victim (Ages)[a]	Behaviors[b]	Duration
A	(1) male neighbor (14)	intercourse, oral sex	1 year
	(2) two neighbors, one female one male (13–14)	sex games, strip poker	2 times (45 minutes each)
	(3) two male neighbors	kissing, fondling	1 for 2 weeks 1 for 6 months
B	daughter (4–9)	kissing, fondling	5 years
C	(1) daughter (9)	fondling, showered together	few years
	(2) great niece, brother and two sisters	fondling	unknown
D	four daughters (0–7)	French kiss, oral sex, tongue penetration	2–3 years (once or twice a month)
E	two daughters (0–3)	French kiss, fondling, humping, finger penetration	2–3 years (daily)
F	two sons (4–13)	fondling, humping, penis penetration	6½ years (once every few months)
G	nephew (9)	oral sex	1 year (twice a week)
H	(1) male (3–4) babysitting	humping	1 time
	(2) female cousin (8–10)	kissing, fondling, finger penetration	1¾ years (3 times a week)
I	two daughters and son (2–5)	fondling (oral sex, finger penetration, sex games, masturbation of kids)	6 months (2–3 times a week)

others in that, for the most part, she chose young teenage male victims. At the time of her offending, she described emotional connections such as being "in love" with her longer-term victims. She stated that she believed the relationships were voluntary and she saw the boys as equal partners.

Bonnie, Carol, Dana, Ellen, and Fran abused their own children over the most extensive periods of time in our sample (from two to six and a half years). With the exception of Ellen, all self-reported the abuse out of feelings of guilt or shame. When asked about the abuse, Bonnie, Dana, Ellen, and Fran all mentioned using drugs or alcohol

Table 13.1

(continued)

Client	Victim (Ages)[a]	Behaviors[b]	Duration
J	neighbor twins (13) male/female	spin-the-bottle, oral sex	2 times
K	two sons, daughter, three nieces	kissing, fondling, penetration, spin-the-bottle	2 years (weekly)
L	three daughters, two nephews	kissing, fondling, penetration, spin-the-bottle	2 years, (3 times a week)
M	two sons, two daughters (4–9)	adult sex in front of kids (fondling, oral sex)	5 years (4–5 times a week)
N	best female friend	fondling, finger penetration	1 time
O	(1) daughter (12) and her girlfriend (12)	put snow on vulvas	1 time
	(2) three daughters (4–12)	oral sex with husband in front of kids	1 time
P	stepdaughter (13–17)	fondling, oral sex, tongue penetration	4 years (once or twice a week)

a. Ages represent best estimates.

b. Parentheses ( ) indicate accusations of behavior that denied by client.

during at least part of the time they were sexually abusing. All lived alone with their children during some, if not all, of the abuse.

Grace and Heather were the youngest in our sample. Neither had children of her own and both abused their closest younger relatives. Their victims at the onset of the abuse were generally older than those of the group of women above except Ann. Neither could stop the abuse on her own; it stopped only when she moved out. Each abused the child of a relative who had taken her in and was providing her support.

The remaining eight women reported that their husbands began the abuse, often long before the women became involved. The majority stated that they were initially coerced or forced to participate. Irene differed in that once she discovered the abuse of her children by her husband, she willingly joined in. Although the abuse was initiated or coerced by their husbands, Irene, Jenny, Kris, Lisa, and possibly Marie eventually initiated sexual behavior with the victims independently.

Table 13.2
Sexual Abuse Data

Client	Abuse Pattern	Responsibility	Rationale	Arousal
A	alone	100	love, attention, acceptance	during and fantasies
B	alone	100	no peers, children safe, fusion love and sex, closeness	during and fantasies
C	alone	100	anger, frustration	during
D	alone and with husband	100	young—no harm, low self-esteem, isolation, power, own abuse	during and fantasies
E	alone	20 80 (H)	own abuse, attention, jealous of husband dating, pornography	fantasies
F	alone	100	male rejection, isolation, attention	during and fantasies
G	alone	100	own abuse	fantasies
H	alone	60 40 (V)	anger, revenge, used by males, low self-esteem, control, pornography	during
I	husband first, client joined	60 40 (H)	lonely, unmet needs, own abuse, love, anger at husband's affair	during breast-feeding
J	husband coerced, later client initiated	80 20 (H)	husband's threats to leave, fear of being alone, obeyed him	denies
K	husband coerced, later client initiated	70 30 (H)	fear of husband, love	during
L	husband coerced, later client initiated	80 20 (H)	beatings and threats by husband, dependency on husband, revenge, low self-esteem, unmet needs	during
M	husband coerced (done with husband)	50 50 (H)	male dependent, isolation, tired of life	denies
N	husband coerced	100	"had to—he hit me," scared	denies
O	husband coerced	50 50 (H)	to end abuse, forced by husband	denies
P	husband coerced	50 50 (H)	"he made me," physical abuse	denies

NOTE: (H) = husband blamed; (V) = victim blamed.

Marie and Olivia differ from the other women in that their main behavior was nontouch—that is, they were sexual with adults in the presence of their children. Nancy stands out in that her victim was an adult, her best friend. Her husband was also sexually abusing their daughter during this same time period, but Nancy was not aware of the abuse and did not participate in it.

Patterns of Denial, Acceptance, and Rationale

Table 13.2 shows additional similarities and differences among the women. The information was gathered from the women during the initial two-hour intake session in response to specific questions about their offenses, their responsibility, and their understanding of their behavior.

During intake, all of the women were asked, "How much are you at fault for what happened?" With the exception of Heather, none of the women projected any blame or responsibility for the abuse onto their victims. Of the women who acted alone in the abuse, six out of eight took 100% of responsibility for their actions. When husbands initiated or coerced the sexual abuse, all but one woman shared responsibility with him. Three believed they were equally responsible; the remaining five women took either all or the majority of the blame.

It is noteworthy that even though they were mostly coerced, the women saw themselves as primarily responsible for their behavior. Of the four women who further commented, each felt that she should have done something more to oppose or respond to the abuse.

Rationale

The women were asked, "Why did you commit the offense(s) and how do you understand your behavior now?" Of the 16, 13 stated that a key factor was either prior or present use by, dependency on, or rejection by males. Those who were coerced by their husbands (7) reported dependency, fear, threats, and physical abuse (4) as reasons for their involvement.

> I was sexually abused as a child from quite young on up, until I was a teenager. Some of the same things that I did to my children, some of the inappropriate boundaries, of growing up, of thinking came from the family. (Irene)

> I didn't want my husband to leave me. I didn't want to be alone. He always threatened to leave; "Do what I say." (Jenny)

I didn't want to be there. He wanted me there in case she woke up. Why? I had to. Didn't say no when I should of. He hit me to make sure I did. (Nancy)

Nine of the women described themselves as being needy or in a low period. They reported needing acceptance, attention, and closeness; having unmet needs or low self-esteem; and feeling isolated. Feelings of anger, revenge, power, jealousy, and rejection (but not by or of the victims) were listed by seven women as reasons for their abusing. The majority reported that their children were safe targets for these displaced feelings. Four of the women believed their acts to be expressions of love, either for the victim (A, B, K) or for the husband.

Arousal

Of the 16 women, 11 (all of whom had initiated some of the abuse they perpetrated) acknowledged either arousal or fantasies during offenses. Of the 4 women who reported that they abused only when coerced by a male, none admitted sexual arousal or fantasies. The majority of the women stated that arousal was not a main motivating factor. These women described fantasizing specifically about their victims, not about children in general. Most also reported that their arousal during the abuse was associated with imagining that the children were adult males, or with having power in relationships, something that was absent in their interaction with adults.

Having sex with my sons was more enjoyable than having sex with a man and that was because I had some control over what was going to happen. (Kris)

I was sexually aroused . . . felt very powerful. (Dana)

Backgrounds

One of the most striking findings of both the therapy group and the research effort was the number of common experiences that the women shared in childhood, adolescence, and adulthood. Even though their crimes varied in kind and degree, many of the women were able to identify factors that motivated their antisocial behavior. Tables 13.3, 13.4, and 13.5 show the childhood, adolescent, and adult experiences of the women.

Table 13.3
Childhood Experience

	Client												
Variable	A	B	D	F	H	I	J	K	L	M	N	O	P
Victim sex abuse within family		X	X	X		X			X	X	X	X	X
Victim sex abuse outside family					X	X	X	X		X		X	
Victim physical abuse		X	X		X	X		X	X			X	
Low status in peer group	X	X	X			X	X	X	X	X	X	X	X
Low status in family	X	X		X		X	X	X	X		X	X	X
Poor school performance	X				X	X	X	X	X	X		X	X

Table 13.4
Adolescent Experience

	Client												
Variable	A	B	D	F	H	I	J	K	L	M	N	O	P
Victim sex abuse within family		X	X	X		X			X		X		X
Victim sex abuse outside family	X			X	X	X	X	X				X	X
Victim physical abuse	X	X	X		X								X
Promiscuity	X	X	X		X		X	X	X	X		X	X
Alcohol/drug use onset		X	X	X	X			X	X	X		X	
Feelings of inferiority	X	X	X	X	X	X	X	X	X	X	X	X	X

Table 13.5
Adult Experience

	Client												
Variable	*A*	*B*	*D*	*F*	*H*	*I*	*J*	*K*	*L*	*M*	*N*	*O*	*P*
Victim physical abuse				X			X	X		X		X	X
Victim rape					X				X	X	X	X	X
Mental health problem	X	X						X					
Drug/alcohol addiction		X		X								X	X
Significant weight problem	X	X	X			X	X	X	X			X	X
Work history	X								X	X	X		
Nonassertive with men	X	X	X	X	X	X	X	X	X	X	X	X	X
Coerced into sex abuse others						X	X	X	X	X	X	X	X
Initiated sex abuse others	X	X	X	X	X	X	X	X					

TYPOLOGY OF FEMALE SEX OFFENDERS

Three types of female sex offenders emerged from this study: the teacher/lover offender, the intergenerationally predisposed offender, and the male-coerced offender. Each will be discussed in turn.

The Teacher/Lover Offender

This type of offender had a difficult time believing that her behavior was criminal, since she has no malice for the children she had abused. She taught children about sexuality in discussions and games, and she fell in love with an adolescent male, who became her sexual partner. She saw him as her equal and believed that he would not be sexual with her unless it was a positive interaction and one that he desired. She believed that her sexual favors were an act of kindness that she bestowed upon the youth because she liked him, and she generally endorsed the widely held notion that sex is so important to adolescent males that they are ready and willing for sexual contact at any opportunity.

Some women in this category, like Ann, have been victims of childhood sexual abuse. All had backgrounds fraught with severe emotional and verbal abuse. Family relationships were stormy and marked by many power struggles and misunderstandings. Barren or inconsistent interaction with parents and caregivers was the norm. Many described indulgent mothers but distant, aloof, and emotionally inaccessible fathers. All reported fearful or strained relationships with adult men at the time of their crimes. Many felt so brutalized by men that they turned to an adolescent male. When they fell in love, many women reverted to adolescent feelings and behaviors. Most hoped that the boy would love her, accept her, and be kind to her in ways that adult males were not. In some relationships this was true for a little while, but usually the boys eventually lashed out in hurtful or rejecting ways.

> We had an affair, a love affair. Isn't that ridiculous? I'm 40 years old! And I had an affair with a 14-year-old kid, which is totally ridiculous. And I was in love—not I loved him—but in love!

Ann's "love affair" went bad, but she subsequently offended in games with other neighborhood children. Ann was placed in a treatment program where all the other participants were male. Because of the numerous times that she had been raped, she found it difficult to trust them. While in treatment she reoffended, again with young males. This time she allowed the boys to touch her when they asked "if we can get experimental." She confessed to her therapy group about the new sexual contact and was temporarily suspended from the group. She would have been allowed to continue, but she decided that she wanted to be involved with a group that consisted of women. She was accepted into and successfully completed the Genesis II Sex Offender program.

The Intergenerationally Predisposed Offender

All of these women acted alone in initiating the sexual abuse. Their victims were family members and their own children (except G and H). There are strong indications that sexual abuse had occurred in their families for years, and other family members, such as aunts, uncles, siblings, cousins, parents, and grandparents were also victims of sexual abuse (B, C, D, and G).

These women reported being sexually abused at very early ages by more than one family member or entrusted caretakers. The abuse usually lasted until they were adolescents (B, C, D) and involved more than one type of sexual abuse, such as fondling, oral sex, and/or intercourse. The women reported being able to extricate themselves from the abusive family relationships as adolescents, but they found it extremely difficult to establish positive relationships with adolescent males. Generally, sex was a part of dating for these women and, as they dated more, they developed a reputation for being "easy." Most were promiscuous even though they did not enjoy sex. Being used sexually was terrible for them, but they continued the pattern partly because, as they stated, they did not know they had a right to say no (B, C, D, E, F, G, H), and the price they were paying for acceptance and human contact was very familiar.

These women generally described the relationships with their families as painful. No one spoke openly about the abuse. They kept silent for various reasons. Some feared that their mothers would be devastated if the abuse came to light. Those who did tell were often blamed and punished. Others believed that they were evil and that all the pain they endured was appropriate punishment from God (B, C, D, F, G). These women reported lashing out and hurting those around them, even as children. They physically abused siblings and relatives, became oppositional, and refused to do schoolwork. Their negative behavior did not make sense to their families, and they became the "black sheep." As such, they shared very few positive experiences with other family members and developed very few strong emotional bonds. Their self-destructive behavior (B, C, E, F, G, H) was viewed by their families with shame, which reinforced their own sense of worthlessness. In adolescence, they discovered that substances such as food, alcohol, and cigarettes could give them comfort.

All the women reported being involved in many unhealthy and dangerous relationships. They reported being so hungry for love and attention that they would do almost anything to keep men around.

The Male-Coerced Offender

These women were very passive and reported feeling powerless in interpersonal relationships. They all endorsed, directly or indirectly, the traditional life-style of husband/father as the breadwinner and wife/mother as the homemaker. Their husbands were feared and in charge. The women felt dependent and tried very hard not to antagonize their husbands. They all married quite young and had very limited work histories and few marketable skills.

All these women reported that their relationships with men had never been good. All had been sexually abused by men as children, some by their fathers and their fathers' friends, some by father surrogates, one by older brothers, and two by strangers. None of the women told about the sexual abuse and all stated that they were frightened of men. At the same time, they yearned for someone to protect and take care of them. They had very little faith that they could do that themselves.

All the women reported fearing that they could not attract a husband, so they felt the need to preserve the relationship they had, even if it was painful and abusive. Many of these women married men they did not care about. They feared being alone and reasoned that marriage with a man they did not love was better than no marriage at all. The men totally dominated these women. Verbal, physical, and sexual abuse were part of their relationships.

The male-coerced offenders reported that their lives became more and more chaotic over time. The demands of their husbands became more extreme as they capitalized on the women's fear of being alone, thereby assuring compliance with their demands.

In all of these cases the man began sexually abusing and then brought the woman into the abuse. Only one (I) participated willingly. One (N) did as she was instructed in spite of great emotional turmoil and sadness. Five of the women (A, J, K, L, O) became involved only after a struggle. Some of the women (J, M, N, O, P) acted only in concert with a male, but others (I, K, L) eventually initiated sexual abuse themselves.

THE WOMEN'S EXPERIENCE OF TREATMENT

The third in the series of interviews focused on the women's experience of the sex offender outpatient program and resulting changes. Of the 16 women, 7 (A, B, I, J, K, M, O) participated in this interview (including one poor-quality recording). Of the 9 not interviewed, 7 were no longer participating in the research and 2 (F, N) had participated in treatment for such a short time that questioning would have been premature.

Since only half the women who completed treatment (two of four) and the majority of the women who failed treatment (three of four) did not participate in this interview, the results are limited. The statements most accurately represent women active in the program who were nearing completion of treatment and those having a successful treatment experience up to the time of the interview.

The interview results discussed below concern the women's insight into sexual abuse and insight into male dependency, and their thoughts on parenting, self-worth, the sex offender program itself, and hopes for the future. All of the women interviewed had either success-fully completed treatment or were in good standing (except I).

Insight into Sexual Abuse

The women distinguished (as if it were new learning) the difference between positive and negative touch. They expressed empathy for their victims and for themselves. They also expressed a belief that no one should be sexually abused. Four of the women (J, K, M, O) spoke of their past pattern of being dependent on or submissive to men. They saw this as undesirable and were committed to change.

> I wasn't a whole person unless there was somebody else with me. That's pretty much what it's been like for a long time. There had to be a male in my life, otherwise I would think I was nobody. Now I'm working on being important to myself. (Marie)

Parenting

Three of the women (M, K, O) talked about their children and the struggle they experienced in either terminating parental rights or fighting to retain custody of their children.

> Wanting my children back. It took me a long time to decide what I wanted. I was very mixed up. Did I deserve 'em? Would I be a good mother? Would I be anything good to them? A lot of self-doubts. And now that I know I can be a good mother, a good person, I feel that I deserve my children back. (Olivia)

Self-Worth

The women were asked to describe how they were when the abuse occurred and how they are now. The theme that emerged was one of increased self-worth and self-respect. They spoke of being whole per-sons, being capable, caring about themselves, and being happy.

> Yeah, it's really different because it's like watching a different person go to work. It's not me, it's another person in there, when I compare to the

way I used to be. It's just different—every feeling with people is different. I can talk, say more what I feel. Say a lot more. I feel like a different person that way. I can get as angry or as frustrated or whatever, and no way. I can't never see myself doing that again. I feel more equal with people. I don't put everybody up on pedestals. I don't know, I guess I just feel like a person. I never felt like a person. I don't know what I was but not a person. (Bonnie)

The Offender Program

In the interview, the women were asked what, for them, was the most significant aspect of treatment. Time and again they spoke of not being condemned for the sexual abuse they perpetrated. They felt the treatment group was a safe place to talk about the abuse. They took great comfort in knowing there were other women who were perpetrators of sexual abuse. They felt understood, accepted, and cared about.

Of all the programs that I've been involved with, this is the one I like to be at. 'Cause I feel accepted here. That I'm not a horrible person, that I'm not being judged. Even though it's hard for me to talk about sexual abuse. "What kind of person is that? Oh, my God! I'm in the same room with her!" But here I don't feel that. No matter what I've done—right or wrong—I'm still me. (Marie)

Future

The women were asked what the future held for them. They spoke of education, work, and children:

And it's just been wonderful. Just having them with me again. Pauline's opening up, telling me about the sexual abuse that Ralph did; what Ralph did to her. Beckie and me are becoming more close. She knows that I'm going to protect her. There's a few points that we have to work out yet. . . . So I see us as working as a family for the next five years, hopefully. (Olivia)

Comments about the impact of the treatment program were made in the other two interviews as well as in case notes, group exercises, and therapeutic assignments. In addition to the changes that the women identified above, they saw themselves changing by virtue of the fact that they could identify in their outlook and functioning increased empathy, increased trust, decreased shame, increased courage and strength, increased awareness of appropriate boundaries, and increased assertiveness.

Analysis of Treatment Impact: A Framework

This study's findings can be viewed in terms of the developmental model offered by Belenky et al. in their book *Women's Ways of Knowing* (1986), in which they identify five "ways of knowing." Women in the "Silence" category experience themselves as mindless, voiceless, and subject to the whims of external authority. Those operating out of "Received Knowledge" perceive themselves as capable of receiving, even reproducing knowledge from all-knowing external authorities, but do not see themselves as capable of creating knowledge on their own. Women evidencing "Subjective Knowledge" view truth and knowledge as based in subjective/personal experience (intuition and knowing). "Procedural Knowledge" is the category representing women who are invested in learning and formal processes for objectively obtaining and communicating knowledge. Women operating out of the final perspective, "Constructed Knowledge," view all knowledge as contextual; they experience themselves as creators of knowledge and value both subjective and objective strategies for knowing.

At the time of their crimes, most of the women in this study described themselves as like the women in Silence. As Belenky et al. reported, these women felt deaf and dumb. They operated out of blind obedience, were passive, subdued, subordinate, and perceived their knowledge of self as lodged in others. They lived in isolation, often with violence. Unlike the women operating out of Received Knowledge, these women were not able to hear the voices of others.

As noted earlier, the women studied had histories of abuse, isolation, feelings of inferiority, passivity, male dependency, shame, and lack of self-development. Test data (MMPI and Tennessee Self-Concept Scales) supported the women's statements regarding their lack of social and self-development. All of the offenders, to some degree, experienced abuse at the hands of others, male dependence, neediness, and isolation as key factors leading to their sexual abuse. The seven who were coerced by men obeyed their husbands' wishes to abuse others sexually.

In describing their offenses some of the women spoke about being unable to hear their children:

> I wasn't paying attention to the children and the other abuse. . . . I didn't see what the kids were needing. (Irene)

The women's statements and changes in pre- and posttesting showed development of other perspectives or ways of knowing, especially Received and Subjective Knowing. Women newly operating within the perspective of Received Knowledge viewed themselves as learners. They actively listened as a way of knowing. They relied on authorities, others, and social expectations for self-knowledge and definition. The women spoke of these movements and developments. The structure of the program, which includes group involvement, helped counter their isolation.

> The biggest thing was I didn't feel like I was alone. . . . There was a bunch of women, all in there for the same thing. It was very comforting. It wasn't threatening. It was women that could understand. (Irene)

The women frequently talked about the importance of learning ("receiving knowledge") about sexual abuse, boundaries, and the abuse they suffered (B, J, K, M, O). For example, Kris learned to view her children differently—as human beings. This led to greater awareness of the impact of her actions and empathy for her victims. The women's insights into sexual abuse indicated a need for education in child development basics as part of the treatment process, even at the beginning of treatment, where it could help establish a foundation for further understanding, change, and growth.

As Erikson's (1963) taxonomy indicates, a self lodged in shame and doubt cannot gain autonomy. The women's statements regarding the offender program consistently stressed that a nonjudgmental, caring, direct, and supportive approach by treatment providers was crucial to their movement out of shame toward change and identity development. Being nurtured and taught facilitated their growth. As many indicated, this was a new experience for them. Three women (A, K, L) indicated that their previous involvement in programs that lacked these ingredients was unproductive (e.g., Ann further offended and Kris acted out sexually with a fellow group member).

As Belenky et al. describe, women's movement out of Silence and Received Knowledge or external authority to Subjective Knowledge is a leap. This transition is a step in becoming self-protective, assertive, and defined. Eventually the woman becomes her own authority or inner expert. Some of the women from all three offender typology groups described their moves to Subjective Knowing (A, B, K, O).

> I've been learning who I am and discovering myself. . . . I've always thought of myself as "I can't do nothing right." And I've given up on myself a lot. And now I kind of feel like I'm a good person and I do have goals and dreams that I want to reach. I've even carried out some of them. (Kris)

Olivia described her changing self: "Just like a flower when it's starting to blossom. . . . First, it's real weak. Then it's open and it sorta becomes stronger and stronger and it sorta reaches for the sun."

Four of the male-coerced offenders (J, K, M, O) also spoke about moving out of submissive, dependent relationships with men and becoming assertive and self-protective, indicative of Subjective Knowledge. As these women asserted, once they began discovering themselves and feeling like whole persons, they were no longer willing to enter into or remain in abusive relationships, especially if hurting others was involved. For the male-coerced offender, becoming her own authority and, therefore, having the option to leave an abusive relationship appeared critical. Without a separate identity, the women could not confront the abuse and leave their husbands, for, as Marie stated, "I would think I was a nobody."

As they developed greater self-definition, those who successfully participated in treatment (A, B, D, and F through P) viewed their past experiences differently. Regarding the abuse she received from her family, Olivia stated, "I just realized that because it happened doesn't mean I deserved it." She, like others in the study (B, D, E, G, H, I), identified a connection between the abuse she received and the abuse she perpetrated. Having worked through her own abuse, Olivia asserted, "The connection's broke, so I know I'd never sexually abuse my children again."

Some realized their limitations. In the process of therapy, Marie, Kris, and Lisa came to the realization that giving up their children for adoption was in the best interests of the children.

DESIGNING PROGRAMS
FOR FEMALE OFFENDERS

The sex offender treatment program at Genesis II was facilitated by women, informed by literature and research regarding gender differences, and specifically designed for women. All three of the women who previously attended sex offender programs designed and attended by males (A, K, L) reoffended or failed while in these programs; all three were successful or in good standing in the Genesis II program. While acknowledging the limited nature of our data, we believe our study raises questions about whether programs for male sex offenders produce effective results for women.

The results of this study are limited in their generalizability to programs employing a different philosophy or approach, such as programs that support highly confrontive, authoritative, nonnurturing, indirect, or objective, goal-oriented approaches. The women clearly and consistently stated that what was most critical to their process of change was care, support, and a nonjudgmental atmosphere, where they felt respected as equal human beings. Indirect techniques (e.g., paradoxical injunctions) in which the therapists manipulate might not facilitate the women's resolution of basic trust versus mistrust issues, the foundation of all growth (Erikson, 1963). Confrontive styles, involving harsh, loud, or inconsistent criticism, patronizing remarks, or sarcasm do not engender trust, respect, openness, or a feeling of safety. Women who had been in other therapy programs reported that these tactics, as well as those encouraging deviant fantasy, harsh and critical confrontation, and an aloof or superior stance by the therapists were therapeutically counterproductive. Based on the women's statements, their progress in treatment was augmented by the therapists' genuine and direct love, care, concern, feedback, acceptance, and respect.

The results of this study provide no support for theories such as those of Samenow (1985) and Yochelson and Samenow (1977), who propose that sexual offenders have a "criminal personality" that therapists must break down. On the contrary, these data suggest that female offenders have little ego development, understand that their behavior is wrong, exhibit empathy for their victims, and rarely project blame onto their victims. There is no evidence to support the notion that these women are intentionally malicious people possessing rigidly structured deviant personalities.

Neither is there much support for the diagnosis of antisocial personality disorder. These women most frequently presented characteristics similar to borderline, avoidance, and dependent personality disorders, some of which appear to stem from other environmental influences in addition to the sexual abuse. While working on past abuse, the women also exhibited characteristics of posttraumatic stress syndrome. Attacking the weak ego that these women show on the MMPI would probably push them to decompensation, stripping them of the few resources for change that they have.

In general, the female sex offenders under study entered into treatment with very little ego or self-development, as measured by the MMPI and the Tennessee Self-Concept Scale. The majority of treatment changes described by the women (trust, identity, and self-worth) showed the importance of a developmental treatment approach. These women viewed a caring, nonjudgmental, direct treatment modality as most helpful in creating change. Through learning about critical topics—sexual abuse, healthy sexuality, and parenting—and being nurtured, many of the women were able to develop a sense of self and to become "real people." This learning and self-development appeared to be instrumental in helping the women reach their treatment goals.

CONCLUSION

Relatively little is known about female sexual offenders. Most of the research has been conducted within the last 10 years and has focused on profiling adult female perpetrators. Through these limited research efforts, tentative preliminary portraits of different types of female sexual offenders are emerging.

More research on the child, adolescent, and adult female sexual offender is needed. Further development and expansion of typologies will provide greater understanding of the dynamics of female-perpetrated sexual abuse. Studies regarding treatment, prognosis, and outcome are lacking, and there is no known longitudinal research on female sexual offenders. Also, little is known regarding the impact (short or long term) of female-perpetrated sexual abuse on male and female victims, or whether the victim's relationship to the offender (e.g., mother, nonrelative) or type of offense (e.g., teacher/lover, predisposed) would bring about different effects.

As our cultural awareness increases, traditional cultural sexual stereotypes will continue to be challenged. Likewise, as perceived power differentials between males and females are confronted, our perceptions of females as offenders, males as victims, and what is considered sexual abuse may change. We hope, as our knowledge of female offenders increases, to be better able to identify this population and to treat its members more adequately.

REFERENCES

Belenky, M. F., Clinchy, B. M., Goldberger, N. R., & Tarule, J. M. (1986). *Women's ways of knowing: The development of self, voice, and mind.* New York: Basic Books.
Brown, M. E., Hull, L. A., & Panesis, S. K. (1984). *Women who rape.* Boston: Massachusetts Trial Court.
Erikson, E. H. (1963). *Childhood and society* (2nd ed.). New York: W. W. Norton.
Faller, K. (1987). Women who sexually abuse children. *Violence and Victims, 2,* 263–276.
Finkelhor, D., & Russell, D. (1984). Women as perpetrators. In D. Finkelhor, *Child sexual abuse: New theory and research* (pp. 171–185). New York: Free Press.
Gilligan, C. (1982). *In a different voice.* Cambridge, MA: Harvard University Press.

Keller, E. F. (1985). *Reflections on gender and science.* New Haven, CT: Yale University Press.

Marvasti, J. (1986). Incestuous mothers. *American Journal of Forensic Psychiatry, 7*(4), 63–69.

Mathews, R. (1987). *Preliminary typology of female sexual offenders.* Unpublished manuscript.

Mathews, R., Matthews, J., & Speltz, K. (1989). *Female sexual offenders: An exploratory study.* New York: Safer Society Press.

McCarty, D. (1981). *Women who rape.* Unpublished manuscript.

McCarty, L. (1986). Mother-child incest: Characteristics of the offender. *Child Welfare, 65,* 447–458.

McCormack, T. (1987). Machismo in media research: A critical review of research on violence and pornography. *Social Problems, 25,* 547–559.

Patton, M. Q. (1990). *Qualitative evaluation and research methods.* Newbury Park, CA: Sage.

Samenow, S. E. (1985). *Inside the criminal mind.* New York: New York Times Books.

Wolfe, F. A. (1985, March 3–5). *Twelve female sexual offenders.* Paper presented at the conference, "Next Steps in Research on the Assessment and Treatment of Sexually Aggressive Persons (Paraphiliacs)," Saint Louis, MO.

Yochelson, S., & Samenow, S. E. (1977). *The criminal personality* (Vols. 1–2). New York: Jason Aronson.

PART IV
SYNTHESIS

14

Patterns, Themes, and Lessons

MICHAEL QUINN PATTON

Taken one by one, chapter by chapter, each of the studies in this book is quite narrow in focus and limited in its contribution to our understanding of family sexual abuse. Taken together, these studies provide a panoramic collage of the tragic phenomenon of child sexual abuse. These studies focus on quite different populations and problems. They cover a full range of issues, from identification of sexual abuse to treatment of both victims and perpetrators, as well as investigation of the causes and correlates of family sexual abuse. That the whole is greater than the sum of the parts is no mere cliché in this instance. The themes, patterns, and insights that cut across these studies emerge as a mosaic that is true to the diversity and complexity of the phenomenon even as it illuminates core motifs and issues. It is the task of this chapter to arrange the distinct pieces so as to reveal the emergent mosaic.

CONTEXT

Though each was conducted as an independent, freestanding inquiry, these studies share a common geographic, historical, and political context—Minnesota in the late 1980s. Chapter 2, by Margaret Bringewatt, established that shared context, including the common framework of the Family Sexual Abuse Project under which these studies were funded. The purposes of the Family Sexual Abuse Project were to support new evaluation and research projects that would advance the state of knowledge regarding intervention and treatment with families who have experienced sexual abuse, and to disseminate findings to a wide range of professionals and policymakers. This book is part of that dissemination commitment.

These research projects were funded through an open, competitive proposal and bidding process. An independent project advisory committee of family child abuse professionals selected the projects for funding based on their collective perception of the importance of the topic, methodological appropriateness, and the proposed project's potential contribution to our understanding of family sexual abuse—its origins, correlates, pervasiveness, effects on families, demands on intervention systems, and amenability to treatment.

That these studies are frontline inquiries conducted collaboratively by practitioners and researchers is especially noteworthy. The principal investigators and senior authors on 6 of the 11 studies are practitioners—physicians, clinicians, program directors, and therapists—who are professionally active at the forefront of family sexual abuse treatment and intervention in Minnesota. The 5 studies directed by researchers could not have been done without the collaboration and cooperation of clinicians, program staff, and prison officials. These research projects epitomize the ways in which practitioners and researchers can work together at the local level to investigate and reflect on important questions of mutual interest, thereby improving local practice and informing local policy dialogues even while contributing to the national research agenda.

Because family sexual abuse research is still an emergent, exploratory field of inquiry mirroring the stage of development of family sexual abuse treatment and policy, it is premature to seek comprehensive explanations, global generalizations, or definitive answers. Far from confidently providing answers, researchers and practitioners are still trying to formulate the appropriate questions and prioritize the research agenda. Given our quite limited understanding of child sexual abuse, practice is necessarily highly situational and policies are still evolving. Those closest to the action—local practitioners and frontline researchers—are in the best positions to capture the diversity that characterizes the field. These 11 studies now take their modest place (Minnesotans being humble by nature) within the burgeoning interdisciplinary field of family sexual abuse research, providing a frontline perspective on some of the problems and issues of national and international import analyzed by Jon Conte in the first chapter.

The overview and synthesis that follows will highlight distinct findings, identify common conclusions and mutually reinforcing patterns across studies, and examine some of the methodological lessons learned from the variety of research strategies employed.

THE SCOPE AND SEVERITY OF THE PROBLEM

The studies show that family sexual abuse is a significant problem in Minnesota. The Children's Hospital study, by Levitt, Owen, and Truchsess (Chapter 3), notes that the number of reported cases of child sexual abuse in Minnesota increased 133% from 1982 to 1984 and another 18.6% from 1984 to 1987, with a total of 8,392 cases reported in 1987 (the last year for which data were available). Children's Hospital of Saint Paul is a primary evaluation site in the Upper Midwest for children who are suspected of being sexually abused. Between 1982 and 1986, more than 900 children were referred for evaluation of suspected abuse to Dr. Carolyn Levitt, director of outpatient services at Children's Hospital. The records of 482 children evaluated in 1985 and 1986 were studied for this project.

Many sexually abused children are quite young. The Hewitt and Friedrich study of preschool children (Chapter 4) reports that 65% of referrals to the Midwest Children's Resource Center, a specialized child abuse program in Saint Paul, are children under age 6 suspected of having been sexually abused, as are approximately 50% of referrals seen in the Section of Psychology at the Mayo Clinic. Of the 111 preschool children assessed, 57% were identified as having a probable history of sexual abuse, 17% were determined not to have been abused, and abuse was uncertain but possible for the remaining 26%.

O'Brien's study of the seriousness of sibling incest (Chapter 5) includes all male adolescent sexual offenders referred to the PHASE treatment program in Saint Paul from January 1985 through June 1987. These 170 offenders admitted to having committed a total of 1,636 criminal sexual acts against 461 victims, a mean of nearly 10 criminal sexual acts per offender and almost 3 victims per offender overall.

The Owen and Steele follow-up study of previously incarcerated incest offenders (Chapter 12) includes data on numbers of victims of the 108 men in the sample. Only 25% of these men were known to have had or were suspected of having had a single victim; 45% had two or three known victims and 30% had four or more victims, including one man who had at least 12 victims. For the majority of victims the abuse went on for more than a year, and in 83% of the cases the abuse included vaginal or oral penetration or oral sex. Minnesota places fewer convicted offenders in prison than all but one other state, so these cases probably represent the more serious incest cases with the best evidence for prosecution.

Carter and Parker's study of family sexual abuse in the American Indian community (Chapter 7) cites statistics from the Division of Indian Work that "80% of American Indian families in urban areas now have a history of family violence including incest, sexual abuse, and battering."

In various ways the findings from each of the 11 studies show that many more people are affected by family sexual abuse than just the victim and the perpetrator. The entire family is involved and affected in ways that create or intensify severe stress and dysfunction. Hewitt and Friedrich (Chapter 4) argue that, given the primacy of maternal and family variables, family sexual abuse research must be conceptualized as ecological and developmental. The ecosystem perspective of Maddock, Gusk, and Lally (Chapter 11) is similarly concerned not only with the possible psychopathology of the perpetrator or the effects of abuse on the victim but also with disturbances in the total family system and the family's interactions with the larger community and society.

In short, the problem of family sexual abuse affects a large number of individuals and family members in Minnesota and affects them intensely, often over long periods of time. Moreover, the data show that severe demands are being made on social services and the criminal justice system as a result of the pervasiveness, intensity, and scope of the problem.

DISPELLING COMMON MYTHS

Each of the studies contributes in an important way to greater understanding of the nature of family sexual abuse and its implications. The Family Sexual Abuse Project included, by design, a commitment to engage policymakers and practitioners in research-based discussions about child sexual abuse. Each year (1988, 1989, and 1990) as research findings became available the project sponsored a one- or two-day workshop at which professionals and policymakers could hear the findings and discuss their implications. More than 100 people participated in each of those conferences. The conference discussions, in small groups and large plenary sessions, often focused on sorting out myths from reality. Each study makes a significant contribution in this regard by dispelling stereotypes and common misperceptions about sexual abuse.

One common misperception is that sexual abuse is primarily a problem of poorly educated, low-income families. Woodworth's follow-up study of the Wilder Family Project (Chapter 8) found that the typical family being treated in that program was fairly well educated (parents with more than a high school education). This program served 22 families; only 1 of the 22 families was receiving welfare at the time of intake. These were middle-class families with well-educated, working parents, yet they experienced problems with family sexual abuse.

The Children's Hospital follow-up study (Chapter 3) is based on a larger sample (N = 220 families). While one-third of affected families fell below the poverty level, the average income was $28,500. The data show that 88% of the parents had at least a high school diploma. A large proportion of these families, then, were middle-class families.

Nor is family sexual abuse only an urban problem. The data show that 25% of the Children's Hospital referrals were from rural Minnesota. Likewise, 25% of the male adolescent offenders in the PHASE program (Chapter 5) were from rural counties.

The data from these studies also show that the problem of family sexual abuse occurs in families of all kinds of compositions: families with both natural parents, families with single parents, families with stepparents, families with foster parents, families with one or two children, and families with a number of children.

In short, like the earlier discovery that problems of alcohol and drug abuse were not limited to poor, uneducated families, we now know that problems of family sexual abuse cut across all sectors of society and involve all kinds of families. This is by no means a problem restricted to the poor, uneducated, and obviously mentally disturbed.

Another common belief dispelled by these studies is that family sexual abuse is primarily a problem between fathers or stepfathers and daughters. Of the 170 male adolescent offenders in the PHASE study, about 30% were *sibling* incest offenders. These were older siblings (at least five years older than the victim) who used force or threats of force, manipulation, and bribery to sexually exploit younger siblings. Compared with other types of adolescent offenders, the sibling incest offenders committed a greater number of sexual crimes, had more extensive sexual contacts with their victims, and were judged to commit more serious sexual offenses than either nonsibling child molesters or nonchild offenders. While sibling incest is often thought by the public and policymakers to be the least serious kind of child sexual abuse, these data depict sibling incest as a very severe and widespread problem, often a manifestation of highly dysfunctional family systems.

The Children's Hospital study found that 29% of perpetrators were natural fathers and 7% were stepfathers; more than 60% of perpetrators, then, were *other than* fathers or stepfathers. Some 12% were natural or nonnatural brothers. Thus it is clear that family sexual abuse involves a full range of relationships with perpetrators, including uncles, grandfathers, mothers, mothers' boyfriends, male babysitters, victims' friends, and close family acquaintances.

The Lino Lakes follow-up study of sex offenders (Chapter 12) reports that in 85% of the cases studied, the offender lived with the victim during the time the abuse occurred. Victims were of all ages, with 19% age 8 or younger at the time the abuse was disclosed. Most abuse had occurred over a period of more than a year.

The Hewitt and Friedrich study (Chapter 4) brings data to bear on the myth that little can be done to substantiate sexual abuse in very young, preschool children. Among 111 preschool cases they were able to substantiate abuse in 57% of the children. They then documented the pervasive and disturbing behavioral effects on both "probably abused" and "abuse-uncertain" children. They conclude that allegations of sexual abuse among preschoolers should be taken seriously:

> Not only is sexual abuse associated with significant behavioral impacts, but using careful observation, extensive history taking, and empirically based assessments, we were able to determine the veracity of sexual abuse allegations in the majority of children.

They go on to lament the fact that "despite our ability to assess the majority of these children, they were almost never given the opportunity to testify and their perpetrators were usually not confronted with their misdeeds."

Another myth is that females are the sole victims of child sexual abuse, with male victims of incest being relatively rare. Yet 10% of the victims in the Lino Lakes offender follow-up study (Chapter 12) were sons or stepsons, most of whom (73%) were victims of anal intercourse. Moreover, 57% of the 110 men in the Lino Lakes study were themselves victims of family sexual abuse. The American Indian study (Chapter 7) found that few males were reported as victims in the case files examined, but the study reports the view of one experienced professional that "Indian males are victims much more frequently than is reported."

O'Brien's study of adolescent male sexual offenders (Chapter 5) leads him to conclude that male offenders' prior sexual victimization is a significant contributing factor in the development of offending behaviors. More than 38% of the 170 male adolescents in his study disclosed that they had been sexually abused; sibling incest offenders had the highest rate of prior victimization (42%). Thus boys as well as girls are victims of family sexual abuse, with male victims at high risk of themselves becoming perpetrators.

Gilgun's in-depth study (Chapter 6) of 48 adults maltreated as children includes 36 men. She found that the boy victims typically lacked a confidant or anyone with whom they could talk about their victimization. They tended to become isolated and their social development was arrested, sometimes severely. Differences in sex role socialization, especially the male tendency to be less disclosing of feelings and pain, may increase the risk that boy victims will become perpetrators.

Another group, like boy incest victims, that stands outside common stereotypes is that of female sexual offenders. Indeed, the victims of female sexual offenders are often, but not exclusively, boys. The study by Matthews, Mathews, and Speltz (Chapter 13) documents in depth and detail the serious and devastating nature of female perpetration of sexual abuse on both male and female children. The researchers' portrayals of 16 female sexual offenders provide important insights into the ways in which females get caught up in and contribute to sexual dysfunction and abuse often, but not always, under male coercion.

EFFECTS ON VICTIMS AND FAMILIES

These studies show the devastating effects of child sexual abuse on victims and family systems. Nearly half of the Children's Hospital study families (Chapter 3) reported significant, identifiable problems for the child as a result of the sexual abuse. Of additional importance, the impact on the family was often perceived by the respondent as greater than that on the victim, with 70% reporting that the abuse caused considerable problems for the family. The study emphasizes the need for service providers and the criminal justice system to acknowledge and respond to child sexual abuse as an event that affects the whole family system, not only the victim. There is considerable evidence of the need for more counseling and assistance to families experiencing the trauma of child sexual abuse. The other studies in various ways corroborate this conclusion.

The study of preschool sexual abuse victims (Chapter 4) analyzes dysfunctional behaviors observed in very young, often preverbal, victims. Hewitt and Friedrich found a variety of negative behavioral effects that led them to conclude that these young children need careful monitoring, specialized attention, and therapeutic intervention. The authors emphasize their belief that the focus of intervention and treatment should be on the whole family while also assuring individual therapy for victims.

The female offenders study (Chapter 13) provides particularly dramatic documentation of the nature of family abuse through the detailed presentation of case data (only a small amount of which could be presented in this book). The case studies take the reader into these dysfunctional families and abusive situations in a way that provides insight into how devastating it is to be involved in and to experience abuse.

The severity and longevity of abuse reported in the sibling incest study (Chapter 5) dispels any notion that sexual abuse among siblings is child's play. The emotionally laden stories told to interviewers in the Children's Hospital study (Chapter 3) provide significant data about the effects of family sexual abuse on family members.

The study of the effects of removing offenders from the home (Chapter 9) shows that removing the offender typically has devastating financial consequences for the families involved. Financial stress adds to already-intense psychological stress and enlarges the scope of total family victimization, anger, and grief. Offender removal also works to weaken family structures further in ways that many of those interviewed perceived as punishing the whole family, not just the offender. "Offender removal seemed to put already shaky marriages more firmly on the divorce track." Especially difficult was the "boundary ambiguity" of dealing with whether the offender was "in" or "out" of the family system. Furthermore, family members had difficulty finding time to deal with each other when additional jobs had to be taken to meet financial hardships, and treatment sessions and being monitored by the system took up time. Many interviewees felt that with more support and time, their marriages could have been saved.

Removing offenders typically increased feelings of safety by reducing the threat of recurring sexual abuse (a major reason for removal being to protect the remaining family members), but it also contributed to other kinds of fears, especially fears of being alone without a man in the house. Family power relationships and other family dynamics are clearly affected by family sexual abuse. This study concludes with recommendations for how to reduce family stress and disruption while providing for safety and change.

The study of families reunited after family sexual abuse (Chapter 10) tells the story of the long-term struggle to deal with the effects on the family. It is clear that there is no simple way for families to put the past behind them. The abuse becomes a pervasive context for family relationships. Victims deal with the continuing anger and mistrust. Mothers deal with guilt, uncertainty, and fear. Perpetrators struggle to find a new basis for relationships clouded by actions for which they know they bear responsibility.

In short, taken in combination, these studies contribute substantially to documentation of the serious nature of the problem, the horror of sexual abuse for child victims, the disruption of the whole family, and the struggle to heal wounds that are deep, painful, and resistant to healing.

UNDERSTANDING THE REASONS FOR CHILD SEXUAL ABUSE

Both the literature cited by these studies and the findings from the studies themselves make it clear that there is no single, straightforward explanation for child sexual abuse. These studies, however, tend to add to and confirm some major patterns and possibilities current in the field of sexual abuse research.

The results show that child sexual abuse is, as commonly suspected, very often an intergenerational phenomenon. All but one of the women studied in the female offenders program (Chapter 13) were victims of childhood sexual abuse, most of them within their own families. They were also typically victims of physical abuse.

In the study of adolescent male offenders (Chapter 5), 38% reported having been sexually abused themselves prior to abusing others. Gilgun (Chapter 6) studied 15 perpetrators of child sexual abuse, all of whom had been abused as children. The Wilder Family Project evaluation (Chapter 8) also found support for the hypothesis that incestuous behavior is learned within the family system and passed on from one generation to another. The Lino Lakes study of child sex abuse offenders (Chapter 12) found that 57% of the men had experienced incest in their families of origin. Hewitt and Friedrich (Chapter 4) found that over 50% of the mothers of sexually abused children had experienced sexual abuse.

Yet, these studies also show that not all victims of abuse become abusers, and that not all abusers have been victims or members of families where abuse had previously occurred. In short, abusers and perpetrators have often been abused or been a part of abusive family systems, but prior abuse is not universal enough to make this the primary explanation for child sexual abuse.

Another major factor often related to family sexual abuse is alcohol and drug abuse. These studies confirm alcohol and drug abuse as major contributing problems to family dysfunction generally and child sexual abuse specifically. Gilgun found alcoholism to be prevalent among both the perpetrators and the fathers of the perpetrators she interviewed. Over half of the adolescent male sex offenders' families reported chemical abuse problems (Chapter 5). Of the Children's Hospital families, 38% had experienced stressful events related to alcohol and drug abuse (Chapter 3). The American Indian community study reported that chemical abuse is commonly a problem for victims and offenders, and that while alcohol cannot be considered a cause of incest, it is frequently present and, "in the presence of alcohol, incest is more likely to occur" (Chapter 7). Of the Lino Lakes male sex offenders, 66 reported current or recent chemical dependency problems (Chapter 12).

Another clearly contributing factor is the social isolation of offenders. Gilgun's study (Chapter 6) and that on female offenders (Chapter 13) provide considerable insight into the early lives of male and female offenders. These data show strong and consistent patterns of childhood social isolation, alienation, and lack of development of interpersonal skills and competence among perpetrators. This appears to lead to an inability of offenders to take into account the effects of abuse on victims. The sibling incest study (Chapter 5) shows strong patterns of social isolation among male sex offenders. The Wilder Family Project follow-up study discusses the importance of establishing friendships and being able to experience love relationships as part of effective treatment and adjustment.

These studies provide independent corroborative data that childhood experiences of extreme social isolation and alienation may contribute to subsequent child sexual abuse in adults. Such a finding, which focuses on the individual psychopathology of offenders, has important implications for treatment and rehabilitation as well as for prevention.

A final motif in the search for understanding why family sexual abuse occurs is that the families in which it occurs are often severely dysfunctional (see especially Chapters 4, 5, and 9 through 13). The nature and severity of the dysfunction vary from family to family, but the roots of family sexual abuse often appear to reside in the internal dynamics and dysfunctional systems of the families where abuse occurs. Hewitt and Friedrich capture this theme succinctly in their summary observations:

Child sexual abuse is not an isolated event for the children in our sample. Their abuse occurs in the context of impaired family functioning. The frequency of such elements as concomitant marital discord, parental battering, financial problems, and physical child abuse is extremely high. We cannot emphasize enough that *these families are highly distressed.*

TREATMENT FOR VICTIMS AND OFFENDERS

A common concern discussed at the Family Sexual Abuse Project conferences was the widespread perception that there is no effective treatment for sexual abuse offenders. Corollary notions are that sexual abuse inflicts permanent long-term damage and inevitably destroys families, with little hope for rehabilitation of perpetrators or lasting assistance to victims. The evaluation studies in Part III of this book provide an array of evidence regarding treatment effectiveness. None of the evaluations used methods that would resolve complex issues of causal attribution, and the validity of outcome measures is open to challenge, especially given the common reliance on self-report data. Nevertheless, when properly understood as exploratory, small-scale evaluations done at the front lines for formative purposes (Patton, 1986, 1990) these studies reveal patterns that are informative, suggestive, and often hopeful.

Contrary to some perceptions that treatment is universally ineffective, the evaluation of the Wilder Family Project (Chapter 8) shows substantial and apparently lasting positive impact. Half of the respondent families were still intact at the time of the follow-up interview and no families (intact or not) reported any recurrence of sexual abuse. The Children's Hospital Study (Chapter 3) also found that many families were coping well: 89% reported no recurrence of sexual abuse, and 86% of victims were reported to be doing "good" to "excellent."

Both the Wilder and Children's Hospital follow-up studies found that mothers often reported more long-term adjustment difficulties than were reported for victims, and entire families experienced at least as much and often more difficulty than the immediate victims. The study of reunited families (Chapter 10) documents how difficult it can be to put family lives back together after treatment. But all five reunited case families showed enhanced coping skills, victims determined not to be abused again (though still experiencing pain, anger, and mistrust), perpetrators taking responsibility for their actions, and couples struggling to make their marriages work through greater openness of communication. Nevertheless, there were no illusions that things would ever again be the same and these remained troubled families in need of ongoing support and counseling.

Hewitt and Friedrich (Chapter 4) assessed the clinical improvement of "probably abused" preschool children over the course of a year. Based on parent data from the Child Behavioral Checklist, they found that 67% of these children improved, 20% deteriorated, and 13% remained unchanged. Improvement was directly related to the length of time the child spent in therapy, leading the authors to conclude that their results support "the utility of therapy with sexually abused children." They further conclude that other family members also need both individual and family therapy.

Maddock and associates (Chapter 11) believe that they have made real progress toward a protocol for evaluating *family* outcomes of incest treatment. More systematic and comparative approaches to evaluating treatment impacts are critical, they argue, to address concerns that current treatment efforts may neglect and/or have a negative impact upon families as a unit. Their preliminary results indicate that incest families display a variety of dysfunctional attributes, with marital relationships often continuing to be strained and unstable after treatment.

The study of the Transitional Sex Offender Program (TSOP) at Lino Lakes Correctional Facility (Chapter 12) shows that 93% of the 43 men interviewed felt that the treatment program was generally helpful, with 84% agreeing that "the treatment program has helped me to avoid sexual behavior with children" and 77% reporting that "the treatment program has helped me to change the kinds of thoughts I have about children." The TSOP study also found that 85% of program participants were free of new felony convictions during the follow-up period. Among those living in the community, 69% had formed households with female partners, including 41% who were also living with minor children (over half of whom were reunited with women and minor children they had lived with prior to their convictions). Recidivism rates were higher for men who began but did not complete the treatment program compared with those who completed all phases of the program (22% versus 6%). While the overall results indicate that treatment for convicted male sexual offenders can be helpful, the researchers suggest that longer periods of community supervision, increased emphasis on family therapy, and additional supportive services may be necessary to reduce the risk of recidivism among treated incest offenders.

The study of women offenders in the Genesis II treatment program (Chapter 13) suggests considerable promise for effective treatment of female offenders when that treatment is specifically designed for and supportive of women and their special "ways of knowing." The data hold out the hope that nearly two-thirds of the women will successfully complete treatment and move on to productive lives. The interviews with these women reveal recognition, responsibility, insight, and determination.

In short, while far from conclusive, these varied preliminary and exploratory findings suggest that victims, families, and offenders can be helped with timely, effective, and professional treatment and support.

Yet treatment is neither easy nor quick, and the outcomes remain uncertain for many. The detailed descriptions of treatment struggles for women in both the female offenders study and the American Indian study make it clear that years and years of shame, anger, fear, and grief cannot be treated or healed easily or quickly. Treatment is made even more difficult among American Indian victims because of the "on again/off again" nature of their contact with services. Incest victims may make or renew contact with a counselor after particularly upsetting incidents, but ambivalence and fear about dealing directly with their incest experiences lead many women to deny or to try to forget. The priority of ongoing family obligations and demands interferes with consistent or long-term treatment. Finally, there are the complications of chemical abuse and financial stress, which can make the victims' lives so chaotic that regular and ongoing treatment commitments are more than they can manage.

The American Indian study provides insight into the treatment philosophy and challenges of Indian counselors and the attitudes of the Indian community toward both incest and the needs for subsequent healing and balance, but no follow-up data on the outcomes of treatment were available or possible to collect. The research makes it clear that any such outcomes study would need to be sensitive to larger cultural issues of Indian victimization and the long-term effects of living in an oppressive environment where survival is an ongoing concern. Treatment for incest victimization also involves treatment for cultural victimization, both of which involve feelings of grief, terror, anger, shame, and withdrawal.

An evaluation of the Rape and Sexual Assault Center Child Sexual Abuse Family Treatment Program in Minnesota (part of the Family Sexual Abuse Project but not part of this book) reveals the difficulties of providing long-term, phased treatment for families. Only 18% of clients in the program completed treatment; 20% were still in treatment; and 62% had failed to begin treatment (following an initial assessment) or complete treatment (including dropouts, transfers to other programs, and other sources of dissatisfaction that led to treatment termination). The evaluation data indicated that the program was effective for those who completed it, but the low completion rate cast a shadow over the whole program. There was also evidence that some family situations deteriorated among the high percentage of dropouts. This study encountered a number of problems and was not sufficiently completed for publication in this volume, but the preliminary results clearly show that keeping clients in treatment long enough to help them can be a major barrier to effective family sexual abuse treatment, particularly because treatment is seldom covered by insurance.

Wright (Chapter 9) analyzed the effects on treatment progress of removing offenders from the home. The results show that situations vary a great deal, and no clear pattern of effects can be substantiated. There were cases where offender removal clearly contributed to family healing. There were also cases where the researchers concluded that removing offenders impaired treatment progress—that is, the removal backfired and made things worse for the family, especially financially, rather than better. The reasons for impaired treatment explored in the study demonstrate how complex, uncertain, and fragile the therapy process is. This study also raises questions, based on family interviews, about the emphasis in therapy on the individual first and the family second. The study documents how the treatment team has struggled—and continues to struggle—with the wisdom, ethics, and effectiveness of offender removal. The results raise questions about any uniform, standardized policy, but also make it clear that the issues are complicated and highly situational. The authors suggest that rigid, inflexible policies requiring absolute offender removal may be problematic.

The American Indian study also addresses the issue of removing male offenders from the home. The American Indian culture values keeping men in the families as well as not subjecting them to oppression by the system. As a result, there is great reluctance to report incest to authorities.

In summary, the research on treatment for victims, families, and offenders holds out hope that treatment can be helpful and effective, but only for those who are willing and able (emotionally and financially) to see it through to the treatment's end. Many in need of treatment are either unable or unwilling, so the potential for impact remains less than fully realized. Much more evaluation is needed, with better instruments and longer periods of follow-up, before more definitive judgments can be made about treatment effectiveness. Several of these studies represent pioneering efforts in this regard, but each is limited and all are exploratory, as are the treatments studied.

"THE SYSTEM"

These studies also provide insights into how the social service and criminal justice systems are dealing with problems of family sexual abuse. The Children's Hospital study (Chapter 3) investigated in some depth families' experiences with various parts of "the system." Nearly one-fourth of the respondents rated services they received in the "less helpful" range. There were complaints of poor communication, lack of coordination, insensitivity to victims' and family needs, lack of support from workers, not enough follow-up or action, incompetence of staff, and inadequately trained personnel.

Wright (Chapter 9) reports that many couples who wanted to work through their family sexual abuse crisis and preserve the family as a unit faced "an uphill battle against the system" because "the people who were controlling their lives, the experts on what was healthy and okay, just didn't think they should stay married."

Hewitt and Friedrich (Chapter 4) express deep concern about how allegations of abuse are investigated, especially the policy in some communities of not investigating allegations of abuse unless the child can talk. They argue against such a policy based on their success in substantiating sexual abuse among preschool children.

Research studies with a system evaluation component (Chapters 3 and 9) found that many respondents did not and could not distinguish among parts of "the system." They complained generally of the system's lack of coordination, lack of consistency and "the seeming endlessness of the process."

The American Indian study discusses the Indian community as outside of and threatened by "the system." Indians are reluctant to report family sexual abuse because the system reacts in culturally inappropriate ways. Shelter personnel are typically white, "speaking a language that is exactly like a white, welfare social worker" and therefore alienating. The study reports the perceptions that "Indian women have little trust in police."

The sibling incest study (Chapter 5) includes insights about the workings of "the system," especially the finding that sibling offenders are treated less severely than other offenders despite the typically greater severity of offenses by sibling offenders.

The Lino Lakes follow-up study of offenders (Chapter 12) reports that about two-thirds of offenders felt they benefited from parole and 58% reported benefiting from a stay in a halfway house. Offenders who complained about halfway houses complained most often about too many restrictions and conflicts with staff.

While many victims, families, and perpetrators find help in "the system," a substantial number experience difficulty, alienation, and disrespect. In particular, the Children's Hospital study raises concern about "victims being revictimized in the court process." Moreover, there was some confusion among many respondents about how the social service and criminal justice systems work, especially how various parts of the court system are related to each other.

METHODOLOGICAL LESSONS

These 11 studies have contributed not only to our understanding of family sexual abuse, but also to our knowledge of how to study the problems of family sexual abuse. This section summarizes methodological lessons learned from these studies. Before doing so it is worth noting that despite the narrow focus, relatively small scale, and limited resources of these research efforts, each produced far more data and many more insights than could be reported in this book. Lengthy and detailed research reports had to be condensed and painfully edited to meet the space limitations of publication. Thus these chapters present no more than highlights of what was learned. In drawing methodological lessons I have included insights discussed in the more detailed methodological sections of these studies' full reports.

Most of the studies used multiple methods, both quantitative and qualitative, to get at the complex and varying dimensions of and perspectives on family sexual abuse. Standardized surveys for follow-up studies of relatively large samples provided systematic data from victims, perpetrators, and other family members, but these surveys also provided opportunities for interviewees to respond to open-ended questions in which they could explain their perspectives in their own words. The combination of closed and open questions worked quite effectively. Other studies combined standardized psychological instruments with in-depth interviews and observations. Still other important methods included systematic coding and analysis of files and records, and interviews with key informants. The use of multiple methods is a form of triangulation in which different types of data provide cross-data validity checks (Patton, 1990: 188). The researchers, in panel discussions at the Family Sexual Abuse Project conferences, strongly agreed that multimethod, triangulated research approaches are especially appropriate in family sexual abuse studies to avoid the limitations inherent in any single and unitary approach.

Telephone interviewing can be used effectively for follow-up studies about the experiences and reoccurrence of child sexual abuse. There was some concern initially about whether family members would be willing to talk about their experiences to strangers over the telephone. The Wilder Family Project evaluation (Chapter 8), the Children's Hospital follow-up study (Chapter 3), and the Transitional Sex Offender Program follow-up evaluation (Chapter 12) each made extensive use of telephone interviews with considerable success. The methods sections of the full reports (not published here) include suggestions for how to use telephones effectively for family sexual abuse follow-up studies.

Interviewers in family sexual abuse studies need special training, skills, sensitivity, and tolerance. It is already well established that providing professional child abuse services is difficult and stress producing. These studies show that it is also difficult and stressful for those who conduct research on this problem. Interviewers need ways of ventilating their feelings, talking about what they hear, and integrating the interview experience.

While refusal rates remain a problem and many people are difficult to find for follow-up interviews, all of these studies shows that people involved with family sexual abuse—victims, family members, therapists, and perpetrators—are willing, even anxious, to tell their stories. Some of the telephone follow-up interviews went on for more than three hours as people poured out their stories, expressing a clear need to be heard. Often they were highly emotional and cried as they told their stories. Gilgun found that male perpetrators had a great need to tell their stories and be understood, a particularly interesting finding given the pattern she discovered that these offenders had childhood and adult histories of social isolation, lacking confidants or others with whom to talk openly. The female offender interviewers found that in-depth, open-ended, qualitative interviews provided a needed catharsis for offenders. While some of the people involved in family sexual abuse remain defensive and protective (e.g., see Chapter 11), the great majority have a need to process the experience and help others understand it. Neither of these studies, however, addresses the issue of how to differentiate between what critics may perceive as offenders' self-serving rationalizations and more genuine catharsis.

In contrast to the willingness of many to tell their stories to inter-viewers when contacted directly, two studies (Chapters 10 and 11) that depended on referrals from clinics and therapists to identify research-able families had major difficulties getting referrals, difficulties suffi-ciently severe to have significantly changed the scope and original intents of the studies. Matthews, Raymaker, and Speltz eventually resigned themselves to being entirely dependent on their own client populations to find reunited families to study, thereby substantially reducing their sample size and sample diversity, and substantially increasing the length of the study. Maddock and associates also expe-rienced difficulty getting clinics to honor cooperative agreements:

> Our efforts to secure subject families taught us an important lesson: Make formal agreements with treatment programs to solicit client partici-pation in the research as a *routine* part of their own intake/assessment process. This procedure requires greater initial effort, including extensive discussions with governing boards, administrators, and entire clinic staffs. However, it builds stronger support for the project, regularizes the recruitment process, and provides better feedback to the participating clinics.

Research and evaluation are highly dependent on the availability of good records. It is critical that accurate and complete records be kept at every stage in the family sexual abuse process from initial identifi-cation through treatment to follow-up. These studies reveal significant data problems in current agency and program record-keeping sys-tems. The lack of good data makes follow-up, evaluation, and research difficult, sometimes impossible.

The best data are collected at critical contact points. Recall data are less valid and reliable than data collected close to the moment of an event. Documenting changes requires baseline data and periodic change data. Our long-term understanding of and intervention in family sexual abuse will need better record-keeping and data collec-tion systems. However, several of the studies (especially those reported in Chapters 3, 5, and 12) show that a great deal of valuable information can be extracted from careful and patient analysis of existing records.

All of the victim follow-up studies rely on self-reports to determine recurrence of abuse. Such data are obviously suspect, especially since interviewers are required to warn respondents that unreported recur-rences will be reported by the interviewer. There are significant meth-odological problems for follow-up studies created by legal and ethical requirements that professionals (including interviewers) report recurring abuse. When interviewees, whether victims, perpetrators, or others, are told that revealing subsequent unreported recurrences will be reported by interviewers, the validity of reported nonrecurrences is cast in doubt. Trade-offs are involved between legal protection and the desirability of accurate and valid research. Before self-report data on recurrences can be trusted, these issues of validity and alternatives to current reporting requirements will need additional discussion.

Maddock and colleagues have identified another important caveat for studies of clinical families being treated for abuse: Clinical families are inevitably interviewed *after* incest has been reported, so their behaviors probably reflect the influences of social intervention as much as the effects of the incest itself—"one of the inevitable limitations of clinical research in the area of child abuse."

Evaluation of treatment programs is hampered by poor conceptualization and inconsistent implementation of treatments. The Family Sexual Abuse Project's proposal solicitation process revealed significant and widespread inadequacies in treatment specification. Moreover, ambiguous intake procedures and high dropout rates significantly complicate research and evaluation efforts.

It can be difficult to evaluate specific agencies or treatments because many families have trouble differentiating separate parts of "the system." They experience a complex array of actors and interventions, complicated phases and stages of treatment, and interconnections between the family abuse crisis and other family crises. These interconnections complicate the research and evaluation task.

Special populations need special research attention. Family sexual abuse is not a uniform phenomenon. Interventions and treatments vary tremendously. Generalizations are to be distrusted at this stage in the field's development. The American Indian study shows the complexity of this issue for one kind of culture. The Wright study (Chapter 9) shows the complexity of studying one fairly concrete policy (removing offenders from the home).

The 11 studies, taken together, provide a mosaic of enormous complexity. A great deal of additional research will be needed over time to identify and verify patterns, consequences, and explanations that can be applied with any confidence from place to place and from group to group.

Finally, these studies illustrate both the strengths and weaknesses of doing small-scale, frontline research with very limited time and resources. As research goes these were small studies, averaging about $25,000 in direct support and conducted within the relatively short time frame of one year. In every case the actual costs in time and effort far exceeded the available financial support, demonstrating why it is so difficult to undertake such research—and why it is so important to do so with the full cooperation and genuine commitment of both practitioners and researchers. That such cooperation and commitment existed is what made these studies and this book possible.

REFERENCES

Patton, M. Q. (1986). *Utilization-focused evaluation* (2nd ed.). Beverly Hills, CA: Sage.
Patton, M. Q. (1990). *Qualitative evaluation and research methods* (2nd ed.). Newbury Park, CA: Sage.

About the Authors

Margaret J. Bringewatt, M.A., is a human services and public policy consultant who has worked in the Twin Cities of Saint Paul and Minneapolis for nearly 20 years. She has worked with issues of child sexual abuse, AIDS, families in poverty, child development, refugee services, and rural issues. Her master's degree in public affairs is from the Humphrey Institute of Public Affairs.

Irl Carter, Ph.D., is Associate Professor in the School of Social Work, University of Minnesota. His primary research area is American Indian policies, and his publications have been in human behavior, community development, and industrial social work. He recently served as Acting Director of the Center for Youth Development and Research, University of Minnesota. He is coauthor of *Human Behavior in the Social Environment: A Social Systems Approach* (Aldine, 1990), now in its fourth edition. He teaches social policy, human behavior, organizations and communities; for two years, he taught at the Chinese University of Hong Kong.

Jon R. Conte, Ph.D., is an Associate Professor at the School of Social Work, University of Washington, Seattle. He is the editor of the *Journal of Interpersonal Violence* and *Violence Update*. He is a frequent lecturer at national and international meetings and a past President of the American Professional Society on the Abuse of Children.

W. N. Friedrich, Ph.D., is a consultant in the Department of Psychiatry and Psychology at the Mayo Clinic, and is Associate Professor in the Mayo Medical School. He is a diplomate in clinical and family psychology with the American Board of Professional Psychology. He has recently authored a book, *Psychotherapy of Sexually Abused Children and Their Families*, published by W. W. Norton in 1990.

Jane F. Gilgun, Ph.D., is an Associate Professor in the School of Social Work, University of Minnesota, Twin Cities. A researcher in child maltreatment for the last 10 years, she was a practitioner in child welfare and family service settings for the 10 previous years. She currently is editing a book of original articles, *Qualitative Methods in Family Research*, with two co-editors, Gerald Handel and Kerry Daley.

S. K. Hewitt, Ph.D., is a licensed consulting psychologist with River City Mental Health, Saint Paul, Minnesota. She is the former Co-Director of Midwest Children's Resource Center, Children's Hospital of Saint Paul. She has been seeing abused children since 1976, with emphasis on preschool children.

Catherine F. Lally, M.A., is a doctoral student in the Department of Family Social Science, University of Minnesota.

Pamela R. Larson, M.A., is a doctoral student in the Department of Family Social Science, University of Minnesota.

Carolyn J. Levitt, M.D., is a pediatrician and Director of Midwest Children's Resource Center, a program for child abuse consultation, evaluation, and treatment. She personally has examined 4,000 children for suspicion of sexual abuse. She holds leadership positions at the state and national levels, including Vice President of the National Child Advocacy Center Board and member of the Executive Committee of the Section on Child Abuse and Neglect of the American Academy of Pediatrics.

James W. Maddock, Ph.D., is Associate Professor in the Department of Family Social Science, University of Minnesota. He has worked as a therapist, trainer, and consultant in the area of family sexual abuse since 1974. He is a former president of both the American Association of Sex Educators, Counselors and Therapists and the Upper Midwest Association for Marriage and Family Therapy.

Ruth Mathews, M.A., is a licensed psychologist and has coordinated the Program for Healthy Adolescent Sexual Expression (PHASE) for adolescent male and female sexual offenders since 1983. In 1985, along with Jane Kinder Matthews, she developed an Adult Female Sexual Offender Program. She also serves on the National Task Force on Juvenile Sexual Offending. She has presented at numerous conferences and workshops on adolescent and female sexual offending, and has provided expert testimony. She is currently completing her Ph.D. dissertation at the Saybrook Institute on the role pornography plays in adolescent male sexual offending.

Jane Kinder Matthews, received her B.S.Ed. degree from Southeast Missouri State College and her M.A. in psychology from St. Mary's College in Winona, Minnesota. She has worked with adult male and female sex offenders and adolescent victims of sexual abuse since 1981.

Michael J. O'Brien is currently Director of Clinical Services of East Communities Family Service, a private nonprofit mental health clinic in Maplewood, Minnesota, and a branch of Family Service of Greater St. Paul. Michael is the founder and director of the Program for Healthy Adolescent Sexual Expression (PHASE). He has authored a number of articles on this topic, has appeared on national network news and information shows, and has lectured and trained across the United States and Canada on the topic of sexual abuse and sexual offenders.

Greg Owen, Ph.D., is a Senior Research Scientist with the Amherst H. Wilder Foundation in Saint Paul, Minnesota. He also serves as Adjunct Professor in Health and Human Services Administration for St. Mary's College of Winona, Minnesota.

Lawrence J. Parker holds an M.A. in public affairs and a master of social work degree from the University of Minnesota, and is a doctoral student in social work. He is a member of the Cree tribe, Rocky Boy's Reservation, Montana. He was formerly Director of Planning and Development, and Interim President, Fort Berthold Community College, in North Dakota, and a staff member of the U.S. Senate Select Committee on Indian Affairs.

Michael Quinn Patton, Ph.D., is a social scientist with the Union Institute Graduate School, Cincinnati, Ohio. He is the author of four major evaluation books published by Sage Publications: *Qualitative Evaluation and Research Methods* (1990), *Creative Evaluation* (1987), *Utilization-Focused Evaluation* (1986), and *Practical Evaluation* (1982). He has served as President of the American Evaluation Association (1988) and as editor of the *Journal of Extension* (1988–1990). His Ph.D. in sociology is from the University of Wisconsin – Madison.

Jodie Raymaker, licensed psychologist, received a bachelor of science in education degree from Mankato State University in 1978. She was employed as a secondary teacher before completing a master's degree in counseling from the University of Wisconsin in 1981. As a primary therapist with the Program for Healthy Adolescent Sexual Expression (PHASE) for seven years, she developed an expertise in working with adolescent sexual offenders, sexual abuse victims and survivors, and sexually abusive families. She is currently in private practice.

Kathleen Speltz received her B.S. in psychology from St. Mary's College, Winona, Minnesota, and her M.Ed. from Boston University. She received a Bush Fellowship to study public affairs at the Lyndon Baines Johnson School, University of Texas, Austin. She is currently Grants Administrator for Criminal Justice Programs at the Minnesota Office of Drug Policy.

Nancy M. Steele, Ph.D., is a licensed clinical psychologist and Supervisor of the Minnesota Department of Corrections Transitional Sex Offenders Program, Lino Lakes, Minnesota. She also serves as a technical consultant for the National Institute of Corrections.

Jeanette Truchsess is a doctoral candidate in family social science at the University of Minnesota. She is a licensed psychologist, licensed marriage and family therapist, and psychiatric nurse practitioner. She teaches and has a private practice, specializing in family dysfunction and abuse.

Deborah L. Woodworth received her Ph.D. in sociology from the University of Minnesota. She has worked primarily in the areas of evaluation and policy research. Currently, she is a Program Evaluation Specialist for the Office of the Legislative Auditor, State of Minnesota.

Sara Wright, Ph.D., is a licensed consulting psychologist and a licensed marriage and family therapist. She works as a clinician, consultant, researcher, writer, and parent.